Starmont Contemporary Writers 2
ISSN 0738 - 0119

Margaret Drabble
Symbolic Moralist

Nora Foster Stovel

Dale Salwak, Series Editor

Starmont House, Inc.
1989

FOR BRUCE

LIBRARY OF CONGRESS
Library of Congress Cataloging-in-Publication Data

Stovel, Nora, 1942-
  Margaret Drabble, symbolic moralist / by Nora Stovel.
    p. cm. -- (Starmont contemporary writers series ; no. 2)
  Bibiography: p.
  Includes index.
              ISBN 1-557-42035-1 : $19.95.
              ISBN 1-557-42034-3 (pbk.) : $9.95
  1. Drabble, Margaret, 1939- --Criticism and interpretation.
2. Moral conditions in literature. 3. Symbolism in literature.
4. Women in literature.   I. Title. II. Series.
PR6054.R25Z93 1989
823'.914--dc19   88-1079
                                                           CIP

Published and copyright ©1989 by Starmont House, Inc. All rights reserved. International copyrights reserved in all countries. No part of this book may be reproduced in any form, except for brief passages quoted in reviews, without the expressed written permission of the publisher. For information, contact Starmont House, Inc., P.O. Box 851, Mercer Island, WA 98040, USA. Printed in the USA.

<u>First Edition</u>

Cover photo by Mark Gerson, FIIP.

Nora Foster Stovel is an Assistant Professor of English at The University of Alberta, where she teaches twentieth-century literature. She received her B.A., M.A, and Ph.D. from McGill, Cambridge, and Dalhousie Universities respectively. Dr. Stovel has published several articles on Margaret Drabble, as well as essays on Margaret Atwood, Margaret Laurence, Rudyard Kipling, and D.H. Lawrence. Following *Margaret Drabble: Symbolic Moralist*, she is at work on *Margaret Laurence, Diviner* and *D.H. Lawrence: From Playwright to Novelist*. She lives in Edmonton, Alberta, Canada, with her husband and two children.

CONTENTS

ACKNOWLEDGMENTS iv

ABBREVIATIONS OF INTERVIEWS v

ABBREVIATIONS OF TITLES vi

CHRONOLOGY vii

One   MORAL VISION AND SYMBOLIC VEHICLE 1

Two   BIRD, BEAST, AND FLOWER: MARRIAGE AND SYMBOLISM IN *A SUMMER BIRD-CAGE* 29

Three   ILLUSION AND REALITY: THE GARRICK THEATRE AND THE RIVER WYE 43

Four   THE IVORY TOWER AND THE MARKET PLACE: ART AND REALITY IN *THE MILLSTONE* 61

Five   IDENTITY AND COMMUNITY: GOLD AND GILT IN *JERUSALEM THE GOLDEN* 74

Six   "SUBLIME BLOOD" AND "SUBLIMATED BLOOD": PASSION AND POETRY IN THE *WATERFALL* 95

Seven   THROUGH *THE NEEDLES'S EYE* 109

Eight   EXCAVATING *THE REALMS OF GOLD* 130

Nine   BRITAIN'S COLD WAR WITH A NEW ICE AGE 149

Ten   THE EXCREMENTAL VISION AND THE AERIAL VIEW OF *THE MIDDLE GROUND* 166

Eleven   QUESTING THE *RADIANT WAY* 186

Twelve   CONCLUSION 205

BIBLIOGRAPHY 207

INDEX 219

ACKNOWLEDGMENTS

I wish to acknowledge the invaluable assistance of Margaret Drabble, Valerie Grosvenor Myer, and Ellen Cronan Rose; the sage advice of Drs. David Monaghan, Rowland Smith, Michael Klug, Keith Wilson and Thomson Sinclair-Faulkner; the editorial skill of Dr. Dale Salwak and Ted Dikty; the understanding of my children, Laura and Grant; and the unfailing support of my husband, Dr. Bruce Stovel.

I also wish to acknowledge the support of the Dalhousie University Killam Predoctoral Scholarships and Research Development Fund Grant, which enabled me to research and compose this study in partial fulfillment of the Dalhousie doctorate; the Calgary Humanities Institute and University of Calgary Postdoctoral Fellowships, which allowed me to revise the dissertation for publication; and the University of Alberta Research Grant, which helped me to finalize the manuscript for the Starmont Contemporary Writers Series.

ABBREVIATIONS OF INTERVIEWS

BBI: Bergonzi, Bernard. "Novelists of the Sixties." London: BBC, 1968.

BFI: Le Franc, Bolivar. "An Interest in Guilt." *Books and Bookmen*, 14 September 1969, 20-21.

JHI: Horder, John. "Heroine in an Empty House." *The Times*, 21 May 1969, p. 12.

NSHI: Hardin, Nancy S. "An Interview with Margaret Drabble." *Contemporary Literature*, 14 (1973), 273-95.

PFI: Firchow, Peter. "Margaret Drabble." *The Writer's Place: Interviews on the Literary Situation in Contemporary Britain.* Ed. Peter Firchow. Minneapolis: Univ. of Minnesota Press, 1974, 102-21.

NPI: Poland, Nancy. "Margaret Drabble: 'There Must Be a Lot of People Like Me.'" *Midwest Quarterly*, 16 (Spring 1975), 255-67.

MGI: Gussow, Mel. "Margaret Drabble: A Double Life." *New York Times Book Review*, 9 October 1977, 40-41.

VGMI: Myer, Valerie Grosvenor. "Margaret Drabble in Conversation with Valerie Grosvenor Myer." London: The British Council, 1977.

BMI: Milton, Barbara. "Margaret Drabble: The Art of Fiction LXX." *The Paris Review*, 20 (Fall-Winter 1978), 40-65.

IRI: Rozencwajg, Iris. "Interview with Margaret Drabble." *Women's Studies*, 6 (1979), 335-47.

DPI: Preussner, Dee. "Talking with Margaret Drabble." *Modern Fiction Studies*, 25 (Winter 1979-80), 563-77.

MPI: Powell, Marilyn. "An Interview with Margaret Drabble." Toronto: CBC, 22 February 1980.

NHI: Household, Nicki. "Love Story: *The Waterfall*." *Radio Times*, 8 November 1980, pp. 23-27.

DCCI: Clark, Diana Cooper. "Margaret Drabble: Cautious Feminist." *Atlantic Monthly*, 246 (November 1980), 69-75.

MFI: Forster, Margaret. "What Makes Margaret Drabble Run and Run." *Guardian*, 28 February 1981, p. 9.

JCI: Creighton, Joanne V. "An Interview with Margaret Drabble." *Margaret Drabble: Golden Realms.* Ed. Dorey Schmidt. Edinburg, Texas: Pan American Univ. Press, 1982, 18-31.

JTI: "Margaret Drabble Interviewed by Gillian Parker and Janet Todd," *Women Writers Talking.* Ed. Janet Todd London: Holmes & Meier, 1983, 161-78.

ABBREVIATIONS OF TITLES

SBC	A SUMMER BIRD-CAGE
GY	THE GARRICK YEAR
M	THE MILLSTONE
JG	JERUSALEM THE GOLDEN
TW	THE WATERFALL
NE	THE NEEDLE'S EYE
RG	THE REALMS OF GOLD
IA	THE ICE AGE
MG	THE MIDDLE GROUND
RW	THE RADIANT WAY
W	WORDSWORTH
AB	ARNOLD BENNETT: A BIOGRAPHY
WB	A WRITER'S BRITAIN: LANDSCAPE IN LITERATURE
JA	JANE AUSTEN: LADY SUSAN, THE WATSONS, SANDITON
TH	THE GENIUS OF THOMAS HARDY
TWF	THE TRADITION OF WOMEN'S FICTION
OCEL	THE OXFORD COMPANION TO ENGLISH LITERATURE
AC	"THE AUTHOR COMMENTS"
WW	"A WOMAN WRITER"
PP	MARGARET DRABBLE: PURITANISM AND PERMISSIVENESS
EF	THE NOVELS OF MARGARET DRABBLE: EQUIVOCAL FIGURES
GR	MARGARET DRABBLE: GOLDEN REALMS
MD	MARGARET DRABBLE
CEMD	CRITICAL ESSAYS ON MARGARET DRABBLE

CHRONOLOGY

1939 Margaret Drabble born 5 June in Sheffield, Yorkshire, England, to John Frederick Drabble, barrister, and Marie Bloor Drabble.
1960 Graduated from Cambridge with a double starred first in English, married actor Clive Swift, and joined Royal Shakespeare Company.
1961 Birth of first of three children.
1963 Published *A Summer Bird-Cage*.
1964 Published *The Garrick Year* and produced *Laura* on Granada television.
1965 Published *The Millstone* (awarded the John Llewellyn Rhys Memorial Prize for Fiction); awarded a Society of Authors Travelling Scholarship.
1966 Published *Wordsworth*.
1967 Published *Jerusalem the Golden* (awarded the James Tait Black Memorial Prize for Fiction).
1969 Published *The Waterfall*, produced *Bird of Paradise* at the National Theatre, and wrote screenplays for *A Touch of Love* and *Isadora*.
1972 Published *The Needle's Eye* (awarded the E.M. Forster Award); separated from husband, and coedited *London Consequences* with B.S. Johnson.
1974 Published *Arnold Bennett: A Biography* and edited *Jane Austen*.
1975 Published *The Realms of Gold* and dissolved first marriage.
1976 Edited *The Genius of Thomas Hardy* and *An Anthology I* and awarded an Honorary Doctor of Literature degree by the University of Sheffield.
1977 Published *The Ice Age*.
1978 Published *For Queen and Country: Britain in the Victorian Age*.
1979 Published *A Writer's Britain: Landscape in Literature*.
1980 Published *The Middle Ground* and named Commander of the British Empire.
1982 Published *The Tradition of Women's Fiction* and married Michael Holroyd.
1985 Reedited *The Oxford Companion to English Literature*.
1987 Published *The Radiant Way*.

Chapter One:

MORAL VISION AND SYMBOLIC VEHICLE

Margaret Drabble no longer requires any introduction on either side of the Atlantic. With ten successful novels, five books of criticism, five editions, four plays, ten short stories, and innumerable articles to her credit, Drabble has clearly established herself as a major eminence on the contemporary literary horizon. Popular from the outset, her domestic novels of the sixties—*A Summer Bird-Cage* (1963), *The Garrick Year* (1964), *The Millstone* (1965), *Jerusalem the Golden* (1967), and *The Waterfall* (1969)—brought her enormous success, as a new generation of educated women identified with her intelligent heroines. With the development of a more public phase of her fiction in her novels of the seventies—*The Needle's Eye* (1972), *The Realms of Gold* (1975), *The Ice Age* (1977), and *The Middle Ground* (1980)—Drabble also achieved critical acclaim, which *The Radiant Way* (1987) has since intensified. Sheridan Baker declared:

> Margaret Drabble is the girl for me. She is Jane Austen modernized, with sex admitted. She seems born knowing what Lessing's Martha is still questing. She accepts life, and all its breakage, with irony, wit, and unerring perception—indeed with a very unobtrusive, almost Shakespearean, wonder at the mysteries of chance and time, at the faint intimations of some greater order sustaining the daily mess, with death just around the corner. Her sense of language, her people and their speech, are true to the bone. She will make you laugh aloud, and bring tears to your eyes.[1]

Not only a popular and critical success as a novelist, Drabble herself is also a critic and editor of note: author of *Wordsworth* (1966), *Arnold Bennett: A Biography* (1974), *For Queen and Country: Britain in the Victorian Age* (1978), *A Writer's Britain: Landscape in Literature* (1979), and *The Tradition of Women's Fiction* (1982), Drabble has also edited *London Consequences* (1972), *Jane Austen* (1974), *The Genius of Thomas Hardy* (1976), and *An Anthology I* (1976). As editor of the new revised version of *The Oxford Companion to English Literature* (1985), Drabble has definitely become a major figure in the contemporary literary establishment.

The recipient of numerous literary awards, including the John Llewellyn Rhys and James Tait Black Memorial Prize for Fiction, whose novels have been translated into all the major world languages, Drabble was made an honorary Doctor of Literature by the University of Sheffield, her home town, in 1976 and named Commander of the British Empire by Queen Elizabeth II in 1980 in recognition of her contributions to the world of literature.

Recent critical enthusiasm has produced a plethora of publications in Europe, America, and Asia, including eight monographs, two collections of essays, and literally hundreds of articles. Despite the burgeoning critical industry, Lorna Sage concluded that "Real criticism on Ms Drabble is sparse"—a judgment which reflects the fact that, until recently, critics have emphasized the topical surface rather than the thoughtful depths and artistic heights of Drabble's fiction.[2] Now that the first shock waves of Drabble's brilliance have been absorbed, it is time to consider the real value of her work.

Heralded as the "Chronicler of Britain," Drabble has been applauded from the outset primarily for the topicality of her fiction.[3] Joyce Carol Oates declared, "It is doubtful that there is any single American writer who represents the diversity and near-chaos of our culture, as Drabble represents the tone of contemporary English culture."[4] Drabble is not simply a journalist, however; she is an artist, and her fiction is distinguished by provocative thinking and evocative imagery, as well as vivid verisimilitude. Her real subject is not just society, but morality, and her method of presenting her moral themes is not simply realism, but symbolism. Drabble's dazzling social accuracy has blinded many critics to both the moral issues and the poetic imagination beneath the surface reportage. Contrary to the prevailing sociological approach, this study will attempt to complement the dominant realist emphasis of Drabble criticism with a more literary approach to the author, focusing on her achievement both as a moral thinker and imaginative artist.

Latterly, Drabble criticism has taken a different sociological tack, as the British realist approach has given way to an American feminist emphasis. She has been called "the first

English woman to give voice to the delusive promise of college life, followed by the cold douche of matrimony and child-bearing."[5] Drabble is not only a feminist, however; she is a humanist, because the questions she debates in her fiction are human issues rather than simply female ones. Despite her commitment to "the tradition of women's fiction," Drabble has affirmed that "None of my books is about feminism, because my belief in the necessity for justice for women (which they don't get at the moment) is so basic that I never think of using it as a subject."[6] Although she acknowledges that "All my first books were written very much from the woman's point of view and they were narrated through the vision, if not by the voice, of women,"[7] Drabble has taken considerable pains in her later novels to shed the label "women's writer," earning the ambiguous labels "cautious feminist" and "double-voiced feminism."[8] In fact, she has announced that she is "fed up with women,"[9] and her recent writer-heroine exclaims to a male friend: "I'm as bloody sick of bloody women as you are, I'm sick to death of them, I wish I'd never invented them."[10] Drabble declares, "I'm a feminist only when I have certain accusations flung at me. But I don't think I write particularly for women. I just happen to be one."[11] We already know that Drabble is a woman writer; it is time now to demonstrate that she is also a good one.

If the traditional criteria for evaluating quality in literature—be it contemporary or classical, male or female—are moral profundity and imaginative artistry, then Drabble is indeed a good writer, not merely a popular one. This study will attempt to demonstrate that Drabble is a major writer on both counts. This introductory chapter will argue, first, that she is a moralist exploring changing values and, secondly, that she is an artist employing symbolism to present her moral themes. Following this introduction, a chapter devoted to each of her novels in turn will elucidate the moral framework of each book through a detailed examination of the patterns of symbolism, leading to new interpretations that may differ significantly from the established ones. This chronological examination of her novels will also reveal a distinct development in the author's moral vision and artistic vehicle that has not yet been fully appreciated by critics. These interpretations will be substantiated by reference to Drabble's own critical writing, the manuscripts of the novels, a score of interviews with the author, and important unpublished material.

The final chapter will conclude the argument, summarizing Drabble's moral and artistic development, and projecting the future direction of her fiction.

I MORAL VISION

Perhaps the most exciting recent development in contemporary fiction is the emergence of the woman's novel—a genre that examines the new female identity and explores the changing status of women in our society. Drabble acknowledges that "I always feel as if I'm living on slightly uncharted territory,"[12] because "women today are finding themselves in situations . . . for which there are no literary guidelines . . . women are charting this ground where the rules have changed, the balance of power has shifted."[13] She believes that "literature is one of the ways of mapping out territories," because "writing fiction is a search for a future in that you are creating, as you go, the images that you can then pursue" (*TWF* 13). Drabble develops these connections between literature and life most eloquently in "A Woman Writer":

> Many people read novels in order to find patterns or images for a possible future—to know how to behave, what to hope to be like. We do not want to resemble the women of the past, but where is our future? This is precisely the question that many novels written by women are trying to answer: some in comic terms, some in tragic, some in speculative. We live in an unchartered world, as far as manners and morals are concerned; we are having to make up our own morality as we go. Our subject-matter is enormous; there are whole new patterns to create. There is no point in sneering at women writers for writing of problems of sexual behaviour, of maternity, of gynaecology—those who feel the need to do it are actively engaged in creating a new pattern, a new blue-print. This area of personal relationships verges constantly on the political: it is not a narrow backwater of introversion, it is the main current which is changing the daily quality of our lives. The truest advantage of being a woman writer now is that never before, perhaps, have women had so much to say, and so great a hope of speaking to some effect.[14]

This comment certainly applies to her own fiction, for Drabble explores unknown landscapes and draws up blueprints for charting the golden realms of the future in her novels. The modern novelist of morals and manners, Drabble is one of the major chroniclers of the recent emergence of women and the new moral problems that liberation has created. As

Bergonzi declared, "It is Margaret Drabble's particular contribution to the contemporary novel to have devised a genuinely new kind of character and predicament."[15] It is now time to examine the exact nature of that contribution.

The new character Drabble has devised is the professional mother, and the new predicament is the conflict between parenthood and professionalism. If the source of conflict in the traditional novel was adultery, the source of conflict in the contemporary novel may be maternity: "Childraising, rather than say sexual freedom or economic parity, is now being increasingly recognized as the central contradiction for women."[16] More than any other novelist, Drabble has recognized that motherhood raises serious ethical and metaphysical questions based on the essential conflict between egotism and altruism. She has shown how the novel's traditional conflict between the individual and society may apply to the microcosm of the family. This conflict becomes sharpest in the case of that recent sociological phenomenon, the professional mother, where the opposition between the demands of a woman's personal life and her professional life becomes paramount. As both mother and professional, Drabble has embodied that conflict in her own life, becoming a novelist rather than an actress as a result of the birth of her first child. Certainly, she has portrayed the distinctively contemporary conflict between the personal and the professional life more dramatically than any other novelist. As Valerie Grosvenor Myer states in *Margaret Drabble: Puritanism and Permissiveness*, "Her heroines were preoccupied with the difficulties of fulfilment and self-definition in a man's world, the conflicting claims of selfhood, wifehood and motherhood, long before the women's lib movement really got going."[17]

Preeminently "the novelist of maternity,"[18] and herself a mother of three, Drabble has affirmed that "Motherhood is the most natural, basic, profound emotion that I have."[19] Indisputably also a successful professional woman—as novelist, critic, editor, teacher, and public figure—Drabble has resolved this dilemma so successfully in her own life that she constitutes a role model for women today. Drabble's account of how she took her typewriter into the labour room, while preparing to deliver the child whose birth inspired *The Millstone*, and proceeded to type out her Wordsworth book, is a vivid illustration of her successful sustaining of both the professional and personal roles.[20]

Each of Drabble's novels explores the female identity by examining one specific feminine role, as wife, mother, lover, daughter, sister, or professional woman—all roles which she herself has played. *A Summer Bird-Cage* focuses on two rival sisters; *The Garrick Year* dramatizes the adulteries of a young husband and wife; *The Millstone* explores the effects of unmarried motherhood on a young academic woman; *Jerusalem the Golden* examines the relationship of a daughter to her mother; *The Waterfall* chronicles the romantic passion of a poet and her lover; *The Needle's Eye* explores a mother's relationship with her children during a custody case with their father; *The Realms of Gold* excavates a woman's maternal heritage in her quest for a spiritual mother; *The Ice Age* examines the relationship of a divorced mother with her intended husband; *The Middle Ground* analyzes the attitude of a feminist journalist to her profession; and *The Radiant Way* follows the friendship of three professional women. So each novel explores one possible relationship of a woman to her community.

Although all of Drabble's heroines attempt to define their individual identity, her real goal is not individuality but community. As Showalter observes, "The ultimate room of one's own is the grave" (297). Ellen Cronan Rose concludes *The Novels of Margaret Drabble: Equivocal Figures* by wishing "to acknowledge and applaud her feminist vision and encourage her to give it freer rein in the future. . . . I want her next novel to be 'not only a book but a future,' an unequivocally feminist blueprint."[21] But Drabble disappoints the radical feminist, for her ideal is not liberation but responsibility. Drabble insists that her heroines "do not seek freedom or liberation. These concepts have little meaning for me. We are not free from our past, we are never free of the claims of others, and we ought to not wish to be. . . . We are all part of a long inheritance, a human community in which we must play our proper part."[22]

Certainly Drabble's own novels do not resolve the conflict of the contemporary woman by emancipation, but rather by recognition of the individual's responsibility to her community: *A Summer Bird-Cage* concludes with both sisters reunited with their lovers and in harmony with each other; *The Garrick Year* finishes with the reunion of husband and wife to care for their children; *The Millstone* ends by reaffirming the passionate attachment of mother to child; *The*

Waterfall celebrates the resurrection of the lovers' affection; *The Needle's Eye* reconciles mother and father with their children; *The Realms of Gold* reunites the lovers and their families; *The Middle Ground* resolves the conflict between the characters and their careers; and *The Radiant Way* reaffirms the friendship of the three female protagonists. Indeed, the only heroine who fails to resolve this conflict in community is Clara Maugham; by evading her true descent, however, Clara also abandons her real identity.

As Gail Cunningham observes, "For the typical Margaret Drabble heroine, then, the forms of modern feminism are acknowledged and, often, consciously embraced, but the complexities of life are repeatedly shown to demand the painful forging of a more personal, individual morality."[23] Drabble believes that "Morality is so relative and writing novels is a constant process of relating shifting morality to shifting society" (*JTI* 174). Joyce Carol Oates declares that Drabble is "attempting the active, vital, energetic, mysterious re-creation of a set of values by which human beings can live."[24] Daughter of a judge (John Frederick Drabble was a barrister who became a circuit judge and, after retirement, a novelist), Drabble is preoccupied with moral questions of justice and virtue. She affirms that "I'm very much a moralist," who is "trying to define the new moral areas."[25] As Angus Wilson has observed, "Miss Drabble's vision is very English and very moral."[26] Her novels are all moral quests, for, as one of her own protagonists declares, "One can't have art without morality."[27]

Drabble comments, "If I am a moral writer, it is not because I want to teach anybody anything. I want to think about it, to write seriously about life."[28] She believes that the function of a novelist is "to explore new territory. To extend one's knowledge of the world. And to illumine what one sees in it. That's a fairly moral concept. . . . Exploring—illuminating—is slightly moral. One wants to see better, clearer, more."[29] She claims that "My only aim is to get my novels as serious as I possibly can" (*PFI* 116). Her insistence on moral intent suggests the influence of F. R. Leavis, whose criterion of "moral seriousness" in *The Great Tradition*[30] had such profound impact on Drabble, when she fell under the shadow of this critical giant at Cambridge. Drabble praises Leavis in her *Oxford Companion to English Literature*, claiming that he "radically altered the literary map of the past and laid out new patterns for the future; but perhaps his most vital contribution lay not in his assessment of individual authors, but in his introduction of a new seriousness into English studies."[31] She acknowledges that, "As a critic, I admire Leavis enormously. I'm sure he's right about the people whom he admires, and the Great Tradition is what I believe in as a novelist. I mean, his preoccupations are my preoccupations. I'm very much a moralist or would think of myself so. So I think he has affected me deeply" (*PFI* 105).

Educated at a Quaker school—the Mount School in York, where her mother, Marie Bloor Drabble, had been an English teacher—Drabble's moral conscience has implicit religious overtones. Although she acknowledges that "I certainly don't belong to any church, and I don't have any creed or dogma," nevertheless, she affirms that "I would call myself religious" (*DCCI* 73). She explains that "one of the themes I was trying to explore was the possibility of living, today, without faith, a religious life" (*AC* 35). As one reviewer observed, "She is not concerned with the difficulties of being a woman but with the difficulties of being good."[32] Certainly, Drabble's goal is never liberation, but salvation. As Myer asserts, "Salvation is what every leading character is looking for" (*PP* 14), and Drabble has affirmed that "My books are not about feminism or babies, but about salvation."[33]

For Drabble, the source of moral salvation is love. All of her heroines are "trying to pursue an image of love and community" (*AC* 37), in the author's own words. The underlying conflict which generates the moral dilemmas in Drabble's novels is the basic opposition between reality and illusion or art and life. Each of her early heroines is an "escape artist" who escapes from social reality and human intimacy into an illusory world of artifice. The dramatic development of each novel then centres on the protagonist's subsequent struggles to escape from her solipsistic prison into the real world of human community through the agency of affection. Drabble's first heroine, Sarah Bennett, living in a no-man's land, divided from her fiancé by an ocean and from her sister by sibling rivalry, has to learn "to live on the level of the heart," to acknowledge that "Blood is thicker than water," and to recognize that love is "the real thing."[34] Emma Evans of *The Garrick Year*, like her namesake in Jane Austen's novel, is the victim of her own ironic self-deception, caught in a web of her own weaving. She must learn to distinguish between illusion and reality, affection and affectation, so that she can live at last in the real world, rather than in a private drama of her own creation. In *The Millstone*, Rosamund Stacey, a research student writing a doctoral dissertation on the Elizabethan sonnet sequence, is imprisoned in the ivory tower of scholarship, but is finally delivered from her solitary confinement through childbirth, which initiates her into the real world of humanity and affection. Only when she learns to feel can she truly understand how literature mirrors life and the Elizabethan sonnet reflects love. In *The Waterfall*, Drabble's most intensely subjective novel, Jane Gray is solipsistic to the point of paralysis, living in her poetry, which she calls "my sublime blood, my sublimated blood" (*TW* 130), rather than in reality. Romantic passion finally melts the frigidity that congeals her blood, making it flow once more, so that the word can at last be made flesh.

No doubt the limitations of the artist's vision in these early novels reflect the limits of the author's own personal life. Drabble is an intensely autobiographical novelist who acknowledges that "The books are expressions of different aspects of me" (*NSHI* 291); as if to illustrate this fact, the American paperback edition features portraits of the artist on the cover of each novel. Drabble affirms that "My earlier novels were written largely from personal experience or from inner experience" (*TWF* 82), and learning to develop within one's limitations is one of the major themes of her early fiction. Drabble admits that "I had a very narrow vision. I had a very narrow life and so I began with one particular situation: like having an illegitimate baby or having to go where your husband's job is. Now, that seems to me very restricting. Too particular" (*BMI* 49).

The Waterfall, Drabble proclaimed, was her "farewell to claustrophobia": she predicted, "I don't think I shall go on writing subjective novels" (*BFI* 20), because "I think I may have grown out of having a single female protagonist."[35] *The Waterfall*, her most intensely subjective novel, was as far as she wanted to go or could go in the direction of solipsism: "*The Waterfall* was the last novel that I wrote while I was still trapped in a life with very small children, and I think this shows in the book. . . . it was my farewell to that kind of claustrophobia, because, after that, my novels have had bigger cast-lists, and they've moved more from place to place, reflecting precisely the fact that I can move more from place to place." She explains her subsequent shift in focus from subjective to objective: "Every book presents a problem, and the writing of the book finishes the problem, in a sense. I now find I have completely different problems, literary and life problems, from the problems that I had when I was writing *The Waterfall*, and to me I seem to have moved a great deal."[36] In fact, we can trace a very significant development in Drabble's moral vision between the early novels of the sixties and the more mature novels of the seventies.

Drabble's first five novels reflect the influence of her early interest in the Romantic poet William Wordsworth, both in the emphasis on the subjective self escaping from oppressive society into a communion with nature and in the use of nature imagery to symbolize the vivid inner life of the psyche. These early novels are primarily psychological in emphasis, with intensely solipsistic heroines who are totally absorbed in their own inner life, which they chronicle in highly subjective first-person confessional narrations. Similarly, in her critical study *Wordsworth* (1966), written in the same decade, Drabble portrays Wordsworth as a psychological poet who explores the impressions of nature on the spirit of the artist. Accordingly, she emphasizes *The Prelude*, subtitled "The Growth of a Poet's Mind," because she believes that "It is more like a modern psychological novel than a poem."[37]

If Wordsworth is the major influence on Drabble's early subjective fiction, the dominant literary influence on her later objective fiction is Arnold Bennett. In *Arnold Bennett: A Biography* (1974), written in the same decade as her more mature novels, Drabble emphasizes this literary idol and kindred spirit as a preeminently social creature in both his life and his literature, asserting that Bennett "was a man who wished to live in society and to make sense of it and work through it."[38] This comment could as easily he applied to Drabble's own mature fiction, for in her four novels written during the seventies, her themes expand to involve economic, political, and cultural concerns. As Lynn Veach Sadler observes, "Passionately resisting solipsism, Drabble has moved from the semiautobiographical to a wider and wider canvas,"[39] earning the title of "central chronicler of contemporary urban middle-class life."[40]

As her heroines develop from claustrophobia to community, Drabble's concept of community also extends to include continuity with the past and future, as well as with the present. Unlike her early heroines, initially intent on emancipation, all of her later heroines, from *The Needle's Eye* to *The Radiant Way*, go home again—as Drabble describes herself doing (*AB* 5)—in order to reestablish their roots so that they can tap the riches of the past required to nourish the future into fruition. *Jerusalem the Golden* marks a transitional point in Drabble's development, for, while Clara Maugham seeks golden worlds in the future, Drabble's more mature heroines search for a golden age in the past. In *The Realms of Gold*, Drabble answers the problem she posed in *Jerusalem the Golden*: whereas Clara Maugham attempted to escape her destiny at the expense of her humanity, Frances Wingate digs into her heritage to excavate the golden treasures of the past to pave the road into the future.

Drabble acknowledges, "It's true that in my earlier novels I wrote about the situation of being a woman—being stuck with a baby, or having an illegitimate baby, or being stuck with a marriage where you couldn't have a job. But I'm less and less interested in that now: one's life becomes wider as one grows older and books reflect one's life. Inevitably" (*NPI* 262). As Creighton observes, her "protagonists have generally followed the course and concerns of her own life," as "her fiction is constantly nourished by her own personal development," for her novels "have increasingly turned to the social scene rather than to the individual psyche" (*JC* 14, 33). Drabble explains the change in her interests from personal to public issues: "I'm not so interested in the issues surrounding marriage now. I have become very offhand about it all and am far more interested in ecology and the decline of Western civilization."[41] She comments, "I'm on better terms with my own interior life. I don't feel the need to write about it. I'm very interested in the way society works" (*MGI* 7).

As her themes progress, so does her technical command; Drabble explains the development of her artistic control from the sixties to the seventies this way:

> The problem in my early novels was that I simply hadn't the ability to express the range of my feeling. I couldn't technically do it. When I wrote my first novel I didn't know how to write a novel at all. I only began to be aware that I could actually write a novel and include some of the things I cared about when I reached *The Needle's Eye*. ... My first novel I just wrote, day after day, like a very long letter, with no conscious sense of form or plot at all. In the second, I had a little

more sense of shape. In the third, yet more. In the fourth, I tried to write (not very successfully) in the third person; in the fifth, I queried this method of narration, and by *The Needle's Eye*, I found I could do what I'd always wanted, which was to write a third-person novel with the point of view spread between various characters. I now have a much better sense of control. (*BMI* 60)

The Needle's Eye certainly marks the beginning of a more mature phase in Drabble's fiction, for it deals not simply with domesticity and romance, but with money and morality in the modern world, as its title so subtly suggests. All of her later novels reflect this increasing scope in her social vision. In *The Realms of Gold*, Drabble employs archaeology, history, and geology to span the evolution of man from the primal slime to the final cinder. She takes the temperature of the times in *The Ice Age*, as she shows England fighting a new cold war with a second age of ice. In *The Middle Ground*, Drabble explores the cesspool of contemporary British society through the multiple viewpoints of an impressive mixture of characters who represent the social, scientific and feminist aspects of society. *The Radiant Way* traces the intertwined narratives of three professional women, each representing various facets of intellectual and social life, to present a panoramic public and private view of contemporary Britain—their harmonizing voices constituting her most polyphonic narrative ever.

II SYMBOLIC VEHICLE

This maturing moral vision requires a more sophisticated artistic vehicle. Drabble's symbolism is the key to the other side of her genius, revealing the moralist beneath the realist and raising her fiction above the level of mere journalism to the golden realms of poetry. In fact, the real key to Drabble's underlying moral framework is the substructure of symbolism in her novels: the reason most critics misinterpret *Jerusalem the Golden*, for example, seeing Clara Maugham as a social success, rather than as the moral failure the author intends, results from their tendency to take the word of the heroine, rather than the word of the author embodied in her imagery. The fact that so many of Drabble's protagonists are self-deceived, like Jane Austen's heroines, trapped in a no-man's land between reality and illusion, means that their interpretation of events is not to be trusted—especially when, like Sarah

Bennett, Emma Evans, or Jane Gray, they are also the narrators of their own tales. Consequently, the reader must look to the subtext provided by the symbolism to comprehend the author's real moral framework.

This is particularly important because Drabble's narrator-heroines, personae of the author, are all symbolists. As Cynthia Davis observes, "All of Drabble's protagonists have this need to connect, to grasp the meaning of events by reference to definitive scenes or symbols."[42] Because they initially confuse the ideal world of art with the literal world of reality, they habitually view everything in figurative terms. Drabble's first heroine, Sarah Bennett, remarks, "perhaps people choose their own symbols naturally" (*SBC* 73), and she employs her acquaintances' self-appointed emblems to characterize them. In *The Garrick Year*, Emma Evans is a self-deceived romantic who believes she is a realist and thinks she has rejected the figurative in favour of the literal: "Poetry is one thing and living another," and so, she explains, "I steered clear of poetry for the sake, or so I thought, of the other thing."[43] Rosamund Stacey, the scholar-heroine of *The Millstone*, is so intellectual that she views her personal predicament in terms of literary models, until reading a fictionalized version of her real-life situation shocks her into a recognition of the differences (and similarities) between literature and life. The narrator-heroine of *The Waterfall* is a poet who consciously employs water imagery to symbolize love, literary models to interpret experience, and the metaphorical ambiguities of language to exploit the ironic interaction of ideal and real in her fictional account of her actual romantic passion. The protagonists of Drabble's omniscient narratives are also distinguished by a symbolic cast of mind. The narrator of *Jerusalem the Golden* characterizes the heroine's literary imagination thus: "The world of the figurative was Clara's world of refuge. The literal world which she inhabited was so plainly hostile that she seized with ardour upon any references to any other mode of being."[44] Drabble's first omniscient narrator underlines the irony of the protagonist's self-deception, for Clara misinterprets her own symbols.

A symbol signifies an analogy, usually, authorities agree, by comparing a concrete thing with an abstract concept.[45] Thus, a character, setting, or even an event may be charged with symbolic significance, and the complex interaction of such emblematic details may constitute allegory. Similes and metaphors, various formulations of analogy, may also be used symbolically, and these terms, along with image and emblem, may therefore be used, as I shall use them in this study, to suggest symbolic significance. Thus, a novelist can debate complex moral conflicts in a realistic and dramatic manner because, as one authority puts it, "an idea which would be difficult, flat, lengthy, or unmoving when expressed prosaically and by itself, may be made intelligible, vivid, economical, and emotionally effective by the use of symbols."[46]

A double, starred first in English at The University of Cambridge, where she was imbued with I. A. Richards' methods of literary analysis, still enshrined in the obligatory Practical Criticism paper of the English Tripos, Drabble acknowledges that she uses symbols deliberately: "You store [symbols] up. . . . and actively seek them" (*JTI* 172). As her fiction matures, we can observe her symbolism develop in sophistication, as she becomes increasingly "conscious of plotting my symbolism" (*TWF* 86). Drabble acknowledges that "Studying literature made me very self-conscious about writing novels," because "most students of literature are tempted to look upon books as texts and images and symbols" (*VGMI* 3-5). As a literary critic in her own right and a teacher of fiction for several years at Morley College in London, Drabble is clearly very conscious of literary traditions and fictional techniques. Since Drabble writes as a "practical critic" in both her critical and creative writing, it is helpful for the critic to approach Drabble's own fiction from a similar viewpoint.

Drabble is a particularly well-read and highly allusive writer. She acknowledges that "my mind is like a rag-bin of quotations," so that "I try to conceal my allusions."[47] Her first heroine complains, "I try to resist the temptation to talk in quotations. Sometimes it seems the only accomplishment my education ever bestowed on me, the ability to think in quotations" (*SBC* 45).[48] Drabble acknowledges, "I think this is one of the serious problems of a writer with a literary education, that one tends to use other men's flowers; you tend to steal and to beg and to borrow, and perhaps you expect people to pick them up. . . . you can't become a primeval writer or a primeval reader—you've eaten of the tree of knowledge, and you know" (*VGMI* 25-26). The resulting intertextuality generates considerable resonance in Drabble's fiction.[49]

A consideration of Drabble's emphasis in her own critical writing on symbolism in the work of other authors can throw valuable light on the importance of symbolism in her own creative work. While the creative and critical aspects of Drabble's work differ, they are related, like the light and dark sides of the moon. She explains, "When I'm writing myself, I'm not critical of it. I just let it grow in the dark and I don't take it to pieces. With one's critical mind, you can let it all be in the daylight" (*MPI*). So her daylight critical mind can illuminate her more mysterious creative writing.

All of the authors Drabble focuses on in her own criticism—including William Wordsworth, Emily Brontë, Thomas Hardy, and Virginia Woolf—are symbolists, and it is always the imaginative aspect of their genius that she emphasizes. Wordsworth's ability to embody the eternal in the diurnal is what Drabble most admires: "He believed in those spots of time in one's life when one is in touch with something slightly beyond the immediate. . . . It's the transfiguration of the everyday, which Wordsworth was so good at. . . . this quality of writing about an everyday incident and making it profoundly emblematic" (*DCCI* 72). The romance of the commonplace and the transfiguration of the everyday, the ability to make the most ordinary detail profoundly emblematic, is also what distinguishes Drabble's own artistry.

Drabble considers that her fiction "works very nicely on a poetic, symbolic level" (*VGMI* 36). For an artist whose vision is so profoundly equivocal, as Ellen Cronan Rose demonstrates so convincingly in *Equivocal Figures*, symbolism is the appropriate vehicle, for it courts ambiguity by its very nature. Symbolism is Janus-faced and defies final analysis merely by turning its other cheek. In "Symbolism and Fiction," Harry Levin suggests that the ivory tower is now "a citadel of ambiguity," and Drabble claims to prefer "the ambiguity of art to the certainty of rhetoric."[50] Of all the creative elements that the artist leaves to grow in the dark, symbols are perhaps the most mysterious: "Symbolism is something that comes so deeply out of you" (*VGMI* 40), Drabble affirms. Sometimes deliberately and sometimes unconsciously employed, symbols serve to articulate the intangible and instinctual in Drabble's fiction, for, as she acknowledges, "I don't know what my images mean, but I know they mean something fairly involved to me and I use them because I don't know what I mean in words" (*NSHI* 287). She explains,

"Once you've got a starting image, the thing just naturally goes on. . . . When you're writing in a certain vein, everything grows out of the same source. . . . It's a natural associative process" (*BMI* 51-59). She comments, "Mary McCarthy has written the most brilliant thing on symbolism. She says that all the leaves on a tree are naturally the same, and of course they are. And that's the way symbols grow" (*DCCI* 73)".

The network of imagery in Drabble's own novels grows out of one central symbol as naturally as the leaves on the tree. Each of Drabble's novels centres on a dominant symbol which presents the major theme of the work through a skillful pattern of imagery. In every case, Drabble selects the central symbol as the title for her novel. She has said, "The titles of my books are like the names of my children: it's impossible to imagine having called them anything else."[51] For example, she explains that she chose the title *The Waterfall* because of the significant use of two waterfalls in the novel to symbolize the romantic passion that forms the subject of the work (*NSHI* 291). In fact, she changed the original title from *A Moving Accident* to *The Waterfall*, because, she explains, "*The Waterfall* was a title that is embedded in the work itself" (*TWF* 93). She also altered the original name of her first novel from *The Teething Ring* to *A Summer Bird-Cage*.[52] In both cases, she changed the title from one that emphasized character or theme to one that underlines the symbolism.

The dominant symbol, reflected in the title, unifies each novel and conveys the author's personal vision. In her introduction to the school edition of *The Millstone*, Drabble emphasizes the emblematic importance of the title, as it represents the development of both character and theme in the novel. And in her lecture, "On My Own Works: The Search for a Future," she explains the symbolic significance of many of the titles of her novels, pointing out that most of them are literary or Biblical quotations (*TWF* 91-93). In every case, the symbolism connects the literal and figurative levels of experience and clarifies the conflict between the internal world of the imagination and the external world of actuality in the novel. As Drabble's fiction grows more complex in both theme and style, the major symbol forms the centre of a skillfully interwoven pattern of imagery that constitutes a moral allegory.

When one considers the titles of Drabble's novels, it becomes clear that the concept of a golden realm is central to her vision.[53]   Referring to her own golden titles, *Jerusalem the Golden* and *The Realms of Gold*, Drabble comments that "gold is obviously a very rich image for the woman novelist. . . . certain images, certain themes stimulate the imagination fruitfully and lead one towards a golden discovery. . . . We are trying to imagine the impossible golden world, and into that we have to try to move" (*TWF* 86-87, 116).   Sir Philip Sidney wrote in his *Defense of Poesy* that Nature's "world is brazen, the poets only deliver a golden."[54]   In Drabble's fiction, symbolism "delivers" the golden world of poetry.   The concept of a golden world is central to Drabble's thought, for it connotes an ideal realm of the imagination, a projection of the artist's personal vision.

Drabble's golden vision is the symbolic embodiment of her new morality, signifying an ideal resolution of the contemporary woman's conflict between her duty to her individuality and her responsibility to her community. For this ideal vision, symbolism is the appropriate vehicle, because the artist's transcendent vision of a possible future cannot be realized on the narrative level, but only symbolized on the ideal plane. Drabble has observed that "in a sense I was brought up in too good a world to understand the real world."[55]   While it is clear from the social realist criticism to date that few contemporary novelists understand the real world better than Margaret Drabble, nevertheless it is true that all her fiction suggests an ideal world while portraying the real one. And all of her heroines strive to bring their real world into closer harmony with their ideal image.   To join these two disparate worlds, metaphor, meaning mediator, is the best medium.

Drabble's symbolism unites the real and the ideal through a technique of significant detail where every aspect of her fiction—characterization, action, and setting—functions on both the literal and figurative levels in an allegorical manner. As Creighton observes, "Drabble's metaphorical, allusive language—her 'artistic self-consciousness'—contributes considerable subtlety and depth to her work," as "the literal again becomes the figurative" (*MD* 30, 104).   Drabble combines emblematic characters with moralized landscapes in a complex allegory reminiscent of Bunyan, an author who has had a profound influence on her thinking, as Sadler demonstrates so convincingly.[56]

Drabble's characters may themselves be emblematic: she explains that "I was seeing Anthony [Keating] as standing for old-world British chivalric imperialism" (*JTI* 175). She insists that in *The Waterfall*, the actual waterfall is "less real than the passions of the characters, who, although fictitious, are emblematic in some way, or true beyond truth. True beyond the material representation. They're not real people, but they're true" (*DCCI* 75). The characters' very names may be emblematic: Drabble comments, "I do quite like names which suggest the qualities of the character," because "the name itself seems to impose an image on the personality" (*TWF* 94). She explains: "Rosamund (and Rose) are faintly symbolic because both are very English (the English rose). Jane Gray is a victim. Frances Wingate, a winner. Simon, an apostle" (*BMI* 55).

Even the action of a novel may signify an abstract truth. For example, Drabble writes that childbirth, the subject of *The Millstone*, is emblematic of the concept she wishes to embody in the novel: "It is this duality of feeling—the feeling that hardship and sorrow can be in themselves a source of great joy—that I wanted to describe. And the experience of childbirth (especially in unorthodox circumstances like hers), which is inevitably a combination of physical pain and physical joy, seemed to me a very good, and very natural image for this."[57] Gestation appears to be an archetypal event for Drabble, who explains, "I tend to work the time span of my novels to be almost exactly the time span I take to write the book, which is nine months" (*DCCI* 73)—perhaps because she wrote her first three novels while expecting her three children.

Settings also have emblematic significance in both Drabble's creative and critical writing. Her study of *A Writer's Britain: Landscape in Literature* is devoted to the symbolic use of natural and architectural settings in English writing. She particularly admires Thomas Hardy's fiction for the way that "Man and nature, the real and the symbolic, blend."[58] Certainly settings have a highly symbolic significance in her own creative work, especially when they are used to suggest a moralized landscape. Goredale Scar, for example, which Drabble holds up in *A Writer's Britain* as a prime example of the Romantic sublime, symbolizes the resurrection of the lovers' romantic passion at the conclusion of *The Waterfall*.[59] In *The Realms of Gold*, Frances excavates her own golden realm, not in the golden emporium that she excavates from beneath the arid Saharan sands in exotic Tizouk, but in the golden age of England which she unearths from beneath the damp Midlands loam in humble Tockley. Architectural settings also have symbolic significance in all of Drabble's fiction, notably in *The Ice Age*, a study of real estate and property development.

Drabble's emblematic use of natural and architectural settings brings us to the question of the sources of Drabble's symbolism. Since the source of moral conflict in her fiction is the basic opposition between reality and illusion, the major sources of symbolism in her novels are, appropriately, nature and art. Drabble has acknowledged that "I'm very interested in the relationship between art and life" (*VGMI* 2); "facts and fiction are very interesting, the relationship between the two is very interesting" (*TWF* 90). In *The Garrick Year*, for example, the River Wye symbolizes reality, as opposed to the artifice represented by the Garrick Theatre, for the theatre involves masks, costumes, and role-playing—all the trappings with which the self conceals its true identity. Opposed to this artificial world of illusion and deception is the real world of natural human passions, symbolized by the powerful river that surrounds the theatre, winding like a serpent through the Festival gardens. The river threatens to uproot the theatre, an alien interloper in the sylvan setting, by a flood of its swollen spring waters. It is no accident that Emma Evans' baptism in reality is symbolized by her immersion in the River Wye.

Drabble's emphasis on nature imagery in her fiction reflects the influence of Wordsworth. In her monograph, Drabble particularly celebrates "Wordsworth the nature poet" for his ability to embody the universal in the particular through natural metaphors of "flowers, birds, stars, and the smaller, prettier details of nature" (*W* 108, 64). Nature represents "the holiness of the heart's affections" (*NSHI* 273) for the contemporary novelist as well as the Romantic poet, for Drabble affirms that her fiction is also full of "imagery of nature, the natural world of species, the flora and fauna" (*BMI* 59).

Drabble frequently employs floral symbols, because she believes that art stores emotion which may be recollected in tranquility, much as seeds store life through the dark days. Vegetation forms a metaphor for affection in all of her fiction, symbolizing the triumphant deliverance of her heroines from their ivory towers of art into the real world of nature. The agent of Emma Evans' salvation in *The Garrick Year*, for example, is her daughter Flora, named for the goddess of flowers. At the end of *The Waterfall*, the lovers discover "Heart's Ease," a floral symbol of their individual salvation through love and the resurrection of their affection. The emergence of the heroine from her paralyzing mid-life crisis in *The Middle Ground* is symbolized by her drive home in triumph with her arms full of the flowers she has bought, like Clarissa Dalloway, for the party to celebrate her newly-rediscovered love of life. Similarly, Drabble had her son drive her to the florist to buy flowers for the party to launch *The Middle Ground*—a case of life imitating art (*TWF* 91).

Fauna also fills Drabble's fiction. The bird forms one of her favourite symbols, for she believes that "The spirit of a person is like a bird trapped in his body" (*NSHI* 291). *A Summer Bird-Cage* is filled with "birds" of all feathers, as Drabble uses her title symbol to debate the theme of marriage in this modern parliament of fowls. Emma Evans envisions herself in *The Garrick Year* as a baby bird about to break out of its shell and take wing, symbolizing her emergence from the repressive chrysalis of marriage into fully-fledged identity. And Simon Camish views his trapped spirit as a bird caught in a net in *The Needle's Eye*. Drabble uses birds to symbolize the heart of her hero and to frame the entire allegory of *The Ice Age*, as the narrative begins with the portentous death of a pheasant and ends with the free flight of a wall creeper over the wall of the hero's prison behind the Iron Curtain in Walachia.

Drabble also observes "imagery drawn from rivers, lakes, inland waters, seas, brooks, and rills" (*W* 85) throughout Wordsworth's poetry, and water figures as a central symbol in her fiction also, for she too believes that "water is symbolic" (*NSHI* 287). *The Waterfall*, the most intensely symbolic of Drabble's novels, is positively saturated with images of water symbolizing love, as the heroine, frozen into paralysis by a frigid marriage, melts in a romantic passion signified by the two waterfalls that inspired the title of the novel.

Opposed to this natural world of flora and fauna is the artificial world of culture. While nature forms a constant standard of goodness in Drabble's fiction, art varies in its image from one novel to another. Often the artifice that constitutes the basic opposition to nature is provided by the profession of the protagonist, which generates artful images that conflict with the natural symbolism—as we saw in the case of the

Garrick Theatre and the River Wye. In *The Millstone*, Rosamund Stacey's academic ivory tower isolates her from the marketplace of humanity, and in *The Waterfall*, Jane Gray's poetry, her "sublimated blood," only flows when her life's blood is congealed. Rose, the flower of nature, is crushed under the heavy yoke of law, in *The Needle's Eye*. And in *The Realms of Gold*, Frances Wingate's professional pursuit of archaeology initially prevents her, ironically, from excavating her personal golden realm. Architecture provides the central metaphor in *The Ice Age*, symbolizing the way property imprisons people in constricting structures that paralyze them spiritually.

Architectural symbolism plays a significant part throughout Drabble's fiction. While Wordsworth's influence on Drabble's artistry emerges primarily in the use of natural imagery to signify psychological states, the influence of Arnold Bennett prevails particularly in the use of architectural settings to symbolize social issues. In her mature fiction, Drabble, like Bennett, employs the traditional social symbol of the house to embody her concept of the continuity of the present with the communities of both past and future. Thus, the symbol of the home eventually reconciles the basic conflict between human nature and culture in Drabble's fiction.

In using houses as social symbols, Drabble is following in a tradition of English fiction distinguished by such predecessors as Jane Austen, Charles Dickens, and Henry James, to name but a few. Commenting on her literary hero and kindred spirit Arnold Bennett, Drabble observes that "Bennett's technique is to describe in loving detail the stability, the solidity of the world in which his characters live" (*TWF* 68). She remarks that Bennett's contemporaries criticized his novels as "a mere catalogue of domestic furniture" (*TWF* 72)—a sentiment Virginia Woolf echoed in "Mr Bennett and Mrs Brown." But Drabble explains, "To Bennett, like Lawrence, houses expressed souls. People were not disembodied spirits, and the houses that they built were as much a part of them as their bodies" (*AB* 31). Critics have disparaged Drabble's fiction for the same reason, complaining that "People are characterized far less by their looks or their talk than by their domestic interiors" (Sage 75). But Drabble says, "I always feel a need in novels to describe precisely where people live."[60]

Drabble could say of herself what she writes about her latest heroine, Liz Headleand in *The Radiant Way*: "Her largest dreams, her most foolish fantasies, had been enacted in bricks and mortar and mantelshelves and tiled floors and plaster ceilings,"[61] for Drabble's family home, a redbrick Edwardian row house overlooking Hampstead Heath and backing onto Keats's garden, is so precious to her that, even after she married literary biographer Michael Holroyd in 1982, they both maintained their separate establishments, spending weekends and holidays together in an eminently modern marriage. Drabble has also bought a country house in Somerset where she can write her novels undisturbed.[62]

Houses symbolize psychological themes in Drabble's early personal fiction. The small warm room at the top of the stairs in the deserted house, where Jane Gray (like Jane Eyre) faces her solitary confinement in *The Waterfall*, is a uterine symbol, a metaphorical womb where mother as well as daughter is delivered. As Showalter observes, "For a Drabble heroine, a room of one's own is usually a place to have a baby" (336), and indeed Drabble commented that she herself had a baby in circumstances very similar to Jane Gray's. In *The Garrick Year*, the Victoriana with which Emma Evans overlays her rented home, to conceal its ugly functional modernity from sight, parallels her attempt to camouflage her character with deceptive theatrical costumes.

However, houses symbolize Drabble's social themes in her mature social fiction. In *The Needle's Eye*, Rose Vassiliou's house in Middle Road is built by faith on the rock of renunciation in order to symbolize in its shabby tattiness her democratic ideal and her freedom from the guilt of corrupt capitalism. In *The Realms of Gold*, Frances Wingate finally discovers that her leaden vision, symbolized by the dour Eel Cottage, is countered by her golden vision, embodied in the enchanting Mays Cottage. The Englishman's castle, High Rook House, is the heart of an intricate network of architectural symbols in *The Ice Age*. In *The Middle Ground*, Kate Armstrong's house—the setting for the party to celebrate her reaffirmation of the joy of life—forms the nucleus of society, for there Kate, at the centre of her family circle, conducts her own domestic symphony with a harmony that echoes the music of the spheres. Liz Headleand is less distressed by her husband's desertion than by the prospect of moving from their Harley Street home to "Menopause Mansions" (258) in *The Radiant Way*.

We can trace a distinct development throughout Drabble's

fictional career in the complexity and subtlety of her symbolic technique as it progresses from simple image to complex allegory. In *A Summer Bird-Cage*, she uses the images of the birds in the gilded cage and the flowers in the summer garden to categorize her characters and symbolize their options regarding marriage in a simply schematic manner. Drabble affirms that "In *The Garrick Year* I became aware for the first time that I was using continuous themes and symbols" (*TWF* 79), for here she employs opposing imagery of nature and artifice to symbolize, in the River Wye and the Garrick Theatre, the heroine's complex internal conflict between reality and illusion. Drabble uses celestial symbolism with subtle irony in *Jerusalem the Golden* to suggest the self-deception and moral failure of her protagonist. In *The Waterfall*, Drabble interweaves her dominant water symbolism with imagery of heat and cold to suggest the way that lovelessness freezes the life's blood of her heroine into frigidity, and affection melts it into flowing fountains of life. Drabble's symbolism constitutes a complex allegory in *The Needle's Eye*, as Rose founds her faith on the democratic dogma of her disciple Simon, but ultimately yields to the capitalist Christopher's creed of love. Drabble excavates a very rich symbolic goldmine in *The Realms of Gold*, where she employs the metaphor of archaeology to generate rich strata of symbolism from the womb of Mother Earth, as her archaeologist heroine delves into the past to excavate the golden age of old England. Drabble affirms, "By this time I was very, very conscious of plotting my symbolism and putting the images in the right place and it was all highly deliberate" (*TWF* 86). In *The Ice Age*, Drabble portrays the golden age of England, excavated in *The Realms of Gold*, frozen over again by a deadly new frost, as property speculators dissect the land and deface the nation, creating a waste land of England's Eden. Drabble explains, "By this time I was very conscious of symbolism and a lot of it takes place in prison" (*TWF* 90); she punishes the perpetrators of this crime against nature by incarcerating them in jails as constricting as the dehumanizing structures in which they have imprisoned the people of contemporary Britain. Drabble's symbolism extends to new heights and depths in *The Middle Ground*, where it becomes both a muckrake for exposing the cesspool of society and a starscan for exploring the cosmos. Kate Armstrong—an alchemist, like the author, who turns "shit into gold" (19)—overcomes her worm's-eye view of social architecture when a bird's-eye view of divine architecture reveals the design in the carpet in an eloquent echo of Mrs Dalloway's rhapsody on London: "The city, the kingdom. The aerial view" (218). Where Drabble's vision was squalid, even excremental, in *The Middle Ground*, her vision in *The Radiant Way* is truly demonic, damning both public and private life, until the characters discover in the darkness of the past the monstrous truth that will enable them to overcome the quagmire of the contemporary and illuminate the radiant way into the future.

Drabble insists, "I'm looking for meaning. I'm looking for guidance or help or illumination" (*NHI* 280). She also acknowledges that "Criticism can quite validly illuminate the meaning of symbols that the writer perhaps wasn't conscious of" (*DCCI* 73). Accordingly, the aim of this study will be to illuminate the artist's moral vision by elucidating her symbolic vehicle.

NOTES

[1] Sheridan Baker, "The Contemporary British Novel," *American Libraries*, October, 1974, p. 489.

[2] Lorna Sage, "Female Fictions: The Women Novelists," *The Contemporary English Novel*, Stratford-Upon-Avon Studies 18, ed. Malcolm Bradbury and David Palmer (London: Edward Arnold, 1979), 66. *Critical Essays on Margaret Drabble*, ed. Ellen Cronan Rose (Boston: G.K. Hall, 1985), demonstrates that Drabble criticism is developing greater critical sophistication in the eighties.

[3] Phyllis Rose, "Our Chronicler of Britain," *New York Times Book Review*, 7 September 1980, p. 1.

[4] Joyce Carol Oates, "Bricks and Mortar," *Ms.* 3 (August, 1974), 35.

[5] Rosalind Miles, *The Fiction of Sex: Themes and Functions of Sex Difference in the Modern Novel* (Plymouth: Vision, 1974), 168.

[6] Quoted by Bernard Bergonzi, "Margaret Drabble," *Contemporary Novelists*, 2nd ed., ed. James Vinson (London: St. James, 1976), 373.

[7] Margaret Drabble, *The Tradition of Women's Fiction: Lectures in Japan*, ed. Yukako Suga (Tokyo: Oxford Univ. Press, 1982), 82.

[8] Virginia Beards, "Margaret Drabble: Novels of a Cautious Feminist," *Critique*, 15 (1973), 35-47, and Joanne Creighton, "Margaret Drabble's Double-Voiced Feminism," in "Margaret Drabble: Feminist Novelist?" a Special Session including Ellen Cronan Rose, Mary Hurley Moran, James Gindin, and Sheridan Baker, organized by Nora Foster Stovel for the 1985 MLA meeting in Chicago.

[9] Mel Gussow, "Margaret Drabble: A Double Life," *New York Times Book Review*, 9 October 1977, p. 40.

[10] Margaret Drabble, *The Middle Ground* (London: Weidenfeld and Nicolson, 1980), 3.

[11] "An Interest in Guilt: Margaret Drabble Interviewed by Bolivar Le Franc," *Books and Bookmen*, 14 (September, 1969), p. 20.

[12] Iris Rozencwajg, "Interview with Margaret Drabble," *Women's Studies*, 6 (1979), 345.

[13] Diana Cooper-Clark, "Margaret Drabble: Cautious Feminist," *Atlantic Monthly*, 246 (November 1980), 71.

[14] Margaret Drabble, "A Woman Writer," *Books*, 11 (Spring, 1973), 6.

[15] Bernard Bergonzi, *Contemporary Novelists*, 372.

[16] "Margaret Drabble Interviewed by Gillian Parker and Janet Todd," *Women Writers Talking*, ed. Janet Todd (London: Holmes & Meier, 1983), 165.

[17] Valerie Grosvenor Myer, *Margaret Drabble: Puritanism and Permissiveness* (London: Vision, 1974), 13.

[18] Elaine Showalter, *A Literature of Their Own: British Novelists from Brontë to Lessing* (Princeton, N.J.: Princeton Univ. Press, 1977), 6.

[19] Marilyn Powell, "An Interview with Margaret Drabble" (Toronto: CBC, 1980).

[20] Bernard Bergonzi, "Novelists of the Sixties" (London: BBC, 1968).

[21] Ellen Cronan Rose, *The Novels of Margaret Drabble: Equivocal Figures* (London: Macmillan, 1980), 129.

[22] Margaret Drabble, "The Author Comments," *Dutch Quarterly Review of Anglo-American Letters*, 5 (1975), 36, 38.

[23] Gail Cunningham, in "Women and Children First: The Novels of Margaret Drabble," in *Twentieth-Century Women Novelists*, ed. Thomas F. Staley (London: Macmillan, 1982), 130-152.

[24] Joyce Carol Oates, in a review of *The Needle's Eye* in the *New York Times Book Review*, 14 June 1972, p. 23.

[25] Peter Firchow, "Margaret Drabble," *The Writer's Place: Interviews on the Literary Situation in Contemporary Britain*, ed. Peter Firchow (Minneapolis: University of Minnesota Press, 1974), 105. Mary Hurley Moran, *Margaret Drabble: Existing Within Structures* (Carbondale: Southern Illinois Univ. Press, 1983), explains how Drabble places the individual within a traditional moral context.

[26] Angus Wilson, "Literary Landscapes," *The Observer*, 17 October 1979.

[27] Margaret Drabble, *The Waterfall* (London: Weidenfeld and Nicolson, 1969), 282.

[28] Nancy Poland, "Margaret Drabble: 'There Must Be a Lot of People Like Me,'" *Midwest Quarterly*, 16 (Spring 1975), 264.

[29] Barbara Milton, "Margaret Drabble: The Art of Fiction LXX," *The Paris Review*, 20 (Fall-Winter, 1978), 59.

[30] F. R. Leavis, *The Great Tradition* (London: Chatto & Windus, 1948), 4.

[31] Margaret Drabble, *The Oxford Companion to English Literature* (Oxford: Oxford Univ. Press, 1985), 557-58.

[32] Anthony Thwaite, in a review of *The Needle's Eve, New Statesman*, 31 March 1972, p. 430.

[33] Margaret Drabble, in a 1974 letter to Valerie Grosvenor Myer.

[34] Margaret Drabble, *A Summer Bird-Cage* (London: Weidenfeld and Nicolson, 1963), 215, 200, 146.

[35] Nancy S. Hardin, "An Interview with Margaret Drabble," *Contemporary Literature*, 14 (1973), 294.

[36] "Margaret Drabble in Conversation with Valerie Grosvenor Myer" (London: British Council, 1977), 7.

[37] Margaret Drabble, *Wordsworth* (London: Evans, 1967), 80.

[38] Margaret Dabble, *Arnold Bennett: A Biography* (London: Weidenfeld and Nicolson, 1974), 342.

[39] Lynn Veach Sadler, *Margaret Drabble* (Boston: Twayne, 1986), 6.

[40] Joanne Creighton, *Margaret Drabble* (London: Methuen, 1985), 14, 33.

[41] Nicki Household, "Love Story: *The Waterfall*," *Radio Times*, 8 November 1980, p. 25.

[42] Cynthia Davis, "Unfolding Form: Narrative Approach and Theme in *The Realms of Gold*," *Modern Language Quarterly*, 40 (1979), 396.

[43] Margaret Drabble, *The Garrick Year* (London: Weidenfeld and Nicolson, 1964), 106.

[44] Margaret Drabble, *Jerusalem the Golden* (London: Weidenfeld and Nicolson, 1967), 34.

[45] *Webster's New World Dictionary of the American Language*, rev. ed., ed. David B. Guralnik (New York: Popular Library, 1979), 606, defines symbol as "a visible sign of something invisible; an object used to represent something abstract"; Myer Abrahams, in *A Glossary of Literary Terms*, 4th ed. (New York: Holt, Rinehart and Winston, 1981), 195, writes, "A symbol, in the broadest sense, is anything which signifies something else"; William York Tindall calls "a symbol an exact reference to something indefinite. . . . a symbol seems the outward sign of an inward state," in "Excellent Dumb Discourse," *The Literary Symbol* (New York: Columbia Univ. Press, 1955).

[46] *The Princeton Encyclopedia of Poetics*, ed. Alex Preminger (Princeton, New Jersey: Princeton Univ. Press, 1974), 833-36.

[47] David Leon Higdon, "An Interview with Margaret Drabble" (1979), unpublished, 14.

[48] The typescript of *A Summer Bird-Cage* in the Mugar Library of The University of Boston shows that Drabble cut out the following statement: "We used to fine each other a shilling each time we used a quotation, one term at college. It used to work out rather hard on me" (44).

[49] See John Hannay, *The Intertextuality of Fate: A Study of Margaret Drabble* (Columbia: Univ. of Missouri Press, 1986).

[50] Harry Levin, "Symbolism and Fiction," *Contexts of Criticism* (New York: Atheneum, 1963), 192; Margaret Drabble, "Personal Matters," *New Statesman*, 89 (14 February 1975), 220.

[51] Margaret Drabble interviewed by Nora Foster Stovel, London, 1980.

[52] The typescript of *A Summer Bird-Cage*, originally titled *The Teething Ring*, is in the Mugar Memorial Library of Boston University. The typescript of *The Waterfall*, originally entitled *A Moving Accident*, is in the McFarlin Library of The University of Tulsa.

[53] I discuss this topic in "Margaret Drabble's Golden Vision," *Margaret Drabble: Golden Realms*, ed. Dorey Schmidt (Edinburg, Texas: Pan American Univ. Press, 1982), 3-17.

[54] Phillip Sidney, *An Apology for Poetry*, ed. Forrest G. Robinson (New York: Bobbs-Merrill, 1970), 15.

[55] Margaret Drabble, in a 1974 letter to Valerie Grosvenor Myer.

[56] See Sadler on Bunyan's influence on *The Needle's Eye*, pp. 55-63. Creighton confirms Bunyan's influence on Drabble: "Deeply influenced as a young girl by *Pilgrim's Progress*, Drabble creates characters, like Bunyan's, who are wending their way through an uncharted 'moral landscape,' a world where old values are no longer tacitly accepted and new views are unclear" (*MD* 18).

[57] Margaret Drabble, "The Author's Introduction," *The Millstone*, ed. Michael Marland (Harlow: Longman, 1970), xiii.

[58] Margaret Drabble, "Hardy and the Natural World," *The Genius of Thomas Hardy*, ed. Margaret Drabble (London: Weidenfeld and Nicolson, 1975), 169.

[59] Margaret Drabble, *A Writer's Britain: Landscape in Literature* (New York: Knopf, 1979), 126-29.

[60] Dee Preussner, "Talking with Margaret Drabble," *Modern Fiction Studies*, 25 (Winter, 1979-80), 572.

[61] Margaret Drabble, *The Radiant Way* (Toronto: McClelland and Stewart, 1987), 18.

[62] Margaret Drabble interviewed by Nora Foster Stovel, Edmonton, 1987. In a 1 November 1988 letter to Nora Foster Stovel, Drabble remarks, "We have bought a house by the sea in Porlock, Somerset. I shall become the person from Porlock."

Chapter Two:

BIRD, BEAST, AND FLOWER: MARRIAGE AND SYMBOLISM IN *A SUMMER BIRD-CAGE*

Margaret Drabble reveals herself as a fledgling symbolist in her very first novel. In *A Summer Bird-Cage* (1963), she employs imagery of birds, beasts, and flowers to symbolize the variations on her theme of marriage. The central symbol of matrimony is the bird-cage of the title; in fact, Drabble deliberately changed the title of the novel from *The Teething Ring*, a name that emphasizes the *bildungsroman* theme, to *A Summer Bird-Cage*, a name that underlines the symbolism.[1] The opening epigraph from John Webster's play, *The White Devil*, explains the significance of the title symbol: "'Tis just like a summer bird-cage in a garden: the birds that are without despair to get in, and the birds that are within despair and are in a consumption for fear they shall never get out."[2] Drabble interprets: "The novel was about two girls wondering whether to marry or not: one married, one unmarried, each envying the other what seemed to be her freedom" (*TWF* 91). For the university-educated woman, the conflict between marriage and career is particularly acute in Drabble's view.[3]

Drabble's *Summer Bird-Cage* is filled with birds of all feathers, appropriately enough, for she uses the title symbol as an organizing principle to debate the subject of marriage in this modern parliament of fowls. The distinctive characteristic of her narrator, Sarah Bennett, is her literary imagination, for she is a recent Oxford graduate with a brilliant degree in English, like the author. Sarah views all the "birdy girls"[4] of her acquaintance figuratively as fowl aflutter to enter the conjugal cage or in a flap for fear they may never escape the tender trap.

Sarah's first marital models are close to home. She views her mother as a bird fluttering helplessly but cheerfully chirping in her domestic prison. Sarah is touched by "poor brave twittering Mama, pretending everything had always been so lovely," but "the courage and desperation of Mama that underlaid the nonsense and fuss and chirruping" leave Sarah feeling "sick with the whole idea of marriage" (21). The discouraging example of her parent's marriage prompts Sarah to leave the nest, but Mrs. Bennett is a mother hen who is loath to see her chicks fly the coop: "you won't want to stay here all your life cooped up with your poor old mother, will you? I shall lose all my little ones at one fell swoop, shall I?" (65), she quavers. Mrs. Bennett's clucking, reminiscent of her namesake in Jane Austen's novel, initially deters Sarah from domesticity.[5]

Sarah's Oxford friend Gill, who has married for love, is a different sort of bird. After a squalid conjugal squabble, an abortion, and a separation, Gill feels like "one of these dead birds that farmers hang in the fields to scare the live ones away" (114)—a scarecrow, warning other young birds away from marriage. Gill's bad example instills in Sarah a wariness about marrying for love: "It was so sad, that a girl like Gill should be beaten simply because she had taken a gamble on love. Because that did seem to be the reason. She had jumped in with her eyes shut, and she had got nowhere. I began to wonder if I myself would ever dare to get married. There were so many dangers" (95).

Sarah's elder sister has done the opposite to Gill: after refusing to marry for love, Louise has made the cynical choice of marrying for money. So Sarah visualizes her predatory, aquiline sister as a bird of prey, soaring high overhead and crowing with satisfaction after pursuing her quarry successfully: "I did not think that the drabness and despair which threatened to ooze over my life in every unoccupied second would ever swamp Louise: she was way off, wealthy, up in the sky and singing" (25). But a mercenary loveless marriage to the owlish novelist Stephen Halifax, author of *The Decline of Marriage*, seems an unattractive alternative. Sarah concludes that marriage for either love or money is undesirable: "I was dimly beginning to formulate the idea that of all the many kinds of marriages, Gill's and Louise's represented some kind of extreme, and that both extremes were to be avoided" (78). Sarah complains, bewildered, "but who did that leave me as my model? My parents?" (95).

Given the unattractive fates of all these married birds, the logical alternative is not to enter the conjugal cage at all. For a woman as independent as Sarah, with her interest in being an Oxford don, a single life does hold some appeal, as she admits to herself while she lies between the tight sheets of her narrow girlhood bed in spinsterish delight. But the condition of the poor birds left stranded outside the cage proves even more pathetic than those caught in the domestic trap, as Sarah realizes when she observes these next two birds in the bush. Sarah's first model of spinsterhood is the Bennetts' *au pair* girl, Kristen, who resembles a goose or seagull to Sarah's lively imagination. Kristen does prove to be a silly goose, and the seagull simile seems an obvious Chekhovian symbol for a young bird doomed to tragedy. Sarah's cousin Daphne, the stereotypical spinster, "a cross between a symbol and a cartoon" (117), is an archetypal ugly duckling. Her sombre fate constitutes an awful warning to Sarah, for this drab bird makes Sarah feel "stagnant and covered in oil and dead feathers" (120), like a dead duck swamped by an oil slick.

Neither fish nor fowl in this matrimonial aviary, Sarah is actually an "angel," a bird of quite a different feather. Sarah's fiancé writes, "I know you must be extravagant, my lovely angel, I wouldn't have you clip your wings and put up with the common good of life, so burn the time away till nightfall" (85-86). As an angel, aloof from the human fray, Sarah is in an ideal position to observe the marital status of others. Temporarily separated from her fiancé by an ocean, the narrator inhabits a no-man's-land, neither caught in the conjugal cage nor shut out of it. In this state of marital limbo, Sarah vacillates wildly between the two marital extremes throughout her narrative, declaring at one moment, "I'm not getting married" (30), and announcing at another, "I'm definitely going to get married when my fiancé gets back" (143). Perched thus on the matrimonial fence, she is in an ideal position to determine on which side the grass is greener. Her judgment, based on the models provided by the various birds of her acquaintance, is pessimistic: inside or outside the bird-cage of marriage, female fate seems equally doomed. Sarah feels that she is on the horns of a dilemma: "What happens otherwise is worse than what happens normally, the embroidery and the children and the sagging mind. I felt doomed to defeat. I felt all women were doomed" (29).

A Summer Bird-Cage is a bestiary as well as an aviary, and wild animals stalk its pages, for Drabble uses both beasts and birds to categorize her characters. The narrator divides human nature into two camps: sheep and goats, herbivores and carnivores. Sarah has always viewed her sister as her opposite, an antagonist or alter ego, so she is surprised to realize that she and Louise are on the same side of the fence for once: "if there is a barrier down the middle of mankind dividing the sheep from the goats I am certainly on Louise's side of it as far as physical beauty goes" (21). Sarah has always considered Louise an arch-predator, but it is a revelation to discover that she herself is one of the carnivorous breed. Louise, the initiate, instructs Sarah, her protégé, in self-knowledge: "you can't pretend you're not one of the most exclusive of all . . . the most predatory . . . for all your fish and chips, SallyO, and your down-at-heel shoes." Their carnivorous nature forms a bond between the two sisters: "you know what I mean, we're in it together, you and I. . . . We're the predatory type, don't you think? The flesh eaters? I'd rather eat than be eaten," Louise declares (171-72).

Louise teaches Sarah the difference between herbivores and carnivores, for Cousin Daphne is the archetypal herbivore: "She reminds me of those tame shabby animals in zoos, odd gnus and cows and things, so docile and herbivorous that they don't even bother to put them behind bars, but let them wander around loose (171). She declares, "Give me the flesh eaters, let them all eat each other up, if they can catch each other, and let the others go on chewing the cud" (174). But the carnivores and herbivores need each other, for the thrill of the hunt is enhanced by the admiring audience provided by the cud-chewers: "we can't live without the herbivores. . . . we live by our reflection in their eyes" (165), Louise explains.

Unfortunately, the carnivores devour the herbivores and have to be enclosed in the conjugal cage to protect their vulnerable victims. As they pace their cages, the predators are watched with fascination by the ruminators who wander at liberty in the garden. While Louise and her lover play at being bears and smugly flaunt their mutual satisfaction before their audience, Sarah ruminates: "They looked by Louise's own definition, very predatory. For some reason they seemed to enjoy my company, and I guessed, from watching them, that they needed an audience to build up the striking, wicked image of themselves. In fact, I was playing at being a herbivore for a while, and gazing with admiration into the dangerous caves of the fiercer breed. I didn't mind. It soothed my conscience. Perhaps I am a herbivore at heart, and only predatory by conviction" (189). Sarah is learning.

The conjugal cage can become a cozy cave, it seems, while

at other times it is clearly a prison. Successful predators like Louise are sometimes caught in their own trap, for a cage, no matter how gilded, is still confining. As she paces the floor with a padding, rhythmic step on the eve of her marriage, Louise looks to Sarah "like an animal in a small cage trying to take exercise" (22). After leaving her sister's matrimonial ménage, Sarah feels liberated, as if she has just escaped from a prison: "I began to run through all the grand spaciousness and calm of the street, as though chains had been loosed from my ankles, as though a burden had been lifted from my back" (139). So Sarah finally concludes that she would rather not enter the conjugal cage at all.

Other kinds of beasts stalk the summer garden, however, ready to pounce on unwary birds who flutter freely outside the cage. Depressed by her separation from her fiancé, Sarah feels hunted like a prey by savage psychological creatures: "I had been crouching inside the walls of my consciousness terrified to move too far or too violently in case they collapsed and left me looking at the wild beasts. In the pre-crisis days I feel like someone living in a paper house surrounded by predatory creatures" (85). But after a declaration of faith from Francis, Sarah "could feel the wild beasts slinking away with their tails between their legs, balked of their rightful prey" (81). Apparently her fiancé, whose name suggests Saint Francis, has the power to tame the savage creatures of Sarah's psyche.

Although Louise finally persuades her sister that she too is just a wolf in sheep's clothing, initially, Sarah feels more like the sacrificial lamb: "I looked at myself in fascination, thinking how unfair it was, to be born with so little defence, like a soft snail without a shell. Men are all right, they are defined and enclosed, but we in order to live must be open and raw to all comers" (29). Although both sisters are clearly carnivorous, Sarah believes that all women are "born to defend and depend instead of to attack." Unsure of which side of the fence she should be on, Sarah vacillates between the camp of the predatory beasts and their vulnerable victims. And it takes her until the end of her tale to realize that beneath her brittle shell her self-contained sister may be vulnerable too.

Vegetation fills the garden surrounding the bird-cage, and Drabble uses flora as well as fauna to symbolize her "panorama of female lives" (*VGMI* 12). The narrator characterizes her acquaintances by their own emblems of flower, fruit, or foliage. She observes: "perhaps people choose their own symbols naturally, for Gill always has in her room vast masses of green leaves, any leaves, chopped off trees or hedges, whilst Stephen and Louise have dried grasses in long Swedish vases" (73). Although Gill is surrounded by foliage, after her separation and abortion, she lacks both flower and fruit. Louise's dried grass is also symbolic of her sterile union. Both emblems suggest to Sarah that marriage for either love or money is fruitless.

The "black twig with one yellow flower like a Japanese painting" that Sarah's spinster friend Simone selects as her emblem reflects her black, twig-like script and symbolizes to Sarah Simone's solitary rootlessness.[6] Sarah reflects, "never since then have I seen her writing without the image of that twig and that leafless, austere yellow flower. It was so like her, so deliberately chosen" (73). Sarah's cousin is a classic virgin, reminding Sarah of her namesake from Greek mythology: "Daphne, who was chased by a god and was turned into a tree to preserve her virginity." Considering her cousin's solid trunk, Sarah reflects: "Perhaps there is some truth in that fable. Something our Daphne had preserved. Who would rape a tree?" (33).

While Gill and Louise warn Sarah off marriage, then, Simone and Daphne illustrate the bleak alternative. Like the fruitless Gill and the sterile Louise, the twiggy Simone and the wooden Daphne serve as awful warnings to budding girls. Sarah realizes that each of her female acquaintances is fatally limited: "Simone, the flower without the foliage, and Gill, the foliage without the flower." Not willing to settle for Simone's flower, Gill's leaf, Louise's grass, or Daphne's trunk, Sarah craves the complete harvest: "I should like to bear leaves and flowers and fruit, I should like the whole world" (73).[7] Sarah's vision of the fullness of life recalls the final image from Yeats's poem, "Among School Children": "O chestnut-tree, great-rooted blossomer, / Are you the leaf, the blossom or the bole?" But only at university can one find the full bouquet, Drabble believes.[8] Spoiled by the collegiate cornucopia, Sarah realizes that she is now merely grasping at straws: "I learned how difficult it was to get anything, let alone the everything that is showered on one in garlands and blossoming armfuls until one faces the outside world" (63). But these youthful laurels have inspired in Sarah a desire for the whole harvest.

Sarah and Louise are both symbolized by individual flowers from the full bouquet of life—the roses and lilies each carries in the wedding procession. Sarah's yellow roses embody her femininity as well as her vulnerability. She realizes that she does not suit Louise's lilies: "I looked too pink and fleshy for the white intactness of those flowers. I looked less intact than Louise, ironically enough. I looked horrifyingly pregnable" (29). The lily, symbolizing Louise, is the major floral emblem in the novel. Louise looks like a lily, and this resemblance is reinforced by her affectation of white apparel. Sarah makes the symbolic significance of the lily explicit when she quotes these lines from "that sinister Shakespearean sonnet, which had come into my head the first time I heard that Louise had chosen lilies for her bouquet":

They that have power to hurt and will do none,
That do not do the thing they most do show,
Who, moving others, are themselves as stone,
Unmoved, cold and to temptation slow:
They rightly do inherit heaven's graces . . .
Lilies that fester smell far worse than weeds. (75)

Louise also reminds Simone of "that piece which begins 'They that have power to hurt and will do none'" (71). Sarah reflects with bewilderment, "But Louise, of course, had the power to hurt and did it."

Louise's resemblance to the lily turns sour on the eve of her wedding, suggesting the festered flower of the sonnet: "Everywhere was littered with ash, little grey worms of it all over the carpet, and Louise herself looked quite fantastic, her long hair all wild and tangled up with two odd curlers stuck in the top, and her skin glistening white and deathly with cold cream" (23). On her wedding day, Louise arises, "looking wax-coloured and stiff" (25), suggesting the funereal associations of the lily, rather than the bridal ones. The narrator emphasizes the sinister significance of Louise's selection: "Louise's bouquet was made of lilies, huge virginal lilies, very formal," which "would have done equally well for an altarpiece." Sarah reflects, "what a nerve, really, to choose flowers like that. There was something theatrical about them, as well as something ceremonious" (28).

The apparently inappropriate associations of the lily symbolize many of the novel's themes: their ceremonious quality implies the formal pretentiousness of Louise's wedding, a façade masking a hollow farce; their theatrical appearance skillfully suggests the deceptive illusion of Louise's marriage, plus the posing of this consummate actress and the stage career of her lover; the lilies' aura of virginity reinforces the impression of Louise's affectation of a traditional role to conceal her unconventional behaviour; and the funereal sense of the lilies, which casts a pall over this strange wedding, suggests the doomed nature of this disastrous union. All of these associations signify the contrast between appearance and reality which Sarah fails to penetrate. The lily symbol implies that Louise is a whited sepulchre, or the White Devil herself.

Although Sarah perceives the pretentiousness of Louise's lilies, ironically, she cannot comprehend the significance of her own symbols, where her sister is concerned, until the resolution of the story. Sarah does realize, however, that, as a bride, Louise is pure symbol, like the lilies she carries, all form and no substance. Observing the admiration of the wedding guests, Sarah concedes, "For them she was the real thing: and for me too she almost was, for that half-hour, as meaningless and pure as the flowers she carried. By virtue of form, not content. Symbol, not moral" (33). This concept, embodied in the formal lily, represents the underlying theme of appearance and reality in the novel. Louise is addicted to appearances, and Sarah laments their power: "How unjust life is, to make physical charm so immediately apparent or absent, when one can get away with vices untold forever" (32). Louise affects veneers that mask reality; she is certainly one of those who "do not do the things they most do show." For example, the white wedding cake façade of the Halifax house on Honeyman Gardens conceals their hollow home. Similarly, Louise employs her hypocritical marriage to camouflage her adulterous affair. But Sarah is unable to penetrate the mystery of Louise's motivation. for this *ingenue* is blinded, not simply by naiveté, but also by prejudice. Sarah is trapped in the psychological cage of her own jealousy: jaundiced by sibling rivalry, like the author, her view of her sister only goes skin deep.[9] While Sarah, the *voyeuse*, is the narrator, and Louise, the *poseuse*, is the heroine of Sarah's story, the real protagonist of the novel is Sarah herself, and Louise is her antagonist. The crucial development of Drabble's novel is Sarah's initiation into reality, as well as Louise's introduction to truth, for Sarah cannot comprehend the significance of her own symbols or penetrate the moral behind the symbol.

The important lesson both sisters have to learn is the difference between appearances and "the real thing." Sarah finally recognizes the motives behind Louise's curious *ménage-à-trois* when she realizes that Louise enjoys provocation and that she is "one of those that enjoy it more than the real thing" (146). Finally Sarah realizes that the real thing is love—appropriately enough for what she calls "such a female love-love-love story as this" (197). Love is the lesson both sisters have to learn. Louise and Sarah both want everything—to "have one's cake and eat it" (63), in their own phrase. In the context of *A Summer Bird-Cage,* this implies both the security of the conjugal cage and the freedom of the garden. Louise demonstrates to Sarah one way a woman can have her cake and eat it, and for a time it seems to Sarah that her sister has indeed achieved everything—a wealthy, famous husband, plus an attractive, devoted lover: "I envied her bitterly at that moment. It seemed that she had everything and love as well. Everything shall be added unto you, as Jesus Christ once said. Seek ye first the kingdom of this world and everything shall be added unto you. What a bribe. And I said to myself, Louise always wins. Whatever she does, she wins. And I lose. I've too much wit and too little beauty, so I lose" (194). It seems to Sarah that Shakespeare was right: "to them that hath it shall be given. . . . They rightly do inherit heaven's graces, / And husband Nature's riches from expense." So Sarah prays initially to her false idol for the cynicism to make her successful: "Louise teach me how to win, teach me to be undefeated, teach me to trample without wincing. Teach me the art of discarding. Teach me success" (25).

Envy underlies not only Sarah's misinterpretations but also Louise's motivations. Louise finally confesses that jealousy of Sarah prompted her decision to marry the neurotic novelist Stephen Halifax for his money, while retaining the attractive actor John Connell as a lover: "I thought I'd be free, to have my cake and eat it. To keep love as a sideline" (211). She teaches her sister more than she intends, however, for Sarah learns from Louise's example that to divide is not the way to conquer. The outcome of the action vindicates Sarah's idealistic values and invalidates Louise's mercenary ambitions. The protégé proves wiser than the pedagogue: when Louise advises, "Don't you ever marry for love, Sarah. It does terrible things to people," Sarah retorts, "So does the other thing"

(212). Shakespeare was right; the garden-variety weed may be more beautiful than the cultivated bloom, as the central lines of the sonnet (that Sarah significantly omits) demonstrate:

> The summer's flow'r is to the summer sweet,
> Though to itself it only live and die;
> But if that flow'r with base infection meet,
> The barest weed outbraves his dignity:
> For sweetest things turn sourest by their deeds;
> Lilies that fester smell far worse than weeds.

Louise admits that in marrying for money instead of for love, "I knew that I was breaking some kind of rule of the heart."[10] The results of this crime against nature impel her to reject "all that money and duplicity"—proving, to Sarah's surprise, that "all these childish idols of truth and honesty were real" (209).

Louise is finally forced to drop her White Devil mask along with her bridal lilies, as she steps out of her false role as conventional wife in an artificial marriage. This symbolic strip occurs at the climax of the story, when Louise's husband surprises her in the bath with her lover. Louise is forced to abandon her *grande dame* pose, not so much by the discovery itself, as by the fact that she is caught wearing a plastic bath-cap. At this point Sarah's love story descends perilously close to sex farce.[11] The plastic bath-cap tale makes Sarah realize that Louise "must at heart be quite fond of both John and me: of John, to have worn it, and of me, to have told it" (216).

Finally, Louise advises Sarah to marry for love: "I think you should marry Francis" (215), she concludes. She admits that her own decision to marry for money instead of love was not the result of sophisticated cynicism, but of timid feebleness: lack of faith in her lover's affection frightened her off a love-match. Sarah also acknowledges that in urging her fiancé to accept a scholarship abroad, she may have just been avoiding the overwhelming question: "It is only now, at the time of writing (or rather, indeed rewriting) that it occurs to me that I may have been simply delaying the problem of marriage" (78).

The parable of *A Summer Bird-Cage* resolves the narrator's initial question about matrimony, as she decides finally to keep faith with love. In a swift *dénouement*, Sarah reveals that she is awaiting her fiancé's imminent homecoming and implies that she plans to end her moratorium on marriage.[12] She also discloses that Louise is living with her lover, who turns out to be genuinely in love with her. Sarah predicts that "she may even marry him in the end, if she can ever face the fact that he really is fond of her" (216). So the narrative ends on an optimistic note, with the hope that it is possible to reap the whole harvest through love in marriage. As Sarah says, "respecting Francis I sometimes think I may be able to have my cake and eat it" (103).

A Summer Bird-Cage has resolved not only the question of marriage, but also the problem dividing the two sisters. Louise's failure demonstrates to Sarah that her sister is human after all, with real blood in her veins. Sarah learns to her surprise that "blood is thicker than water" (200), and Louise discovers that they are indeed sisters under the skin. Blood sisters, they are bound by their idealistic imagination:

> I saw for her what I could never see for myself—that this impulse to seize on one moment as the whole, one aspect as the total view, one attitude as a revelation, is the impulse that confounds both her and me, that confounds and impels us. To force a unity from a quarrel, a high continuum from a sequence of defeats and petty disasters, to live on the level of the heart rather than the level of the slipping petticoat, this is what we spend our life on, and this is what wears us out. (215)

Both moralists and symbolists then, the two sisters learn to live on the level of the heart, uniting both the security of the summer bird-cage and the liberty of the garden where they may gather their laurels.

While the narrator has used symbolism in a simply schematic manner to categorize her acquaintance in terms of her dilemma about marriage *versus* career, Drabble has employed symbolism much more skillfully and ironically, for Sarah has failed, until the climax of the novel, to comprehend her own symbols or to penetrate the moral behind them. This failure to interpret reveals her own prejudices towards her sister, her delusory view of reality, and herself—deception regarding her own character. In fact, the two sisters are both moralists and symbolists, as they finally discover, bound together by their shared values and figurative imaginations. But they cannot understand themselves or each other until they learn to comprehend each other's symbols; nor can they comprehend each other's symbols until they learn sympathy, trust, and affection for each other. Thus, the fledgling symbolist demonstrates in her first book the ironic and subtle use of symbolism that she will develop more fully and skillfully in her next novel, *The Garrick Year*.

NOTES

[1] The typescript of *A Summer Bird-Cage*, bearing the original title, *The Teething Ring*, is in the Mugar Memorial Library of Boston University. The author's maiden name, Drabble, is also replaced in the manuscript by her married name, Swift. The typescript includes twenty-five pages of a canceled romantic subplot which Drabble says her editor made her cut out (*WFI* 116). Drabble used the slight episode with Jackie Almond (196-201) to replace the cancelled subplot, which chronicles Sarah's fling with Tony, the estranged husband of her flatmate Gill, including an overnight trip to Brighton.

[2] John Webster, *The White Devil*, I, ii, 44-48.

[3] Drabble states that *A Summer Bird-Cage* was about "the purpose of education for women and the choices it offers" (*BMI* 45). She explains:

> I'd just left university and I was pondering on the problem of what women were expected to do in society, what kind of roles they were expected to fulfill . . . women were supposed to be educated, highly educated, as the characters in that novel are. They are then supposed to leave home and get a job, but they are also supposed to get married and these things seemed to be pointlessly combined in society, and I think that's what I was writing about in that book. (*VGMI* 1)

[4] Margaret Drabble, *A Summer Bird-Cage* (London: Weidenfeld and Nicolson, 1963), 7. Subsequent references to this edition will be given in the text.

[5] Drabble comments, "When I began writing, in my innocence I called my characters after Jane Austen characters. In *A Summer Bird-Cage* the characters are called Bennett which is the Bennett from *Pride and Prejudice*" (*TWF* 93). Certainly Mrs. Bennett is silly and nervous, like her namesake, and Mr. Bennett is superior and sarcastic, like his. The Bennett sisters are, true to form, obsessed with marriage,

and their contrasting characters recall Austen's two central sisters. Even the prejudice of the main character, Sarah, is similar to Elizabeth Bennet's. Drabble's rather arch style in this early novel is also reminiscent of Austen's playful wit. The name Bennett reflects Drabble's interest in Arnold Bennett as well.

[6] Rose opines that Simone is "a kind of cartoon representation of Simone de Beauvoir. . . . in Sarah Bennett, Drabble has dramatized the situation of the young girl, as de Beauvoir describes it in *The Second Sex*" (*EF* 5-6).

[7] Myer observes that "Flowers for Sarah mean fulfillment, achievement and abundance," but judges that "vegetation symbolism had been used over-explicitly" in this early novel (*PP* 163).

[8] Drabble comments that "One of the big changes in my life was from university to non-university. . . . at Cambridge I was always busy, constantly employed, constantly the center of a little bit of somebody's attention—and then, suddenly—absolute nothingness for the rest of one's life" (*IRI* 343). "The Month," *Twentieth Century*, 168 (1960), 73-78, the first article Drabble ever published, written during her last week at Cambridge, is about the same subject as her first novel, namely the shock of coming down from university and facing the freedom of the future.

[9] Drabble confesses, "I had a sister, of whom I had been jealous for a long time, and that was what I wrote about" (*VGMI* 13). Her sister, novelist and critic A. S. Byatt, wrote a novel called *The Game* (1967) which appears to be a reply to *A Summer Bird-Cage*.

[10] Drabble comments, "A lot of the plot was based on *Middlemarch*, with the two sisters and the honeymoon in Rome, where she realizes that she has married a terrible man"—quoted by Bernard Bergonzi in *The Situation of the Novel* (London: Macmillan, 1970), 22.

[11] Drabble observes that "I was very keen on tragedy. But when I wrote my first novel and decided that it was going to have a funny ending (the beautiful older sister caught by her husband in the bathtub with her lover) I thought, 'I'm really going to be a different kind of person!' This is wonderful, I felt. Life is going to be good, not bad" (*BMI* 56).

[12] Drabble comments retrospectively on the prospective marriage which concludes *A Summer Bird-Cage*:

I got married in 1960, and everybody got married, you see; you just rushed from university to the wedding ring and then you huddled your babies in and out of the cradle, and ten years later people don't do that. . . . If that character in that first novel had been leaving university now, she certainly wouldn't have got married in that blind and foolish way. She doesn't get married, actually, in the novel, but you can tell she's going to, as soon as that man gets back. (*VGMI* 12)

Chapter Three:

ILLUSION AND REALITY:
THE GARRICK THEATRE AND THE RIVER WYE

Margaret Drabble has stated that "*The Garrick Year* is very much an account of my own experience in the theatre" (*TWF* 78). After graduating from Cambridge University, where they acted together, Margaret Drabble and her first husband, actor Clive Swift, married in 1960 and launched joint theatrical careers. Drabble explains that "*The Garrick Year* was about a year we spent in Stratford-on-Avon with the Royal Shakespeare Company" (*NSHI* 291). "It was very much a novel of sour grapes" (*BBI* 7), she acknowledges: bored with her role as Vanessa Redgrave's understudy, Drabble wrote *The Garrick Year* in her dressing room while waiting to go on stage and babysitting her firstborn, Adam. Motherhood soon forced Drabble to forego acting altogether in favour of writing, although theatre continued to provide food for her fiction. Nancy Poland has commented that "Theatre people fill her books, and she impaled the life in a novel called *The Garrick Year*" (*NPI* 258). The stage provides more than the backdrop for this novel, however; theatre is the central symbol of Drabble's major theme of illusion in *The Garrick Year*.

The Garrick Year (1964), like its predecessor, *A Summer Bird-Cage*, is about marriage. But whereas Sarah Bennett was merely contemplating marriage, Emma Evans is already married and a mother, as Drabble herself was when she wrote the novel. In *The Garrick Year*, Emma is facing the first major conflict of her marriage, as she and her actor husband go to the Garrick Theatre Festival, where they are both unfaithful to their marriage vows.

Since the surface subject of *The Garrick Year* is secret infidelity, the underlying theme of the novel is the opposition between appearance and reality, as the characters are deceived about the true nature of their marriage. This conflict between illusion and truth is symbolized by the opposition between the Garrick Theatre and the River Wye. Drabble's themes and symbols are rooted more organically in the action of *The Garrick Year* than they were in *A Summer Bird-Cage*, arising naturally out of the situation of the novel. Drabble has observed that "In *The Garrick Year* I became aware for the first time that I was using continuous themes and symbols" (*TWF* 79). Let us consider first Drabble's use of the metaphor of theatre to represent the theme of illusion and secondly her contrasting use of nature imagery to symbolize reality.

The Garrick Theatre of the title is the major symbol in the novel of the mutual deception that threatens to destroy the Evans marriage. Theatre is an appropriate emblem of duplicity, for it involves masks, costumes, and role-playing—all the trappings with which the self conceals its true identity. Drabble makes skillful use of all these facets of professional theatre to dramatize the characters' personal pretensions.

The Garrick Theatre actually causes the couple's marital conflict, for Emma foregoes a lucrative new job as a television announcer in London in order to accompany her actor husband to the Garrick Theatre Festival in the hinterlands of Hereford, exacerbating the struggle for domination that characterizes their highly competitive union. The couple resolve this conflict by a curious covenant: Emma accedes to the Garrick proposal in exchange for her husband's agreement to a moratorium on their marital relations. So the Garrick year actually embodies the stalemate in their marriage.

Drabble portrays this deadlock symbolically: Emma's rejection of her husband's sexual advances and her insults to his acting profession incite him to drive his fist through the William Morris wallpaper of their bedroom (the pride of Emma's life), causing a crack to spread through their fragile Victorian home and plaster to rain down on their bed. Emma recalls the symbol of "Our marriage bed, pushed out into the middle of the room, stranded there far from the harbour of the walls, and filled with grit, with David and myself far from unhappy in it. That was perhaps the beginning of the Garrick year, for me."[1] Emma is right about the shipwrecked marriage launching the Garrick year, because this leaky vessel finally founders at the festival. Nature abhors a vacuum, and both spouses initiate love affairs at the Festival directly after this sexual stalemate.

The Garrick Theatre provides more than the location and provocation for these adulteries, however. Drabble uses theatre as a metaphor for the mutual deceptions which endanger the marriage. Both affairs take place under the Festival umbrella with members of the theatre company, all adept at duplicity: Emma has a flirtation with the famous director, Wyndham Farrar, and her husband David has an affair with his fetching leading lady, Sophy Brent. It is appropriate that Emma is deceived by an actor, for there is a "verbal and social association of actor and hypocrite," as Drabble points out in "The Unheroic Mode," a long undergraduate essay on drama which was instrumental in winning the author the starred first in English at Cambridge; Drabble also observes that "The theatre is one huge confidence trick," for it is essentially "a form which involves deceit."[2]

In *The Garrick Year*, Drabble enforces the metaphor of theatre to symbolize the duplicity that threatens the Evans union by comparing the cast's onstage action with the characters' offstage activities in an ironic counterpoint, for the lovers' trysts are staged during rehearsals of *The Clandestine Marriage*. This comedy by David Garrick (in which David plays "Brush" to Sophy's "Fanny," and in which Drabble's own husband acted at the Chichester Festival) is an appropriate choice to inaugurate the new Garrick Theatre, as well as the characters' first infidelities.

The dramatic irony of *The Garrick Year* is intensified by the fact that the deluded heroine recounts her own deception in this first-person confessional novel. The entire narrative consists of Emma's retrospective view of this first major crisis in her marriage, as she recalls "that strange season, that Garrick year, as I shall always think of it, which proved to me to be such a turning point" (7). The Garrick year marks a turning point both in her marriage and in her own development, for Emma has yet to learn the crucial difference between reality and illusion, affection and affectation. Emma states the major theme of the novel: "Appearances are misleading" (114). But so far is she from seeing through deceptive surfaces herself that it takes a domestic disaster to open her eyes to the underlying truth. Like her namesake in Jane Austen's novel, Emma deceives herself most of all.[3]

Before Emma can comprehend her own nature or the nature of her marriage, she must understand her relationship with the major symbol of illusion in *The Garrick Year*—theatre itself. The Garrick Theatre is a crucial character in the novel, and Emma's relationship to the theatre is very complex. Her contempt for theatre in general and the Garrick Festival in particular is both cause and effect of the conflict in her marriage. Although she protests (perhaps too much) that she is related to the theatre only by marriage, she looks like an actress—so much so, in fact, that she decides, "I felt it my duty to end the walking misrepresentation which is myself" (83). While she insists that she has no ambitions for the stage, she admits that she does have aspirations towards gloss, which can be mistaken for the same thing. A comparison between the solid moral substance of her old school friend Mary Summers and the superficial media gloss of the actress Sophy Brent, both extroversions of conflicting aspects of Emma's character, forces Emma to acknowledge the streak of flippant gloss in her own nature. Emma has, in fact, been a fashion model in her pre-marital career, and she confesses that "my appearance has always obsessed me" (120). Moreover, the celluloid drama of television, in which she is so keen to play a part, is actually just an extension of theatrical illusion.

Nevertheless, Emma despises theatre for its unreality: "What was the theatre itself but one huge irrational sham, made for fantasy and fiction, not for fact? To me it hardly seemed to touch reality at any point" (76). She is particularly contemptuous of the Garrick Festival as an extreme example of unreality, because it has been financed by a Mrs. Von Blerke, a rich American widow who fancies herself related to David Garrick and who has actually been an actress of sorts before the mercenary marriage that provided her with the fortune she uses to found the Festival. Emma contemplates the Garrick's bizarre origin: "The theatre must I think be peculiarly prone to romantic aberrations of this kind, for in it people are always discarding the checks of common sense and allowing the more ridiculous elements in human nature to take over, the elements of gross vanity, of jealousy, or even generosity" (61). The question is, which ridiculous element in human nature has taken over Emma?

Emma sees herself as a practical woman, or at least a factual one. Her philosophy is stoical and her standards are puritanical. She has rejected the figurative in favour of the literal: "Poetry is one thing and living another," and so, she explains, "I steered clear of poetry for the sake, or so I thought, of the other thing" (106). The daughter of a Cambridge don, Emma has grown up with a passion for facts.

Even while she is breastfeeding her baby, Joseph, she studies typed lists about the Angevin Empire and events preceding the Sicilian Vespers. Emma's self-image clearly contains a large dose of self-deception, for these facts are far stranger than any fiction.

Emma and David appear to represent opposing principles in the debate between truth and illusion which constitutes *The Garrick Year*: David is devoted to drama, whereas Emma thinks she is a realist. Certainly David is the quintessential Thespian, like his namesake David Garrick: a mere "selfish, drama-besotted actor" (30) in Emma's words. He personifies the artificial illusion of the stage, for David is a sham as a man: his rugged pretensions mask his wishy-washy nature. Emma pities "poor David, who has no more self than a given quantity of water, and who is always trying to contain his own flowing jelly-like shapelessness in some stern mould or confine, because he is I think afraid of the aimlessness of his own undirected violence" (75). That, of course, is why he is an actor. In fact, David's acts of violence (such as hurling Emma's bust of Mary Wortley Montagu downstairs, narrowly missing their sleeping infant son Joseph) create the vivid dramatic tableaux which highlight critical turning points in the narrative—and in the marriage.

Emma, on the other hand, despises acting as sloppy emotional self-indulgence by a pack of megalomaniacs. She declares that it "isn't even an art, it's just entertainment at its highest and prostitution at its lowest" (20). In the relationship between audience and performer that comprises personal interaction in Emma's view, she prefers the role of spectator to that of actor. While David is spectacularly active, Emma is emphatically passive. She camouflages herself in order to preserve her anonymous role as passive observer in the dangerous guerilla warfare that constitutes social intercourse in her view. Like the observer-narrator of *A Summer Bird-Cage*, Emma Evans is indeed a *voyeuse*.

But Emma is actually an inveterate role-player as well. As Dee Pruessner observes, Drabble employs "the metaphor of life as theatre, where everyone plays a part or observes others playing parts" in *The Garrick Year*.[4] Emma herself embodies this principle, for she plays parts in order to conceal her true identity, even from herself.[5] By the Garrick year, Emma has grown bored with her old roles of wife and mother. In fact, she begins to suspect that she has been miscast, and so she decides to try her wings in the new role of television personality. Her rejection of the role of wife is represented by her repeated repulsion of her husband's sexual advances. Sloughing off her maternal role is represented by weaning her baby: "I had had enough of maternity.... I was sucked dry" (81). Balked of the role of professional woman, Emma is doubly frustrated to find herself (like Fanny Price in *Mansfield Park*), the only person with no part to play in the drama.[6] So she decides to cast herself in the role of mistress of the "Master Builder" of the Garrick Theatre, Wyndham Farrar, the powerful director who holds her husband's future in the palm of his hand.

Emma and David do represent opposing relations to theatre and reality, then, but they are the opposite of what they appear. Husband and wife declare themselves in an argument about the art of acting which is at the heart of *The Garrick Year* (73-75).[7] David believes in the contemporary philosophy, "Be yourself," whereas Emma advocates the traditional art of imitation. David declares, "I don't believe acting has anything to do with imitation." He believes, rather, that the whole art of acting is actually a question of truth, as the actor discovers his own character through playing dramatic parts.[8] Whereas David uses his stage roles to reveal his true self, Emma hides behind her life roles in order to conceal her real identity. David protests, "I don't want to spend my life covering myself up in wigs and muck," while Emma dresses up for a party in a scene that has all the significance of the ritual arming of a knight for battle in mediaeval romance. Emma even overlays her home with the same decorative Victoriana which she uses to camouflage her person, whereas David, like the big ugly wardrobe that embodies functional modernity, represents modern life. The real difference between David and Emma, then, is the fact that he is honest with himself about his histrionic impulses, whereas she is grossly self-deceived.

Emma's addiction to theatrical illusion is actually instrumental in inspiring her infatuation with both David and Farrar, because she has fallen in love with each man as an image on the screen, before ever laying eyes on him in the flesh. The subliminal memory of Emma's glamorous image on the glossy cover of a fashion magazine has also influenced both men's infatuation with her. So Emma's marriage and her love affair are both proof of the power of dramatic illusion. Drabble stage-manages each romance in an extremely theatrical manner, with highly dramatic deployment of lighting: being in the limelight with her lover (under a streetlamp with David at lights-out and in the glimmer of a match with Wyndham during a theatre blackout) prompts Emma to fall in love both times.

Although she believes she is a realist, Emma is actually an incurable romantic. She prefers the prospect of romance to real love in the here and now. Her addiction to anticipation accounts for both the success of the Evans courtship and the failure of their marriage, as well as the appeal of her affair with Farrar. Initially, David represents a romantic prospect to Emma: "All I wanted was this feeling of terror with which he inspired me: with him, I felt that I was on the verge of some unknown and frightful land, black desert, white sand, huge rocky landscapes, great jungles of ferns" (30). But the romantic landscape that looked so glamorous in anticipation is less enchanting in reality: "In the case of our marriage, perhaps the rocks and the speed and the dust that I had foreseen were exactly what I had found, though under one's tired feet the aspect of a distant landscape changes, and becomes endowed with human exhaustion, with blisters and sweat and broken nails" (37).

Emma's repeated provocation of David is actually a futile attempt to revive the delicious terror he first inspired: "I have never been so frightened in my life and perhaps the whole of my effort since has been nothing but a struggle to repeat that fright" (29). Once she has succeeded in provoking his to an act of violence, such as driving his fist through the bedroom wall, she is satisfied, and he is strangely appeased: "We were both awestruck; I was so impressed that I was not even angry, for this seemed to be a manifestation of the David I had known, the man at whose approach graves opened, fountains leapt out of rocks, and trees and women gathered to listen" (22). As reality replaces romance, Emma laments, "the only thing which never returned was my first rocky terror" (34).

The failure of the Evans marriage is the old story of "Passion choked by domesticity (32), for Drabble believes that "Real passion cannot thrive in domestic harmony" (*NHI* 23). By the Garrick year, Emma realizes that the romance of their relationship has faded beyond recall. Marriage has deprived her, along with her twenty-two-inch waist, of hope and expectation, the comfortable illusions by which she lives.

Consequently, Emma has to look to a new love affair with Farrar for the titillation of that uncertain feeling which constitutes romance for her: "Doubt being the essence of excitement, I was excited and happy . . . for we were both regarding, with a little awe, the unpredictable" (117). Initially, Wyndham appeals to Emma because "his very manner promised duplicity . . . concealing rather than revealing what he had to say" (61). But reality is always a letdown for someone with her great expectations: "After so much expectation, I was overcome with doubt when I actually set eyes on the man" (146). Inevitably, their romance becomes deflated, like Emma's breasts. Eventually Emma realizes, "Poor old Wyndham, I think he is basically a sham, he has all the attributes of quality without quality itself" (220)—the quintessential man of the theatre.

The distinctive feature of Emma's affair with Farrar is its artificiality. They drive around and around in circular futility, failing to consummate their infatuation. Emma uses the images of "a fly in amber, or a sour black walnut, or a dead brown rose that I once saw trapped in a block of cut glass" to symbolize "the strange pickled charm" (120) of this curiously dispassionate affair. The deception involved in their clandestine trysts is precisely what appeals to Emma: "I had embarked upon deceit" (123), she declares with delight.

In fact Emma does not want a real affair at all, but merely the appearance of one, as symbolized by her preference for rehearsals to performances and *hors d'oeuvres* to *entrées*. When Wyndham accuses her of preferring prawn cocktails to juicy red steaks, Emma admits, "It's just that I connect love—well, lying on beds and so forth—I connect that with babies. And being tired. And wanting to go to sleep. And I don't want all that, I just want to have a good time" (172).[9] It is revealing that Emma is never willing to consummate the affair—"I simply could not bring myself to do it" (168)—and only does so at last as a means of concluding the relationship. The truth is that Emma wants the façade of an affair with Farrar to protect her from real love with David: she declares to Wyndham, "I don't know you. I don't want to know you. . . . I only know one person, and that's David, and I don't want to know anyone else. It's horrible, quite horrible, knowing people" (172).

As soon as their secret liaison becomes public knowledge (before it has even taken place), its function is fulfilled for role which she rejected in favour of the false role of mistress. It forces her to recognize that "the kind of romantic, self-centred indulgence that an affair with Wyndham had promised" is "against my nature and against my situation" (220). Emma's immersion strips off all of her false pretentions at last, leaving her literally exposed. Significantly, it forces her finally to remove her artificial costume and don garments belonging to the natural Sophy. So Flora effects Emma's salvation by proving that maternity is her natural role and true passion.

Not everyone is saved, however: Emma's friend Julian is drowned by the treacherousness of the sylvan Wye.[14] Like Emma, Julian has been uncertain of his true sexual nature and his real role in life, but lacking Emma's terrestrial roots (since the young homosexual actor has no offspring to bind him to life) he has gone under. Emma realizes, "Indecision drowned him. I used to be like Julian myself, but now I have two children, and you will not find me at the bottom of any river. I have grown into the earth. I am terrestrial" (221). Considering "the sylvan Wye, which got Julian and made a bid for my Flora" (222), Emma realizes that she has become, quite literally, an earth mother. Emma is the first of Drabble's heroines to find the source of her survival, and indeed salvation, in maternity.

Although motherhood has saved her from death by water, Emma has suffered her own sea change, for these disasters have taught her sympathy for human suffering. As a result, she has learned compassion for the uninflated truth of literary accounts of human tragedy, like Wordsworth's "The Idiot Boy."[15] She acknowledges, "I weep partly as an apology for my past ignorance, from which I might never have been rescued" (222).

Comparing Julian's fate with her own prompts Emma's self-knowledge: "I being different, and being what I am, am made for survival. . . . The truth was that I could survive anything, that I was made of cast iron" (220). Self-knowledge involves not only being aware of her own strength, however, but also becoming conscious of her human limitation. In accepting their real limits, paradoxically, Drabble's early heroines discover their true strength.

Recognizing her natural limitations also causes Emma to acknowledge that parenthood necessitates marriage, for children require a father as well as a mother: "David is necessary too" (209), as even Farrar realizes. Typically, Emma cites philosopher David Hume as her authority for her new conviction: "'Whoever considers', Hume says, 'the length and feebleness of human infancy, with the concern which both sexes naturally have for their offspring, will easily perceive that there must be a union of male and female for the education of the young, and that this union must be of considerable duration'" (222).

Emma has already recognized the economics of affection that bind herself and David together, but acknowledging her personal limitations makes her realize that she and her husband must also be united in caring for their children. Although they are conflicting characters, their unity of enthusiastic tenderness for their offspring proves that "We had too much in common by now, David and I, ever to escape" (219). Even before the Festival, Emma knew that in "the anatomy of our marriage, there remained something that could not be dissected, for it was still alive: and it was this live thing that made it impossible for us to part" (24). No autopsy then, Emma's narrative is a vivisection, for the crises that conclude her tale prove that the living bond between the couple has survived the duplicitous adulteries of the Garrick year. Emma keeps repeating, "'I love you David,' for quite a long time, not particularly because I meant it or felt it, but because I knew that in view of the facts it must be true" (219). And so Emma finally abandons her false, "theatrical" affair with Farrar in favour of her real relationship with her husband.

As autumn falls and the artificial theatre season draws to an end, *The Garrick Year* concludes with a family excursion into the countryside to celebrate the revival of the Evans marriage. True to the reassertion of reality at the climax of the novel, however, their happiness is not unadulterated, for Emma dreams beforehand of an ideal love for Julian which reflects in an ironic manner on her real relationship with David. She imagines that she and Julian are soul-mates who fuse in an ecstasy of spiritual love, far removed from the down-to-earth slap-and-tickle of the Evans adulteries. Their idealized love is set in the Edenic gardens of ancient England: Islington is portrayed in a state of grace, before its natural vegetation is overlaid by human artifice, and human nature is depicted in a prelapsarian state of innocence, unadulterated by sexuality.[16] "It was like a scene out of a book, a passion out of a poem, it had all the pure intensity that never occurs in life, the dizzy undistractedness, with no rivers, no children" (205).

This idyllic vision prefigures the concluding scene of *The Garrick Year* in an ironic manner, for it emphasizes the difference between Emma's fictional passion and her actual marriage and points up the contrast between ideal nature in a state of innocence and real nature which contains within itself the seeds of evil. The rural reunion represents a partial paradise also, for, in this pastoral setting, with domestic peace restored, Emma and David come as close as they ever can to perfect happiness: "Had David and I been two entirely different people we might well that afternoon have been entirely happy," Emma concedes; "and even being what we were, we did not do too badly" (223).

But there is always a snake in the garden, even in Eden. Drabble concludes *The Garrick Year* with a startlingly symbolic scene which reflects all the nature imagery of the novel and culminates the theme of appearance and reality. In this apparently paradisal setting, the author reveals the real presence of concealed evil in the potent image of a serpent. Emma espies with horror a wild snake curled up and clutching at the belly of an innocent sheep. Like the treacherous river, the snake symbolizes the potentially destructive power of nature, as well as the sexuality which has threatened domestic peace. The image suggests the serpent in the Garden of Eden, symbolizing knowledge of evil. Emma actually acknowledges the significance of the snake, conceding, "the Garden of Eden was crawling with them too" (223). Although she perceives the snake, she pretends not to, keeping up appearances for the sake of the children. Emma's ambivalent attitude to this archetypal symbol of sexuality implies some uncertainty on the author's part about the permanence of the reunion. The ambiguity of the concluding emblem suggests that, while Emma has been initiated into maternal affection, she has not yet fully acknowledged sexual passion. In *The Garrick Year*, Drabble reaffirms reality and restores the natural order in the traditional manner of comedy, but the sinister symbol of the serpent suggests beneath the comic mask the horror of mortality.[17]

NOTES

[1] Margaret Drabble, *The Garrick Year* (London: Weidenfeld and Nicolson, 1964), 22-23. Subsequent references to this edition will be documented in the text. The typescript of *The Garrick Year*, a gift of February, 1966, is in the Mugar Memorial Library at Boston University. It includes what Drabble labels "one or two false starts," involving a brief scene, written previously, in which Wynden Mortwood (an early version of Wyndham Farrar), rehearses Sophy Brent.

[2] I wish to thank Margaret Drabble for giving me this unpublished paper which exhibits such interesting connections with *The Garrick Year.*

[3] Drabble observes that "Emma in *The Garrick Year* is also a Jane Austen character" (*TWF* 93).

[4] Although Preussner observes the metaphor of life as theatre in "Patterns in *The Garrick Year*" (*GR* 117), she does not pursue this motif, but rather focuses on Emma's identity, concluding: "In rejecting the possibility of playing active roles and in hiding behind various disguises, including motherhood, Emma also refuses the possibility of journeying toward an integrated, whole self" (126).

[5] Drabble comments in "An Interview with Margaret Drabble" by Joanne V. Creighton (*GR* 18-31): "She's displaying herself; and he's not telling the truth most of the time. She's much more of a performer" (22).

[6] Drabble compares her own attitude to theatre to Emma's:

> I wrote [*The Garrick Year*] while I was living in Stratford, and almost in the theatre world, but just outside it, which is a rather unhappy position when one is keen and does want to act, as I did. And I wrote it not exactly to get my own back, but to establish myself outside it in a sense. Not wanting to be part of it. And I wouldn't identify myself with the heroine's really very malicious and satiric view of actors. I like actors very much. I think obviously the novel did spring out of mixed feelings. But the heroine in the novel doesn't like the theatre at all, and never has, whereas I was a kind of an outsider who wished she was inside. In a sense it's become more real to me since I wrote the book. When I wrote the book I was definitely on the side of the theatre, and I've now become more critical and am very glad I didn't become an actress. I was prevented by circumstances from doing it. (*BBI* 7-8)

[7] This debate on the art of acting is one of two excerpts

from *The Garrick Year* that Drabble chose to read aloud on the 1967 BBC Radio programme, "Novelists of the Sixties."

[8] It is ironic that the role in which David declares himself is the part of Flamineo, a character whom David describes as "A rotten bastard and a social climber and a pimp" (42). The play in question is *The White Devil* by John Webster, from which Drabble took the title, epigraph, and central symbol for *A Summer Bird-Cage*. The typescript of *The Garrick Year* shows that Drabble cut out the following interesting passage about the play, which has intriguing parallels with the themes of the novel:

> David was going to be very good. I had also been unwillingly impressed by the play. It still seemed an extraordinary choice for a festival season, but what I had at first thought to be a mere incoherent sequence of dazzling phrases, which had delighted in a shallow fashion my eclectic taste, had begun to emerge as a real play, a real thing about something, decadence, infidelity, or that strange last-ditch courage which makes such strong dramatic material: 'Contempt of pain, that we may call our own,' as one of Webster's characters cries in another play. Even in a cosy English shelter contempt of pain is often enough called upon; it is a virtue as much of decadence as of violence, and the presentation of it moved me. (20)

[9] In discussing Emma as a victim of *anorexia nervosa*, Rose concludes that, "by rejecting steak, Emma is symbolically and unconsciously rejecting sex" (*EF* 10).

[10] Drabble says, "I tend to work the time span of my novels to be almost exactly the time span I take to write the book, which is nine months" (*DCCI* 75).

[11] Preussner observes that "Drabble means the river as a symbol of life and abundance . . . on a symbolic level, we can see Emma's fear of this life-force . . . . When Emma finds a decayed apple on the river bank, it becomes clear that the place is a kind of fallen, mutable Eden" (122-24).

[12] Several critics, including Myer, Beards, and Rayson, have observed that Drabble heroines combine sexual frigidity with passionate maternal feeling. Drabble herself commented in a 15 October 1974 letter to Myer: "The motherhood/frigidity syndrome I find enthralling as a problem."

[13] This is the other scene that Drabble read aloud in "Novelists of the Sixties." Myer comments, "Her salvation comes, apparently, after she has jumped into a flooded river

to rescue the child from drowning. There are hints that she has been baptised by her total immersion in the flood-waters and has found rebirth" (*PP* 19).

[14] Drabble has explained that *The Garrick Year* is "all about drowning" (*NSHI* 281), and consequently culminates with an actual drowning (*TWF* 79). Rose comments, "On the symbolic level, to drown means to yield, to assent to, one's own sexuality" (*EF* 113).

[15] Drabble writes that "The Idiot Boy" demonstrates that, even in such a situation, "The instinct of normal motherly love will survive" (*W* 56).

[16] In "The Pastoral Vision," Drabble writes, "Behind these images of pastoral idylls lies the concept of natural nature, the Garden of Eden of unfallen man" (*WB* 49).

[17] A version of this chapter, entitled "Staging a Marriage: Margaret Drabble's *The Garrick Year*," appeared in *MOSAIC*, XVII/2 (1984), 161-74, reprinted in *"For Better or Worse": Attitudes Towards Marriage in Literature*, ed. Evelyn J. Hinz (Winnipeg, 1984).

Chapter Four:

THE IVORY TOWER AND THE MARKETPLACE: ART AND REALITY IN *THE MILLSTONE*

The Millstone (1965) is a novel about a single woman having a baby. This topical subject has made *The Millstone* the most read, translated, and analyzed of all Drabble's novels.[1] It was also the first to be broadcast (on *Woman's Hour* in 1966), the first to be filmed (as *A Touch of Love* in 1969), and the first to be published in paperback in the USA (as *Thank You All Very Much* in 1969).[2] More notorious than famous at first, however, *The Millstone* caused a great uproar when it was first broadcast on the BBC, "because I had mentioned an illegitimate baby," Drabble confesses, and "I had to make a broadcast explaining and apologizing" (*TWF* 11-12).

Childbirth, not illegitimacy, is the subject of *The Millstone*, however. Drabble wrote an introduction to the 1970 English school edition of the novel to correct this popular misinterpretation.[3] Far from intending *The Millstone* as a feminist tract advocating unmarried motherhood, Drabble makes it clear that she simply omitted the usual circumstances of husband and home in order to emphasize the influence of motherhood on her heroine's development. She explains that she used childbirth in *The Millstone* as a symbol of the paradoxical effect of experience on character:

> It is this duality of feeling—the feeling that hardship and sorrow can be in themselves a source of great joy—that I wanted to describe. And the experience of childbirth (especially in unorthodox circumstances like hers), which is inevitably a combination of physical pain and physical joy, seemed to me a very good, and very natural image for this. (xiii)

The symbol of this paradox, Drabble explains, is the millstone itself:

> The millstone of the title has a double significance—in one sense it is the baby itself, which is a source of pain, expense and social disgrace to its mother, but in another, far more significant sense the word refers to

the verse in the Bible where Christ says that those who harm little children should have millstones tied round their necks and be sunk in the bottom of the sea. (xii)

Drabble explains this apparent contradiction: "It was a kind of double reference. The child was both a millstone and a salvation because once it became obvious to Rosamund that she couldn't suffer any more harm from the child, the millstone was lifted from her" (*NSHI* 280). Tracing this change in the significance of the millstone symbol from punishment to salvation will measure the extent of the character's development in the course of the novel.

The heroine of *The Millstone*, Rosamund Stacey, is in desperate need of development: more solipsistic than her predecessors, she is alienated from reality, from humanity, and even from her self. The first-person narrative method, which Drabble uses for the third and last time in *The Millstone*, is perfectly suited to the self-absorption of this highly introspective character. Rosamund's confessional narrative is really a form of self-analysis, as she strives to unify her divided self. She actually characterizes herself as a split personality at the outset of the novel, declaring in her opening statement, "My career has always been marked by a strange mixture of confidence and cowardice: almost one might say, made by it. . . . Confidence, not cowardice, is the part of myself which I admire, after all."[4]

The world in which this career woman is confident is her professional work, and the realm in which she is cowardly is her personal life, for she is unable to love. She quotes the old adage, "Lucky in work, unlucky in love," and challenges Byron's chauvinist maxim: "Love is of man's life a thing apart, 'tis woman's whole existence—as Byron mistakenly remarked" (9). While Rosamund is an efficient professional, she is a personal incompetent, since love eludes her: "Eventually the idea of love ended in me almost the day that it began. Nothing succeeds like success, and certainly nothing fails like failure. I was successful in my work, so I suppose other successes were too much to hope for" (8).

Since Rosamund is a research student writing a doctoral dissertation on English poetry, the dichotomy she experiences between professional and personal signifies a division between literature and life. In *The Millstone*, Drabble dramatizes a debate between art and reality. Rosamund embodies this conflict perfectly, for she is completely divided between the literal and figurative realms of experience. Terrified of love and life, she habitually escapes from the marketplace into the ivory tower of academe.

Rosamund's research intensifies the division in her character between reality and artifice, for she has deliberately selected an artificial, escapist luxury subject: "I'm a dilettante, I mean to say, Elizabethan sonnet sequences, it isn't as though I were even doing nineteenth-century novels or something worthy like that. . . . There's no moral worth in an Elizabethan sonnet sequence, you know" (32). Rosamund's reference to correcting "the proofs of an article of mine on an article on a book on Spenser and Courtly Love" (192) makes it clear that her critical approach to her subject is particularly artificial, being at several removes from the real thing. The irony, of course, is that love is the sole subject of the Elizabethan sonnet sequence, and Rosamund is totally ignorant of love. Since she does not know life, she cannot comprehend literature, for literature reflects life.[5]

Rosamund habitually hides from life in the womb of the British Library. She evades every personal crisis in her life by burying herself in some Elizabethan sonneteer or other. Even her pregnancy fails initially to break her out of her academic cocoon: "My Elizabethan poets did not begin to pale into insignificance in comparison with the thought of buying nappies" (78), she assures us.

So literary is Rosamund that she identifies herself with famous fictional models of fallen women, such as Hardy's Tess of the D'Urbervilles and Hawthorne's Hester Prynne: "I walked around with a scarlet letter embroidered upon my bosom," she confesses. Rosamund wears her scarlet letter with a difference, however, for in her case, "the A stood for Abstinence, not for Adultery." Her sin is not one of commission, but one of omission: "I was guilty of a crime, all right, but it was a brand new, twentieth-century crime, not the good old traditional one of lust and greed. My crime was my suspicion, my fear, my apprehensive terror of the very idea of sex" (20). Crime deserves punishment, and Rosamund views the pregnancy that results from her one and only sexual encounter as a natural form of retribution for her sin of lovelessness. Chastity, a Victorian virtue, is a contemporary crime, and so, she says, "being at heart a Victorian, I paid the Victorian penalty" (21).

Pregnancy, the scarlet woman's nemesis, is a logical fate for Rosamund, however, because she has been playing the role of a scarlet woman all along. Rosamund is a puritan in permissive clothing, for she conceals her embarrassing chastity behind the false mask of a libertine. She pretends to be promiscuous, dating two men at once, but in fact her dual escort system is a clever camouflage for protecting her virginity, for both men assume she is sleeping with the other, and so she is spared "their crusading chivalrous sexual zeal." Both platonic relationships are modeled on the formal courtly love of her Elizabethan sonnet sequences, and in return for this romantic idyll, she boasts ironically, "All I had to sacrifice was interest and love" (21).

Since Rosamund views her pregnancy as the natural nemesis for her prolonged abstinence, she places her story in the tradition of all those harsh tales of fallen women in literature, with "their overhanging grim tones of retribution, their association with scarlet letters, their eye-for-an-eye and Bunyanesque attention to the detail of offence" (19). She presents her narrative as a moral fable for young women in the tradition of her literary namesake in "The Complaint of Rosamond" by the Elizabethan poet Samuel Daniel.[6] Rosamund Stacey's story is a distinctly modern moral fable, however, for it is a warning, not against love, but against lovelessness. She even views the gin she drinks to effect an abortion as a punishment for her abstinence: "It was so thoroughly nasty undiluted that I felt the act of drinking was some kind of penance for the immorality of my behaviour" (17). The bitter draught recalls the poison that Daniel's Rosamund is forced to drink by her lover's vengeful queen.

Drabble's Rosamund does feel positively suicidal when she discovers she is pregnant, and compares her condition to traditional tales of village maidens drowned in duck ponds. She is tempted to imitate the example of all those seduced and abandoned heroines who throng English literature by drowning herself with a millstone as well. Rather than killing herself, however, she decides on another solution for ridding herself of her millstone—abortion. Since her abortion attempt is not based on practical knowledge, however, but on information gleaned through the years from popular fiction, naturally it is ineffectual. When the attempt fails, Rosamund acknowledges that she is trapped inescapably by her natural nemesis, pregnancy. Her ultimate punishment for her isolation is, of course, her solitary confinement. Paradoxically, it is this very confinement which will deliver her from her prison of solipsism.

Before her pregnancy, Rosamund lived in fiction rather than in fact. Her first love affair, for example, is based not on real feeling, but on cheap fiction. No wonder it is unsuccessful and even unconsummated. Rosamund and all of her literary milieu confuse the literal and figurative levels of experience, viewing life as mere fodder for fiction. Pregnancy teaches Rosamund to separate life and literature at last, however, for the experience of childbirth is so real to her that she is unwilling to have it transformed into fiction. She refuses, for example, to allow her novelist roommate, Lydia Reynolds, to accompany her to the hospital for the delivery: "I did not fancy the idea of the details of my labour becoming available to her professional curiosity: she could have a baby herself, I thought, if she really wanted to know what it was like" (111).

Childbirth teaches Rosamund the real difference between art and reality. Previously, she had taken "an Aristotelian and not a Platonic view of fact and fiction" (169), for she has always considered art truer than reality. When she and Lydia debate the literature versus life issue, however, Rosamund realizes that her own ironic situation has taught her that literature, while distinct from life, reflects it: since her own "present predicament would certainly qualify . . . as one of life's little ironies," she realizes that Hardy's "Life's Little Ironies" actually presents a "profound attitude to life" (75-76).

Lydia's novel reveals to Rosamund just how accurately literature can reflect life, for, like Drabble's own novel, it is a fictional version of Rosamund's situation. This novel-within-the-novel device reinforces Drabble's theme of art and reality, for the factual and fictional versions reflect each other's images like a hall of mirrors.[7] Reading Lydia's novel about a girl having an illegitimate baby, Rosamund realizes to her horror that "It was nothing more or less than my life story" (107). The portrait of a research student as an escape artist is all too accurate:

> She hinted that the Rosamund character's obsession with scholarly detail and discovery was nothing more nor less than an escape route, an attempt to evade the personal crises of her life and the realities of life in general. She drew a very persuasive picture of the academic

ivory tower; whenever anything unpleasant happened to this character, as in the course of the extant ten chapters was too frequently the case, she would retire to bed or the British Museum with a pile of books, as others retire perhaps with a bottle of gin. (108)

Reading this fictional version of her own life represents the first time that Rosamund has seen herself objectively: "I thought how unnerving it is, suddenly to see oneself for a moment as others see one, like a glimpse of unexpected profile in an unfamiliar combination of mirrors" (112). The shock of seeing herself as she really is results in her literal delivery by inducing labour. In a figurative sense, it also delivers her from the sterile womb of scholarship.

The child who is born as a result of this revelation avenges her mother's resentment by literally devouring Lydia's undigested version of Rosamund's childbirth: "there was a certain poetic justice in having an exposition of me and Octavia ripped up by Octavia herself" (171), Rosamund realizes. Through this humorously emblematic vignette, Drabble suggests that the child is already subsuming Rosamund's fictional existence and transforming it into real life.

Even before the baby is born, Rosamund has a premonition of the new world it will introduce her to:

> At times I had a vague and complicated sense that this pregnancy had been sent to me in order to reveal to me a scheme of things totally different from the schemes which I inhabited, totally removed from academic enthusiasms, social consciousness, etiolated undefined emotional connexions, and the exercise of free will. It was as though for too long I had been living in one way, on one plane, and the way I had ignored had been forced thus abruptly and violently to assert itself. (77)

Rosamund is introduced to this brave new world by her first trip to an ante-natal clinic: "That visit was a revelation: it was an initiation into a new way of life, a way that was thence-forth to be mine forever. An initiation into reality, if you like" (41).

Rosamund has been reared by her Fabian parents on "the iron rations of atheism, non-conformity, progress and social justice. Flesh, blood and the milk of human kindness have been excluded from her diet."[8] The National Health Service introduces her to the social verities through the broad segment of society and the variety of human misery represented by the mothers at the clinic:

> The facts that I now discovered were precisely the same facts that my admirable parents had always firmly presented to our childish eyes: facts of inequality, of limitation, of separation, of the impossible, heartbreaking uneven hardship of the human lot. I had always felt for others in theory and pitied the blows of fate and circumstance under which they suffered; but now, myself no longer free, myself suffering, I may say that I felt it in my heart. (78)

Drabble explains, "It is into this world of awareness that Rosamund is born—a painful world, but a real one. . . . She learns to notice in her flesh things that hitherto she had noticed only in the intellect" (xii). Thus, giving birth, Rosamund is herself reborn.[9]

Drabble explains, "Through the baby she is brought into contact with the rest of society instead of being shut into the 'ivory tower' of the academic life" (*TWF* 14). Even before the birth, pregnancy makes Rosamund part of the human community, for it compels her to shed her literary masks and fictional poses, along with her courtly lovers, since pregnancy is one condition she cannot conceal forever. Pregnancy also forces her to outgrow her childish illusions of freedom: "it was a question of free will: up to this point in my life I had always had the illusion at least of choice, and now for the first time I seemed to become aware of the operation of forces not totally explicable, and not therefore necessarily blinder, smaller, less kind or more ignorant than myself" (77). The inexorable biological mechanism of pregnancy makes her realize that she is trapped in a human limit for the first time in her life, and that she is going to have to live inside it. Another mother at the clinic impresses Rosamund "like a warning, like a portent, like a figure from another world. . . . I saw that from now on, I like that woman was going to have to ask for help, and from strangers too: I who could not even ask for love or friendship" (82).[10] This is how Rosamund's millstone brings her down from the ivory tower of academe into the marketplace of humanity.

Delivery gives birth to a new emotion for Rosamund: "Love, I suppose one might call it, and the first of my life" (118). She even acknowledges that it must have been in expectation of this love that she had insisted upon having the child. Motherhood teaches Rosamund that love, unlike scholarship, transcends logic: "Before Octavia was born, I used to think that love bore some relation to merit and to beauty, but now I saw that this was not so" (158). Childbirth has taught Rosamund to understand love, the true subject of her literary study.

But love makes Rosamund vulnerable to the fate that she was protected from in her academic cocoon. Octavia embodies Rosamund's new vulnerability—"this small living extension of myself, so dangerous, so vulnerable, for whose injuries and crimes I alone had to suffer" (170). "Children are hostages to fortune,"[11] as Drabble reminds us, and Octavia's congenital heart defect seems to Rosamund a natural form of nemesis for her former lovelessness: "I could not rid myself of the notion that if Octavia were to die, this would be a vengeance upon my sin" (146). Rosamund states, "I felt bitter resentment against Octavia and against the fate that had thus exposed me; up to this point, I had been thoroughly defended and protected against such onslaughts, but now I knew myself to be vulnerable, tender, naked, an easy target for the malice of chance" (139). In sum, Rosamund has become part of the human community.

Overcoming the painful trial of Octavia's illness gives Rosamund new confidence in her own ability to cope with real experience: "I felt, for the first time since Octavia's birth, a sense of adequacy. Like Job, I had been threatened with the worst, and, like Job, I had kept my shape" (164). In bearing her millstone, Rosamund has proved her powers of endurance, and so her millstone is lifted from her, like the Ancient Mariner's albatross.[12]

Now that Rosamund knows something of "the quality of life," she is able at last to comprehend literature. During her painful vigil on the eve of Octavia's operation, Rosamund comes to appreciate the relevance of Ben Jonson's poem, "On My First Son," written in 1603, after the boy's death on his seventh birthday:

> Towards morning I began to think that my sin lay in my love for her. For five minutes or so, I almost hoped that she might die, and thus relieve me of the corruption and the fatality of love. Ben Jonson said of his dead child, my sin was too much hope of thee, loved boy. We too easily take what the poets write as figures of speech, as pretty images, as strings of bons mots. Sometimes perhaps they speak the truth. (147)

Experience has taught Rosamund that literature is not an escape from life, but a reflection of it. She realizes at last that even her Elizabethan poets were writing from the heart.[13]

Now that she has resolved the false dichotomy that she had erected between art and reality, Rosamund is ready to heal the schism in her own nature. During her enforced separation from Octavia following the surgery, motherhood compels her to overcome her habitual diffidence and assert herself for the first time: "It was no longer a question of what I wanted: this time there was someone else involved. Life would never be a simple question of self-denial again" (152). Rosamund's new sense of community has liberated her from her repressive chrysalis at last.

When her way to Octavia is blocked by an officious hospital matron, Rosamund overcomes the obstacle by the effective expedient of losing her temper. Her hysteria represents the turning point in her development, the ultimate battle between the two sides of her nature, her rationality and her passion. She feels her divided self threatening to split apart, annihilating her altogether: "I remember also the clearness of my consciousness and the ferocity of my emotion, and myself enduring them, myself neither one nor the other, but enduring them, and not breaking in two" (155). Under duress, her character proves strong enough to survive this eternal war, and she emerges whole at last, unified by the refining fire of passion, and cured forever of her split personality. Thus Rosamund is "destroyed and created" (vii) by motherhood, in the author's words.

Rosamund's confrontation with bureaucracy marks the climax of the novel, as Drabble's definition of her millstone symbol is finally fulfilled. Rosamund, who initially viewed the baby as the archetypal millstone and tried to abort it, deserved drowning with a millstone herself for attempting to harm the infant, according to Christ's dictum. Ultimately, however, she completely reverses her position and achieves self-realisation by punishing the matron with public humiliation for trying to separate her from her child. The transformation is complete, and the total reversal is a measure of Rosamund's development as a result of bearing her millstone, for the child effects the mother's salvation. Thus, the child is mother of the woman, to vary Wordsworth's statement.

A more literal measure of Rosamund's development is George Matthews, who has been reduced to a disembodied

BBC voice ever since the very brief encounter that resulted in the almost immaculate conception of Octavia. George is an alter-ego figure: Rosamund says, "he was myself, the self that but for accident, but for fate, but for chance. but for womanhood, I would still have been." Rosamund's accidental meeting with George at the end of the novel measures their hopeless distance, for "There was one thing in the world that I knew about, and that one thing was Octavia. I had lost the taste for half-knowledge. George, I could see, knew nothing with such certainty" (199). Thanks to her womanhood, which she has finally realized through maternity, Rosamund has outgrown her male counterpart so far that there is no longer any hope of reunion.

The Millstone concludes, thus, not with marriage, but with matriarchy. A Swedish magazine which published the novel in serial form under the title, *The Baby You Gave Me*, substituted for Drabble's starkly contemporary conclusion a conventional romantic ending in which Rosamund and George marry and live happily ever after.[14] But Drabble's heroine not only dismissed George, she also lies to him about Octavia's birth date so that he has no conception that he is the baby's father. She chooses the child over the man simply because "It was no longer in me to feel for anyone what I felt for my child" (199).

Drabble has affirmed that "Motherhood is the most natural, basic, profound emotion that I have" (*MPI*), and Rosamund clearly prefers maternity to romance.[15] At the end of the novel, Rosamund, maternally melted, is still sexually frigid, "a typical English frigid miss" (*VGMI* 18), in the author's own words. Her own image of a fish, embalmed in the frozen river, suggests her "total maladjustment with regard to sex" (191), recalling Emma Evans' ultimate self-knowledge. Frigidity has the last word in *The Millstone*, when Rosamund concludes, "There's nothing I can do about my nature, is there?" (199).[16] Not until *The Waterfall*, in fact, will a Drabble heroine truly realize her sexual nature.

The final reunion of infant, virginal mother, and ghostly father on Christmas Eve is a distinctly contemporary Nativity, with its single mother and girl-child named for Octavia Hill, a heroine of feminism and socialism. Certainly the mother-daughter unity at the end of the novel is a kind of *egoisme à deux*, with the baby an extension of the mother's personality, for, as Rosamund acknowledges paradoxically, "Love had isolated me more securely than fear, habit, or indifference" (199).

At the conclusion of *The Millstone*, Rosamund expresses her preference for maternal over romantic love in a significant image: "compared with the perplexed fitful illuminations of George, Octavia shone there with a faint, constant and pearly brightness quite strong enough to eclipse any more garish future haze" (199). Rosamund's comparison of her child to a glowing pearl suggests that her millstone has been transformed into a precious jewel, just as the irritant of a grain of sand or a scarlet letter can produce a pearl, symbolizing the way that affliction can create joy and adversity development.

NOTES

[1] Drabble says that "The one that is most read abroad is *The Millstone*" (*VGMI* 18), and "It's much the most translated into other languages" (*BMI* 60). As these notes will indicate, there are over half a dozen articles devoted to *The Millstone*, more than to any other single Drabble novel to date.

[2] Drabble wrote the screenplay for *A Touch of Love*, which starred Sandy Dennis, Eleanor Bron, and Ian McKellen. The title for the American paperback edition, *Thank You All Very Much* (New York: Signet, 1969), came from a scene in the film in which, following a prenatal pelvic examination by an entire class of medical students, Rosamund says precisely that.

[3] Margaret Drabble, "The Author's Introduction," *The Millstone*, ed. Michael Marland (Harlow: Longman, 1970), vii-xiii. Subsequent references will he given in the text.

[4] Margaret Drabble, *The Millstone* (London: Weidenfeld and Nicolson, 1965), 5. Subsequent references will be given in the text. The typescript of this novel, showing comparatively few authorial or editorial changes, is in the Mugar Memorial Library of Boston University.

[5] Sarah Bennett conceives of "a library as an image of the womb" (*SBC* 193). Drabble wrote her early novels in the British Library, before renting a bed-sitter in Bloomsbury for the purpose.

[6] Nancy S. Hardin, "Drabble's *The Millstone*: A Fable for Our Times," *Critique*, 15 (1973), 22-34, and Peter Firchow, "Rosamund's Complaint: Margaret Drabble's *The Millstone*,"

Old Lines, New Forces: Essays on the Contemporary British Novel, 1960-70, ed. Robert K. Morris (New Jersey: Assoc. Univ. Presses, 1976), 93-108, compare *The Millstone* to Daniel's "Complaint of Rosamond."

[7] This is one of the two sections of *The Millstone* that Drabble read aloud on the 1967 BBC programme, "Novelists of the Sixties." She comments, "I think that what I was doing in *The Millstone* by having this relationship between the novelist and the narrator was apologizing for using other people's lives and other people's material. I think that writing novels is a parasitic pursuit" (*BBI* 5).

[8] Quoted from the *Evening Standard* review of *The Millstone*, excerpted in Marland's edition. Ellen Cronan Rose, "Margaret Drabble: Surviving the Future," *Critique*, 15 (1973), 5-21, observes that Rosamund's "Fabian parents are the representatives, in *The Millstone*, of the limits of artifice. Rosamund moves from that crystalline world toward 'reality' through bearing her child" (12).

[9] Firchow comes the closest of all the critics who have written on *The Millstone* to appreciating the symbolic significance of childbirth in the novel:

> It is as if, being impregnated with Octavia, Rosamund had been filled with meaning [for she] gains new life thereby. Giving birth, she is herself reborn. It is not merely that she gains additional knowledge, but that she knows what she knows differently—with the heart and the body, not merely with the head. This is symbolically rendered, in an almost Wordsworthian fashion. (104)

[10] Colin Butler, "Margaret Drabble: *The Millstone* and Wordsworth," *English Studies*, 59 (1978), 353-60, considers this portentous figure "Drabble's own version of the leech-gatherer" (360). This scene, in which Drabble quotes Wordsworth's *Prelude*, is the other section of *The Millstone* that she read aloud on "Novelists of the Sixties." She acknowledges the influence of Wordsworth on *The Millstone*, which she wrote while composing *Wordsworth* and expecting her third child (*BBI* 13).

[11] Margaret Drabble, "Midway through Motherhood," *Parent's Magazine*, April 1974, 66. In "Child Abuse: When a Public Inquiry Isn't Enough," *Sunday Telegraph*, 2 August 1987, p. 14, Drabble explains the source of Octavia's illness: "Crisis came when we discovered that our eldest had a heart lesion: for years the threat of illnesses, infections and opera-

tions hung over us, displacing normal anxieties about everyday disasters as my imagination leapt to the worst possible scenarios."

[12] Susan Spitzer, "Fantasy and Femaleness in Margaret Drabble's *The Millstone*," *Novel*, 11 (1978), 227-45, considers that this development "more logically evokes the Ancient Mariner's albatross than the millstone of the Gospel" (228).

[13] Emma Evans makes a similar discovery of the "uninflated truth" of poetry (regarding Wordsworth's "The Idiot Boy") at the conclusion of *The Garrick Year* (222). Jane Campbell, "Margaret Drabble and the Search for Analogy," *The Practical Vision: Essays in English Literature in Honour of Flora Roy*, ed. Jane Campbell and James Doyle (Waterloo: Wilfrid Laurier Univ. Press, 1978), 133-50, states that Drabble's heroines "reach through their experience an appreciation of the meaning of literature which is a measure of their growth in imaginative sympathy" (138).

[14] Eleanor Wikborg, "A Comparison of Margaret Drabble's *The Millstone* with its Vecko-Revyn Adaptation, 'Barnet Du Gav Mig,'" *Moderna Sprak*, 65 (1971), 305-11, comments on this adaptation. Drabble says, "We are moving into a kind of matriarchy, where the woman keeps the children" (*NPI* 259).

[15] See Ann Rayson, "Motherhood in the Novels of Margaret Drabble," *Frontiers*, 3 (1978), 43-46, and Ruth Sherry, "Margaret Drabble's *The Millstone*: A Feminist Approach," *Edda: Nordisk Tidsskrift for Litteraturforskning*, 41-53, for further discussion of these issues.

[16] Drabble comments, "I intended that book to show her changing from this hard, cold, self-involved person into a warm, loving, tender, outgoing person. But, in fact, I haven't done it, because she's just the same at the end as she was at the beginning. Not just the same" (*VGMI* 6).

Chapter Five:

IDENTITY AND COMMUNITY:
GOLD AND GILT IN *JERUSALEM THE GOLDEN*

Jerusalem the Golden (1967) is intriguing because it is ironic. On the surface, Drabble's fourth novel is the success story of a small-town girl who makes good in the big city. But beneath the entertaining account of a provincial's progress is a serious moral judgment. For although the protagonist succeeds socially, she fails morally. Initially, the reader sympathizes with the youthful aspirations of this spirited heroine, as she strives to escape from her repressive puritanical environment. But finally she forfeits our sympathy by her selfishness in purchasing emancipation at the expense of her humanity.

Clara Maugham, the protagonist of *Jerusalem the Golden*, is the only one of Drabble's heroines who fails to transcend her solipsism. Despite the sentimental education chronicled in the novel, Clara refuses to learn Drabble's primary principles of affection and community. Drabble declares that "It's a very reactionary book, *Jerusalem the Golden*" (*VGMI* 14)—a reaction against the sixties emphasis on self-fulfillment.

Jerusalem the Golden, which Drabble says, "I had based on my childhood experiences of Sheffield" (*AB* 5), is the most autobiographical of all her novels, for she explains that "[Clara's] background contains more of my own than any of the others."[1] The only one of Drabble's protagonists who is considerably younger than the author, Clara Maugham represents a retrospective view of a past persona which the mature author views in an ironic light.

Symptomatic of this dissociation of sympathy with her protagonist, *Jerusalem the Golden* represents Drabble's first use of the omniscient third-person narrative method, as opposed to the confessional first-person technique of her previous three novels. The switch to another character's point of view midway through the novel also effects a subtle shift of sympathy. So the increased artistic distance afforded by this narrative method allows the novelist to view her protagonist with unprecedented objectivity and to invite moral judgment from the reader.

Drabble's irony in *Jerusalem the Golden* has confused critics from the outset. In the 1967 BBC programme, "Novelists of the Sixties," Bernard Bergonzi expressed disappointment in the novel, disturbance over Drabble's intentions, and disapproval of her heroine, because "it was a puzzle to know how far one was supposed to endorse her selfish and facile attitudes to life" (*BBI* 17). Bergonzi's puzzlement was prophetic, for critics have persisted in applauding Clara's self-advancement, while ignoring her inhumanity. In the only article to date on *Jerusalem the Golden*, Lee Edwards concludes: "Clara is allowed to be young, misguided, even willfully mistaken, and, far from being punished for her errors, is celebrated for the energy which animates her."[2] Michael Harper judges: "The third-person narrator has maintained a slightly ironic, mocking tone, encouraging the reader to see Clara's progress as a decadence, a falling-away, a betrayal of identity. Yet this view of Clara is quite wrong, as the reader should already know."[3]

Drabble makes it quite clear in various interviews, however, that she disapproves of Clara: "I don't like her very much, I think she's my most unsympathetic heroine" (*IRI* 338), and "I very much mistrust her. She's the worst side of one's nature" (*BFI* 20). But it is not necessary to go outside the novel for the author's intentions, for she skillfully directs our judgment within the novel by her artful use of symbolism.

Symbolism is especially significant in *Jerusalem the Golden*, for the distinctive characteristic of the protagonist is her habit of visualizing her aspirations in imagistic terms: "The world of the figurative was Clara's world of refuge. The literal world which she inhabited was so plainly hostile that she seized with ardour upon any references to any other mode of being."[4] Clara finds an escape from repulsive reality in the golden world of the imagination provided by the hymn, "Jerusalem the Golden," the source of the novel's title, and by *The Golden Windows*, a Sunday school book of moral fables. These golden realms, both rooted in Clara's Methodist background, generate the celestial and vegetation symbolism which forms a moral framework for judging the protagonist, because the major irony of the novel is that Clara misinterprets her own symbols. The distance between the true moral significance of the symbols and Clara's willful misinterpretation of them measures how far the protagonist's values fall short of the author's standards.

The fable of "The Golden Windows" symbolizes for Clara the contrast between her view of her grim reality and her vision of her golden dream:

> The title story told, with some charm, of a little boy who saw from a hillside while out walking a house whose windows were all of gold. He searched for this wonderful house, but could not find it, and was returning home disappointed when he realized that the house was his own house, and that the gold was merely the reflection of the sun. The moral of this story was, she assumed, that one must see the beauty in what one has and not search for it elsewhere; but it carried with it, inseparably, the real sadness of the fading windows, and the fact that those within the house could never see them shine. (38)

Clara clearly comprehends the moral of this fable, for, like the author, she has already experienced its truth: "Clara knew from first hand experience the moral truth of the story told in *The Golden Windows* about the house with the golden windows, for she had once admired from a friend's house the whole dazzling, distant, smoky layout of her own hillside" (45).[5] But Clara deliberately rejects her comprehension of the allegory and the principle it symbolizes, interpreting the parable instead as signifying that the grass is greener on the other side of the fence. So her goal is to search for greener pastures, rather than to cultivate her own garden.

Clara employs other nature fables to symbolize her own situation. She is particularly appalled by the Biblical parable of the sower:

> As a child, she was always deeply affected by the story of the sower who sowed his seeds, and some fell by the wayside, and some on stony ground and some fell among the thorns, and some fell upon good ground and bore fruit. . . . and long before she could see it as a parable, she already felt shock before its injustice. The random scattering of seeds, and how much worse, of human souls, appalled her. As she grew older, she looked upon herself, tragically, defiantly, with all the helplessness of fourteen years, as a plant trying to root itself upon the solid rock, without water, without earth, without shade. (29)

The parable of the sower symbolizes to Clara her own

desperate situation in the stony ground of Northam: "It always amazed her to see that other people could live so comfortably upon such barren territory. Northam was to her the very image of unfertile ground" (30). Clara is determined to defy her fate, "Because she would live, she would survive." Clara clearly understands the meaning of this parable also, but she is unwilling to accept its harsh moral: that the person, like the plant, must flourish where destiny places it or not at all. Sensitive plant that she is, Clara would rather reroot in richer soil.

The fable of "The Two Weeds" in *The Golden Windows* collection symbolizes to Clara her choice between the puritanical way of life of her reality and the permissive life style of her dreams:

> In this tale, two weeds grew on a river bank; one of them conserved its energy, and grew low and small and brown, with its sights set on a long life, while the other put forth all its strength into growing tall and into colouring itself a beautiful green. During the summer, these two weeds reviled each other, as fabulous creatures will; the lowly weed accused its brother of grandiose, spendthrift ambitions, and the tall weed called the low weed mean and miserly. At the end of the summer, a beautiful girl passed and she saw the tall weed, and plucked it and put it in her dress, where it blushed a glorious red and died content; the weed on the bank saw it die, and laughed, and reflected that it would live till the next year. And it did. (38)

Clara concludes that "The curious feature of this tale was its moral ambivalence," for, "incredibly enough, it seemed to end with a choice." Once again, Clara does understand the obvious moral intent of this nature allegory, but perversely emphasizes the opposite import. She wants to interpret the tale as conceding the appeal of a life of pleasure over a life of virtue, because, being more a product of her puritan upbringing than she acknowledges, she needs to feel that her choice of a hedonistic future has the moral sanction of her repressive past. So "The Two Weeds" fable represents for Clara "the new contained and expressed in the framework and the terms of the old" (39).

These three fables of fate inspire Clara to search for her own golden windows through which to view her future. First she seeks her golden dream in fiction: "She searched in vain in these golden childish worlds for the true brittle glitter of duplicity, for the warm shine of wider, more embracing landscapes; she looked for half-truth, for precious qualification, for choice, for possible rejections, and she could not find them" (37). Instead, she finds the vistas she seeks in Biblical maxims such as, "'Straight [sic] is the Gate and narrow is the way which leadeth unto life.' . . . not because she had any faith in their message, but because they were phrased with some beauty; they were made up of words that seemed to apply to some large and other world of other realities" (35). Paradoxically, Clara finds the food for her imagination in the religious imagery of the puritanical environment she loathed, rather than in the saccharine fantasies of escapist fiction, simply because the latter "did not sufficiently approach the reality that she knew, whereas the threat of the straightness of the gate seemed unfailingly significant." Similarly, "The advertisement life was better than her own, but it was crude, amoral: it lacked both virtue and vice" (37). Ironically, Clara appreciates the vistas revealed by the imagery of the Biblical maxims, while blatantly ignoring the moral truths they symbolize, even though it is that very moral basis which gives their poetic vision validity for her. Clearly, there is a large dose of self-deception in Clara's symbolic vision, just as there was in Emma Evans'.

Clara finally discovers the perfect formulation of her golden dream in the hymn, "Jerusalem the Golden": [6]

>Jerusalem the Golden
>With milk and honey blest
>Beneath thy contemplation
>Sink heart and voice oppressed.
>I know not, oh, I know not
>What social joys are there
>What radiancy of glory
>What light beyond compare. (36)

"Jerusalem the Golden" inspires Clara's golden vision and thus provides, through the protagonist's own imagination, the major symbol pattern of the novel by generating celestial images of a golden heaven radiant with bright light and peopled by angelic creatures.

But "Jerusalem the Golden" also provides the major irony of the novel, for Clara misinterprets it. The hymn clearly signifies a spiritual heaven, but Clara, deceived by the ambiguous word "social," envisions a secular paradise: "She pictured, even at a most tender age, not the pearly gates and crystal walls and golden towers of some heavenly city, but some truly terrestrial paradise where beautiful people in beautiful houses spoke of beautiful things." This heavenly vision fuels the fire of Clara's social ambitions: "The combination of the words and the music of this hymn could unfailingly elevate her to a state of rapt and ferocious ambition and desire." Clara blatantly ignores the spiritual values that the hymn really signifies for the social goals that it apparently suggests. The narrator carefully points to the key word to ensure that we understand both the true meaning of the symbol and Clara's false interpretation of it: "It must have been the word 'social' that created for her this image, a word judiciously expunged from later versions of the verse." Clara takes the heavenly image literally and hopes to discover a new Jerusalem in England's green and pleasant land—not a golden City of God, but a gilt metropolis.

"Jerusalem the Golden" inspires Clara to view reality in Manichean terms: she sees the "soul-destroying grim industrial perspectives" (*AB* 5) of her hometown as a hell on earth and everywhere else is a potential heaven: "all the people who were not from Northam seemed at first sight equally brilliant, surrounded as they were by a confusing blur of bright indistinct charm" (9). The heart of this hell is the miserable Maugham home on Hartley Road, and the witch who casts her evil spell over this "narrow, joyless, constricted family" (*TWF* 80) is Clara's repressive mother. Of all the unpleasant mother figures who abound in Drabble's fiction, Mrs. Maugham is surely the most repellent. If this novel has a flaw, it may be that Mrs. Maugham is just too bad to be true.[7] Certainly Clara's desire to escape from what Drabble terms this "unpleasant, hard, bitter, life-denying" (*NSHI* 279) woman is utterly understandable at this point. Mrs. Maugham is symbolized by ashes throughout—from the Christmas stocking filled with ashes from the grate in her youth to the "ashes to ashes and dust to dust" of her death (34)—suggesting both the fire and brimstone hell of her Methodist background and the dark Satanic mills of her industrial home.[8]

Mrs. Maugham's meanness of spirit blights even her garden, where lethal flowers of evil symbolize Clara's fatal environment: "The garden's sole glory was a laburnum, which blossomed wonderfully each year: but even that she associated more with its dry black fatal pods than with its flowers, so often and so rigorously had she been warned of its poison"

(115). Not gold but plastic reigns in the Maugham home. In a curious inversion of values that Drabble views as characteristic of non-conformist religion,[9] Mrs. Maugham is "so devoted to the principle that beauty is a frivolity and a sign of sin that she would have been ashamed to have it in the house" (49). So she fills her home with ugly utilitarian gadgets that naturally impel Clara to a passionate preference for the purely decorative over the simply functional. Clara's *bête noir* is a tulip-patterned slop bowl: "To Clara, it was always painfully conspicuous, an indictment of a way of life ... an eccentricity erected into a symbol of the traditionally correct" (50).

The nadir of Clara's life in Northam is the death of her father. She weeps, not so much for his loss, as for "the meanness and the lack of love, and for the fear that she would die in so ugly a hole and so unloved." The domestic duplicity of her hypocritical home inspires in Clara "a vision of some other world where violent emotion could be a thing of beauty" (32). After her father's funeral, Clara is vouchsafed a vision of this grander world, thanks to a school trip to Paris. Envisioning Northam as hell and Paris as heaven, Clara views Northam train station as the pearly gates, for its strait and narrow way seems a fitting passage for God's Elect, "travelling through their narrow channel into some brighter birth, and into some less obstinately alien world."[10] Drabble presents Clara's vision in terms of a Bunyanesque religious allegory:

> It occurred to her to wonder why she should so suddenly feel herself to be peculiarly blessed, and a dreadful grief for all those without blessings took hold of her, and a terror at the singular nature of her escape. Out of so many thousands, one. Narrow was the gate, and the hillsides were crowded with the serried dwellings of the cramped and groaning multitudes, the ranks of the Unelect, and she the one white soul flew dangerously forth into some glorious and exclusive shining heaven. (67)

And indeed, "Paris, with its angelic cornices and its pale and flowery stones, its classical statues, its draperies and its trees and its gilt" does seem heavenly, compared to "the blackened bricks and the dirty windows and the non-conformist architecture" of Northam (209). This rather disappointing trip to the celestial city merely whets Clara's appetite for her terrestrial paradise, however. "Obsessed with escape," in the author's words,[11] Clara views her intellectual and sexual assets as a "bargaining power rather than a blessing" (9). Men are the Jacob's ladder and sexual favours the coin of passage for this little angel: "I shall get further if I'm pulled. I can't waste time in going first" (87), Clara declares. Walter Ash, though not a prestige catch, like the glamorous but infinitely tedious Higginbotham, is cultivated by Clara simply because "he promised connexion" (59). Although his name relegates him to the ashen wastes of Northam, Walter Ash prefigures Gabriel, Clara's real angel of deliverance, because he affords her a "painfully beautiful vision" of the social life she seeks: "Her desire for such a life was so passionate, and her gratitude to Walter for this glimpse of it was so great that she could have kissed him in the street, and later that day she did in fact allow him to undo her brassiere strap without a word of protest" (61).

Her intelligence too, once a source of shame, becomes the source of the first power of her life, as the Arts and Science teachers at her Grammar School fight for her favour. Her brightness miraculously delivers her from infernal Northam to heavenly London by means of a scholarship which validates Clara's golden vision, for "the cash payment spoke to Clara's industrial heart decisively" (9).[12] Clearly gold is an ironic symbol in *Jerusalem the Golden*, suggesting both lofty ideals and filthy lucre.[13]

Clara discovers that, in order to reverse her fortunes, she merely has to exchange her social milieu for one where her former liabilities are transformed into assets. Her old-fashioned name symbolizes this principle of inversion in the opening sentence of the novel: "Clara never failed to be astonished by the extraordinary felicity of her own name." Her name appears to connect her with her puritanical background, since her mother maliciously christened her Clara, "not in the vanguard but in the extreme rearguard of fashion, after a Wesleyan great aunt . . . as a preconceived penance for her daughter, whose only offenses at that tender age were her existence and her sex" (7). But the name "Clara," which means "bright light" actually fits her more for the "radiancy of glory" of her golden Jerusalem.[14]

Clara does discover her social heaven in the Denham family, who are all saints in her eyes.[15] Her golden vision is vindicated when she first meets Clelia Denham: she "watched the felicity of her own invention, and experienced the satisfaction of her recognition" (22). Clara emulates her idol in the kind of understudy relationship (perhaps based on Drabble's experience of understudying Vanessa Redgrave) that many Drabble heroines have with their closest friend or sister. Through this alter-ego relationship with her look-alike spiritual sister Clelia, Clara discovers a surrogate mother and father in the cultivated Candida and the sophisticated Sebastian, and proxy brothers and sisters in their brood of children—Clelia, Gabriel, Amelia, Magnus, and Annunciata—in fact, the entire substitute family which she has dreamed of. The Denhams become Clara's cultural mentors: "They taught her, they instructed her" (171), introducing her to a brave new social world.

Clara believes that the Denhams, with their famous poet father, an even more famous novelist mother, and their brilliant brood, are "the real thing" (14)—a phrase which always connotes authenticity in Drabble's fiction. The radiant intimacy between parents and children is illuminating to Clara, and the relationships between the brothers and sisters are also a revelation to her, compared to the alienated individuals of the Maugham family in their "silent pockets of isolated, self-contained, repellent activity" (117). The Denhams even seem to be illuminated by some subtle golden radiance, in contrast to the crude glare of the bald plastic-shaded lightbulb of the Maugham home.

The emblem of the Denhams' wealth is the family photograph album, containing pictures of Candida, with her books and babies "in a lovely heap of human shape," or arm in arm with Eliot or Fitzgerald. Clara concludes that "love, surely, was at the source of such conventional efforts; there had been love and at every stage" (121). But she "wondered uneasily if expense were not after all the key to so much charm," for the album reflects "a small rich world, a world of endless celebration and fame. . . . Advantages blossomed on its pages, and it seemed at moments as though love (and why not?) might be a forced plant, an unnatural flower that could not grow in thinner soil" (122). Money, Clara concludes, must fertilize the rich soil in which love can flourish.

The Denham house is also the real thing in Clara's eyes, and in it, she discovers that "The aristocratic ideal was vindicated" (107). The golden eagle of the Denham dining room is a far cry from the plastic place mats of the Maugham table.

When she first enters the house, Clara is delighted to see a "marble fire place, and under it was a large pot of dying flowers and a very beautiful rocking horse" (100). The fact that the hearth is cold, the rocking horse unused, and the flowers dying, with their petals "spilled brown and carelessly over the floor," is suspicious, however. The fact that Drabble stage-manages Clara's first meeting with the Denhams in the changing room of a theatre—an emblem of illusion, as we saw in *The Garrick Year*—is also sinister. Things are not what they seem in the Denham home: "Houses were not houses, gardens were not gardens: plants grew along picture rails, stone tables stood in the garden, and Gabriel with his three children was much loved by a man" (133).

The Denhams' garden is actually more unnatural than the Maughams' lethal laburnums, for artifacts flourish there instead of flowers. Clara is impressed by a pretentious statue impersonating a tree, for "inside the block swam sadly a drowned lady, some seaweed, and an orange" (113). It is actually Clara, overwhelmed by the Denhams, who is symbolized by the drowned lady, as "Whole concepts, whole reorganizations of thought swam drunkenly through her head, and lurched and revolved like the drowned woman and her orange: and she no longer knew what gardens and houses were for, and their distinctions, once clear, had grown confused" (116).

There is actually something unnatural about the passionate affection and radiant intimacy of the Denham siblings, something incestuous about its mingling of the generations. The prolonged nursery associations of Clelia's room, full of ancient toys, suggest an arrested development. Apparently the Denham home is crippling: Gabriel declares, "Look at Amelia, she went mad through the shock of waking up in the outside world, out of the golden nest, and she only married to get away from us, you know, to escape from our amorous family clutches, and when she got out, when she breathed the cold air of Essex, she went mad" (186).

But "Clara found her craving for the bizarre and she involved richly satisfied [in] the complication of Clelia's family" (91). The extreme complexity of the Denham ménage, which includes Clelia's live-in non-lover and his baby, is symbolized by Clara's Japanese wooden egg puzzle: Clelia dismantles the puzzle, while telling Clara the story of her life and family, and then cannot reassemble it. Clara "liked any promise of the eternal devious possibilities of the human passions. . . . How infinitely preferable was such a world to the world where Walter Ash had grabbed her, sternly, singleminded, with undeflecting simplicity of purpose, among the buttercups" (132-33).

The transition from friendship with her alter ego Clelia to an affair with her look-alike brother Gabriel is a smooth one for Clara. She and Gabriel both relish the sense of being sexually related by proxy to Clelia. When Gabriel reappears in Drabble's later novel, *The Middle Ground* (1980), he confesses that he was always "in love with his sister Clelia" (196). In this incestuous trio, Clara believes that she has finally found "the true thick brew of real passion." The fact that Gabriel is married is "an added enticement, for she had always fancied the idea of a complicated, illicit and disastrous love," and had deliberately complicated several perfectly straightforward relationships "in the hope of discovering just such a spirit of confusion" (125). The clandestine quality of their secret trysts particularly appeals to Clara, as it did to Emma Evans. Their first "secret kiss, in its dangerous angle, with its back to the wall, a few inches from discovery and surprise was for her the lofty classic height of passion" (152).

True to Clara's bent for sexual barter, their liaison is an unabashedly amorous bargain: Clara confesses, "All you are to me, you know, is a means of self-advancement," and Gabriel responds, "I knew that. For all you were to me was a means of escape" (222). Their mock wedding under the arch of Gabriel's desk, with paper punchings for confetti, expresses exquisitely the tawdry quality of the relationship.

Gabriel is appropriately named to escort Clara up her Jacob's ladder to her social heaven: "Gabriel, what a name, Gabriel," Clara exclaims; "Did you know that the Italians call their children Paradise and Heaven and such things?" (182). The golden-haired Gabriel does seem divine in Clara's starry eyes—her ideal man, combining the attraction of Higginbotham, the sophistication of Walter Ash, the cultivation of Peter Harronson, and the sensuality of the unnamed Italian soldier. Even Gabriel's ambivalent sexuality, "perpetually blessed by the possibility of choice" (132), suggested by his ambiguous name, connects him with the androgynous angels.

Gabriel becomes Clara's guide to her social heaven: he introduces her to a tinsel heaven of pop stars—"a celluloid paradise: a paradise from which Gabriel had perhaps fallen, for she might surely never ascend?" So far, "she had kept well away from a closer vision of the locked and pearly gates. But Gabriel stood there in front of her, smiling, accessible, full of good will, as mortal as she was mortal, or acknowledging her too as divine" (126). Either Gabriel is a fallen angel, or she, God's one Elect, has ascended into the ranks of the blessed.[16] And Gabriel does transport Clara to her terrestrial paradise, Paris.

The trip to Paris is the turning point in Clara's fortunes, for the divine Gabriel, her ideal man, and celestial Paris, her ideal city, both disillusion her. As Gabriel's mistress, she is once again disappointed in her ambition of seeing the Paris interiors which would be open to her as Gabriel's wife. Realizing that she does not want marriage to Gabriel, however, she begins to doubt her own ambitions: "It was not one man that she needed, but through one man a view of other things, a sensation of other ways of being, she wished to feel herself attached to the world. . . . She wished to see in the eyes of others the dim, narrowing, receding vistas, the arches and long corridors through which she had travelled. She wished to set, through him, a value on herself. . . . She bowed her head, sadly, saddened, staring into her small bitter black cup, seeing there the bitter limits of her own hitherto illimitable designs" (185).

The limits of Clara's designs are actually the limitations of her own character. Her disillusionment stems from her inability to love: "I am all nerve, I am hard, there is no love in me, I am too full of will to love," Clara confesses to Gabriel, for "love, desperately, eluded her; she had not been taught to love, she had lacked those expensive, private lessons" (181). The lack of love which has stunted her affections is symbolized by the portrait over the bed in their bordello-like Paris hotel room, from which a "woman stared coldly down upon them, through the stiff wrinkles of age," radiating puritanical disapprobation, just like Clara's mother. Looking at the repressive portrait, Clara despairs: "I am chased, I am pursued, I run and run, but I will never get away, the apple does not fall far from the tree" (180).[17]

The trip to Paris marks the turning point, not only in Clara's fortunes, but also in our sympathies. The disaffection initiated by the shift to Gabriel's viewpoint in Chapter Seven is completed by Clara's crass conduct in Paris, where she engages in a perverse flirtation with Gabriel's brother Magnus, its perversity symbolized by the grotesque hag who urinates in the gutter before them. Clara's flirtation with Magnus, who confesses that he used to be in love with Gabriel's wife Phillipa, is initiated by a secret kiss just around the corner from Gabriel, echoing the first time that Gabriel kissed Clara around the corner from Phillipa. But Magnus remonstrates with Clara: "No, no, I said give me a kiss. Open your eyes. It is better to give than to receive." This perverse application of the Christian maxim penetrates Clara's puritanical defenses, and she realizes that she has never kissed anyone in her life. She rises to the challenge, feeling that in kissing Magnus "she was forcing her nature beyond the limits of its spring, that it could not bend back, that it would break rather than bend so far, or bend so far that it would bear the shape of the curve for life" (200-01).

As a result of this pivotal act, Clara feels as if she has torn up her puritanical repression by the roots, as if "a whole moral inheritance of doubt had dropped away from her." Abandoning Gabriel in Paris, she flies home to London, feeling as free as the seed of the sower: "she had cut herself off forever, and she could drift now, a flower cut off from its root, or a seed perhaps, an airy seed dislodged, she could drift now without fear of settling ever again upon the earth" (207).

Retribution awaits, however, in the form of a telegram informing her of her mother's illness—a bitter irony, since she had fabricated an illness of her mother's as the reason for her trip: "She felt faintly guilty about taking her mother's name in vain in this way, but she could not think of any other valid excuse for her absence, and felt, in her heart, a faintly pleasurable, guilty revenge, as though she were plucking her pleasures directly from the thorny tree itself" (178). Clara's Calvinistic sense of original sin inspires her to read the fatal telegram as a message of heavenly retribution:

> I have killed my mother. By willing her death, I have killed her. By taking her name in vain, I have killed her. She thought, let them tell me no more that we are free, we cannot draw a breath without guilt, for my freedom she dies. And she felt closing in upon her, relentlessly, the hard and narrow clutch of retribution, those iron fingers which she had tried, so wilfully, so desperately to elude; a whole system was after her, and she the final victim, the last sacrifice, the shuddering product merely of her past. (208)

Alone in the Maugham home, Clara has the courage to confront her absent mother's spirit in her empty room for the first time: "no longer averting her own eyes from her own shame before it, no longer blind with vicarious grief, no longer clouded by the menace of her own lack of love." Feeling that her mother is already dead, she rifles through her things, searching "for some small white powdery bones, for some ghost of departed life" (212). And she does unearth a lost spirit in a cache of photographs of the young May Maugham, in which "she smiled bravely, gaily, a smile radiant with hope and intimacy" (213).

Clara is even more enlightened by her mother's poem, "O let us seek a brighter world / Where darkness plays no part" (213), which anticipates her own golden dream.[18] Reading it, Clara feels "a sense of shocked relief, for she was glad to have found her place of birth, she was glad that she had however miserably pre-existed, she felt, for the first time, the satisfaction of her true descent" (214). Long ago, Clara realized that "She must have fallen happily upon some small dry sandy fissure, where a few grains of sand, a few drops of moisture, had been enough to support her trembling and tenacious life" (30), and now she recognizes that the fragment of fertile soil which nourished her own dreams was her mother's youthful hopes. Identifying with this new-found kindred spirit, Clara dreams that it is she herself who is dying (220). Significantly, she looks at herself in her mother's mirror, for her own kin, not her proxy family, is the true source of her vision of Jerusalem the Golden.

The Golden Windows fable is validated too, for, thanks to the distant vantage-point provided by her travels, she can now see her home in a better light. She wonders if her jaundiced view of Northam was merely the result of her own prejudices, "if her whole vision of Northam might not after all have been a nightmare, and that the whole city might have been filled with warm preoccupations, a whole kind city shut to her alone, distorted in her eyes alone" (219). Now that the wicked witch has been disenchanted, the spell cast over the Hartley Road home is broken. Even Clara's *bête-noir* is debunked: she looks back at "the sad, much-hated objects of her infancy, the tulip-patterned slop bowl," more in sorrow than in anger, regretting "how much violence she had wasted upon such harmless things," for "What chance had there ever been, ever, that she would have been condemned to them for life? What immense folly had ever made her fear such a fate?" (211-12).

When Clara visits her mother in hospital the next morning, she is appalled by her death's-head appearance, as "The bones of the head, once sunk deep, now reached forth through the skin to their final revelation" (215). Seeing the few roses withering by the bedside, symbolizing the way the woman is wasted by the cancer which gnaws her, Clara is embarrassed to have come empty-handed. Her failure to bring flowers, always an emblem of affection in Drabble's fiction, is a symbol of her failure to love. Clara is ashamed because she had thought of bringing flowers, but "she had been afraid, afraid of rejection, afraid of that sour smile with which so many years ago her mother had received her small offerings. . . . She had been afraid of the gesture; she had learned nothing, she could not give, and yet she knew that without gestures there was no hope that love might fill the empty frames, the extended arms, the social kisses, the proffered flowers. She had brought nothing, and her meanness dismayed her. She had not wished to be mean" (216).

When her mother taxes her for her tardiness, declaring "with all her ancient venom, 'If I were on my deathbed, you wouldn't care,'" Clara is tempted to make a desperate final appeal to that young woman leaning on a gate forty years ago, but such an appeal was impossible, against nature. "Freedom abandoned her, the pitiful ineptitude of freedom, and she found herself once more, as of old, basely prevaricating, terrified into deceit." Finally, Clara "dispelled the hope, which had sprung in her the night before, that some reconciliation, some gleams of sympathy or need might show themselves, and she saw, as she had always known, that understanding is never anything but fitful" (216-17).

Clara has always been terrified of any insight into her mother's bitterness: "when, occasionally, she glimpsed some faint light of cessation, she recoiled from it and shut her eyes in horror, preferring the darkness to such bitter illumination" (62). When Mrs. Maugham acceded to her adolescent daughter's desire to visit Paris, Clara was furious, because "the truth was that this evidence of care and tenderness was harder to bear than any neglect, for it threw into question the whole basis of their lives together." Perhaps it would take a saint indeed to love such a hard woman, but even the adolescent Clara realized that "perhaps a better daughter might have found a way to soften such a mother" (64). Listening to her mother's deathbed venom, Clara "found herself watching anxiously, fearfully, for any sign of feeling, for any chink in the stony front, because it was in truth the last thing that she wanted, the last thing that she could have borne. And there was nothing, nothing at all: with relief she saw that there would be nothing, that she would not be called upon to give, that she could merely answer meanness with meanness" (217).

Although the "brighter world" poem instilled sympathy into Clara's soul, another verse of her mother's struck terror into her heart:

> I wait here for my life, and here I must wait
> While all the world rolls on and passes by;
> Surely my expectations have a date,
> And I will find the answer ere I die? (213)

Clara concludes, "It was possible, then, to go disastrously astray; tragedy was possible, survival was no certainty, there was no reason why anyone should escape" (214). She determines to avoid a like fate: "Her mother was dying, but she herself would survive it, she would survive even the guilt and convenience and grief of her mother's death, she would survive because she had willed herself to survive, because she did not have it in her to die. Even the mercy and kindness of destiny she would survive; they would not get her that way, they would not get her at all" (224).[19]

So, when faced with "the final, often imagined (and yet how final, and therefore possibly endurable) martyrdom," of caring for her dying mother during the last few weeks of her life, Clara succumbs gratefully, guiltily, to the surgeon's superior knowledge of the limits of human effort, when he reassures her, "you've got your own life to live, you won't want to be looking after her yourself, let's face it, will you?" (215). And despite her protests, she does not even last out the weekend. Clearly Clara would rather continue to view her golden windows from a distance.

Clara prefers to drift through life as a floating seed or tumbling tumble-weed, rather than remain rooted in her native soil. So she abandons her mother forthwith, escaping from intimacy and affection into the safely superficial frivolity of her London life, and into "the nostalgic connexion more precious, more close, more intimate than any simple love" (224) of her clandestine flirtation with Gabriel—"safe and warm once more, back at home in the realm of human treachery and love and infidelity" (221). Clearly Clara would rather be worn briefly as a cut bloom in Gabriel's lapel than nourish her roots.

The novel concludes with a tinsel fantasy that creates an ironic contrast with Drabble's own golden vision:[20] Clara, still star-struck, envisions "a tender blurred world where Clelia and Gabriel and she herself in shifting and ideal conjunctions met and drifted and met once more like the constellations in the heavens: a bright and peopled world, thick with starry inhabitants, where there was no ending, no parting, but an eternal vast incessant rearrangement" (224). Brazen as ever, Clara clearly continues to prefer gilt to gold.

This is the conclusion that most critics persist in interpreting as Clara's ultimate success, rather than her final failure. Edwards concludes, for example: "The novel's final lines herald Clara's survival."[21] But Drabble values moral salvation above mere survival. The author clarifies the "conflict between feeling a loyalty to one's past and a desire to escape from it," which she dramatizes in *Jerusalem the Golden*, by explaining: "If you become cultured and leave your roots, have you betrayed something in yourself that can never be reborn? Have you killed a vital part of yourself? And I think when I say that Clara was getting harder and harder throughout the book, I'm suggesting that she was killing something in herself" (*VGMI* 16). Clearly Clara's is "A Pyrrhic Victory" of the sort that Drabble depicts in her story of that name, for in order to win her liberty, Clara loses her humanity.[22]

Drabble has affirmed that Clara is "the only one of my characters that I wouldn't have wanted to know in twenty years time" (*VGMI* 14), and so her recent suggestion of "reintroducing Clara into another novel and saying what happens to her next" (*TWF* 94), is especially intriguing, since she has previously prophesied that "She's going to turn into something fearsome, I think. I rather dread her future" (*NSHI* 278). The fact that both author and readers alike continue to debate Clara's moral status testifies to Drabble's artistic triumph. Whether or not Clara has failed morally, Drabble has succeeded artistically in her skillful manipulation of symbolism to reveal moral complexities in *Jerusalem the Golden*.

NOTES

[1] Margaret Drabble in a 10 December 1974 letter to Valerie Grovenor Myer.

[2] Lee Edwards, "*Jerusalem the Golden*: A Fable for our Times," *Women's Studies* 6 (1979), 317-34, adds: "the triumph in *Jerusalem the Golden*, Margaret Drabble's perhaps even more than Clara's, is the victorious discovery of a form adequate to contain both the hero's aspirations and the surrounding world" (333-34).

[3] Michael Harper, "Margaret Drabble and the Resurrection of the English Novel," *Contemporary Literature*, 23 (1982), 145-68, explains:

> Identity does not consist in Clara's remaining true to the appalling context into which she was inserted by birth, history, circumstance; the "self" she flees is a function of a social practice which was inflicted upon her and which, if she remains within it, will first stunt and then kill her as surely as it first stunted and is now killing her mother. The self she achieves is, of course, just as surely a function of a social context, but it is every bit as genuine as the one she leaves and in some sense more so since she actively constructs it and does not simply suffer it. (160-61)

[4] Margaret Drabble, *Jerusalem the Golden* (London: Weidenfeld and Nicolson, 1967), 34. Further references will be documented within the text. The original typescript of *Jerusalem the Golden*, purchased from the Manuscript Exhibition Appeal Committee in London in March, 1970, is in the Mugar Memorial Library of Boston University.

[5] Drabble explains her own "Golden Windows" experience:

> I had a startlingly similar experience when writing *Jerusalem the Golden*, which I had based on my childhood memories of Sheffield. I wrote the book from memory, and then decided I'd better go back and check up that I'd remembered right, so I went up for a night, arriving after dark and staying in the Station Hotel. In the morning I was expecting to look out of the window and see those soul-destroying grim industrial perspectives, but in fact I looked out, the sun was shining, the hillsides were glittering, green fields fringed the horizon, it was all bright and sparkling and beautiful. I felt as though I had maligned the place in my memory. After the flat dull overbuilt sprawl of London, it was Sheffield that looked like Jerusalem. (*AB* 5)

Jerusalem, of course, is always somewhere else.

⁶ "Jerusalem the Golden" was translated from Bernard of Cluny by John Mason Neale. It was Drabble's favourite hymn at school (*TWF* 93).

⁷ Drabble explains that Clara's "background was similar not to my own but to my mother's. My mother read this book and said it was too true, she didn't like it" (*TWF* 80).

⁸ Drabble says, "It's about being culturally deprived. And it's also about the particular kind of dour northern life that I was brought up on. . . . I still have this feeling that something in me was permanently squashed by that environment, and those attitudes" (*VGMI* 14).

⁹ Drabble criticizes "Methodist frugality, a virtue become a sin," claiming that "its greatest hypocricy, its most profound double-thinking" was its "extreme dourness and repression . . . repressing all disturbing manifestations of energy: sexual, social or political" (*AB* 277, 13).

¹⁰ Drabble comments, "The other thing that runs through my books is the Calvinist idea that some are elected to grace and some aren't. But I can't really believe this. It's intolerable, especially if one is bound to believe that one is among the elect" (*NSHI* 286).

¹¹ Drabble uses this phrase in comparing Clara to Bennett's first hero, Richard Larch, in *The Man from the North*:

> I should acknowledge at this point my own debt to Bennett, in my novel, *Jerusalem the Golden*, which was profoundly affected by his attitudes, though as they are of course also a part of my own background I can't quite distinguish what come from where. The girl in *Jerusalem the Golden*, like Bennett's first hero, is obsessed with escape, and she too is enraptured by trains and hotels and travelling. . . . my novel is almost as much an appreciation of Bennett as this book is meant to be. (*AB* 48)

Drabble wrote *Jerusalem the Golden* when she went to Paris in 1965 on a Society of Authors travel grant to research her Bennett biography. Rose discusses Bennett's influence on Drabble's novel (*EF*, Ch. 2).

¹² Drabble comments: "*Jerusalem the Golden* is about how far you can lead yourself out by education, the welfare state, the grammar school, lucky encounters, happy relationships with other people. Can you get away from this particular kind of background?" (*VGMI* 14).

¹³ Rose comments: "Drabble uses light imagery to define Clara's aspirations and then undercuts them by associating with the dominant light imagery a verbal motif of coinage, which underscores Clara's ruthlessness in the pursuit of her golden dream" (*EF* 31).

¹⁴ Drabble comments: "My grandmother was called Clara," and "Clara in the book feels that she has been picked out by her peculiar name for a peculiar destiny, and indeed so I suspect it proved to be" (*TWF* 94).

¹⁵ The Denhams, who may be based on the Redgraves, recalls Lady Denham, who also adopted a Clara, in Jane Austen's *Sanditon*, which Drabble edited for Penguin in 1974. Drabble comments on the proxy family: "one has to escape from one's own family and find substitute families or substitute patterns of living. Clara Maugham is certainly looking for another pattern of life that she can go into, and in the book I have ambivalent feelings myself about whether she's found a good one. Clearly not" (*NSHI* 278). This section of the novel, in which Clara is introduced to the Denhams, is headed "Part Two" in the typescript of the novel, which is in the Mugar Memorial Library at Boston University.

¹⁶ This is the segment of *Jerusalem the Golden* (126) which Drabble read aloud on "Novelists of the Sixties" on BBC in 1967 (*BBI* 15).

¹⁷ Drabble remarks, "I often think of the phrase which I use in my own novel *Jerusalem the Golden* (which was very closely modelled on Arnold Bennett): 'The apple does not fall far from the tree,' meaning however hard you try to escape your destiny you will end up where you began" (*TWF* 74).

¹⁸ This verse fragment was inserted into the typescript of the novel in the author's handwriting.

¹⁹ Bernard Bergonzi, *The Situation of the Novel*, 23, says, "Miss Drabble also observed that a scene in her novel, *Jerusalem the Golden*, in which the heroine reads a diary dating from her dead mother's youth, has analogies in Arnold Bennett's *Hilda Lessways* and in Maupassant's *Une Vie*." Drabble comments, "There is a good deal of Hilda Lessways in [Clara] too, for like Hilda she relished adventure and irregularity, and like Hilda she is summoned to her mother's death bed by telegram and does not respond in quite the right spirit" (*AB* 48).

²⁰ For a discussion of this concept, see Nora Foster Stovel's "Margaret Drabble's Golden Vision," *Margaret Drabble:*

Golden Realms, ed. Dorey Schmidt (Edinburg, Texas: Pan-American Univ. Press, 1982), 3-17.

[21] Edwards, 333. Ellen Z. Lambert, "Margaret Drabble and the Sense of Possibility," *University of Toronto Quarterly*, 49 (1980), 237-41, concludes: "There have been many accounts in recent years, in both fictional and non-fictional form, of women hard at work, like Clara, on their own self-advancement—or, if you prefer, self-development. But I know of no other so full of a genuine admiration for that labour and for the hope that fuels it, so tender toward the labourer" (240-41).

[22] Margaret Drabble, "A Pyrrhic Victory," *Nova* (July, 1968), 80-84. Rose concludes: "Drabble suggests that [Clara's] refusal to learn from her experience, to reappraise her values, is a shortcoming rather than a virtue" (*EF* 35).

Chapter Six:

"SUBLIME BLOOD" AND "SUBLIMATED BLOOD": PASSION AND POETRY IN *THE WATERFALL*

"*The Waterfall* is a wicked book," Drabble acknowledges, because it suggests that "one can be saved from fairly pathological conditions by loving a man" (*NSHI* 293). Jane Gray, the pathological protagonist and poet-narrator of *The Waterfall*, desperately needs saving, for she is a self-confessed victim of "schizophrenia or agoraphobia," cut off from reality and humanity and even from her self, "imprisoned in her solipsist universe."[1] *The Waterfall* (1969), Drabble declares, is her "farewell to claustrophobia" (*VGMI* 7), for none of her subsequent heroines is so intensely subjective, isolated, or solipsistic as Jane Gray. Art and life are so divorced in this protagonist that her poetry—which she calls "my sublime blood, my sublimated blood" (130)—can only flow freely when she is virtually paralyzed and utterly alienated from reality, whereas when she is fully alive and in love, the fountainhead of her poetic fluency is dried up at its source. In *The Waterfall*, Jane Gray recounts how love—first maternal affection and finally sexual passion—saves her by reuniting her psyche with her physique, ultimately delivering her from her ivory tower of art into the real world of humanity—like Rosamund Stacey in *The Millstone*.[2]

The Waterfall is as schizoid as its heroine, for the narrative method alternates between Jane Gray's poetic novel about her sublime romance, recounted in the objective third person, and her intimate first-person confessions to the reader, acknowledging how far the fictitious version falsifies the truth of her real-life love affair. Drabble insists that this schizoid narrative was not premeditated but evolved naturally out of the character of the protagonist and the difficulties of producing an account of romantic love both fictional and truthful.[3] The typescript of the novel, full of scissored and taped pages repeatedly reshuffled and renumbered, looks like a living creature, as it bears the scars demonstrating Drabble's dilemma. Even the structure of *The Waterfall* reflects the divided self of the protagonist, for it too is separated into two halves which mirror each other closely: just as Jane's lover James saves her initially from a living death by love, so she subsequently revives him through her faithful affection. Not only are the themes reflected exactly, but even the symbols are precisely parallel as well.

The Waterfall is the most intensely subjective and symbolic of Drabble's sixties novels, because she uses symbolism as a psychological tool for probing the psyche's individual vision and for tracing its development, as the self is delivered from the artistic womb of the imagination into the real world of reason. Symbolism has a special significance in *The Waterfall*, for "the language of *The Waterfall* is poetic," Drabble explains, because "Jane Gray is a poet" (*VGMI* 27), who is "partially based on the poet Sylvia Plath" (*NHI* 24). As a poet-narrator, Jane Gray self-consciously explores the metaphorical resources of language, exploiting the ironic ambiguity of "delivery" and "deliverance," for example, "sublime" and "sublimated," to suggest the intrinsic connections between art and life, the discrepancies between the sublime ideal and the ridiculous reality.

Jane Gray uses water as her central symbol of love because love nourishes humanity just as water refreshes vegetation. Water or blood can also be frozen into ice by the chill of lovelessness or melted into flowing fountains of life by the warmth of affection and the heat of passion. "Water is symbolic" (*NSHI* 291), Drabble declares, for it traditionally signifies the flood of feeling and female nature. Water symbolism positively saturates this novel as a metaphor for the love in which the lovers gladly drown. They are saved, paradoxically, by drowning. Sinking into the depths of passion signifies the lovers' baptism in life, just as immersion in the River Wye symbolized initiation in maternal affection for Emma Evans in *The Garrick Year*.

Drabble introduces the drowning image emphatically at the outset in the epigraph of *The Waterfall*:

>Drowning is not so pitiful
>As the attempt to rise.
>Three times, 'tis said, a sinking man
>Comes up to face the skies,
>And then declines forever
>To that abhorred abode,
>Where hope and he part company—
>For he is grasped of God.

> The Maker's cordial visage,
> However good to see,
> Is shunned, we must admit it,
> Like an adversity.

Emily Dickinson's poem suggests the hopelessness of fighting one's fate. Drabble reinforces this concept in the opening statement of *The Waterfall*: "If I were drowning I couldn't reach out a hand to save myself, so unwilling am I to set myself up against fate." Jane Gray expands her own image at the beginning of her novel:

> If alone, quietly, going under, submerging, she would reject the opportune branch, and fail to make for the friendly bank. Unless cast up there by the water itself, she would drown. There was something sacred in her fate that she dared not countermand by effort. If the current chose to rescue her, it could: providence could deal with her without her own assistance. If she was chosen, she was chosen: if not, then she would quietly refrain from the folly of asserting her belief in her election, in the miraculous interventions of fate on her behalf. (7)

"Jane Gray is a victim" (*BMI* 55), Drabble declares, like her namesake, the pretender who lost her head, but Jane's extended metaphor of drowning and the intervention of fate suggests confidence in her own ultimate salvation.

The most significant symbol of salvation in the novel, of course, is the waterfall of the title. "*The Waterfall* was a title that is embedded in the work itself" (*TWF* 93), Drabble explains; she chose the title deliberately because of the central significance of the two waterfalls to symbolize the lovers' parallel resurrections (*NSHI* 291). In fact, Drabble changed the original title of the novel from *A Moving Accident*, a name that emphasizes the action, to *The Waterfall*, a name that reinforces the symbolism.[4] The watershed of the novel is a card trick called a "waterfall," performed for Jane by James with "sinister dexterity" at the first climax of the narrative (158-59).[5] His "*coup de grâce*" symbolizes James' skill as a lover which effects Jane's "sexual salvation" (161). The second waterfall is Goredale Scar which Drabble offers in *A Writer's Britain: Landscape in Literature* as a traditional example of the Romantic sublime. This actual waterfall symbolizes the romantic passion of the lovers, as they make a pilgrimage to the waterfall to celebrate James' revival and the renewal of their love at the conclusion of the novel.[6]

As *The Waterfall* opens, Jane Gray's blood has been frozen by a frigid marriage into an ice age of alienation: "The temperature of her life seemed to be cooling into some ice age of inactivity, lacking the friction of a dying marriage, lacking even the fragile sparrow-like warmth of her child" (8). Nature reflects Jane's paralysis, shrouding the world with snow.[7] Isolated in the decrepit house which embodies her moribund marriage, connected to society only by the contemporary umbilical cord of the telephone, Jane awaits her delivery, reflecting that delivery seemed at hand. By concentrating all the fires of the cold house into the delivery room, convincing Jane that the close heat would surely generate its own salvation, the midwife transforms Jane's warm, moist, enclosed birth chamber at the top of the stairs into a metaphorical womb in which mother as well as child is delivered.[8]

Childbirth thaws Jane's frozen self into a triple fountain of blood, sweat and tears: "Jane let her whole body weep and flow, graciously, silently submitting herself to these cruel events, to this pain, to this deliverance" (11). Just as the fire melts the snow, so delivery melts Jane's hardened heart and congealed blood. Her liquefaction is proof of her humanity, just as lactation is proof of her femininity. She interprets the sign of her blood on the sheets as a symbol of her renewed vitality: "I am wounded, therefore I bleed. I am human, therefore I suffer" (28), she declares rhetorically, varying Descartes' rational proof of existence with a sentient verification of life.[9]

Paradoxically, Jane's "solitary confinement" delivers her from her solipsistic prison, as it did Rosamund Stacey in *The Millstone*, by immersing her in community. Childbirth heals the classic schizoid state of this contemporary Crazy Jane by rending her: "As I bore Bianca, I think I could feel that I was coming together again, that I could no longer support the division, that my flesh and mind must meet or die" (111). Jane's delivery is both catalyst and symbol for her own deliverance, as it was for Rosamund, because in giving birth, she is herself reborn. Although she names her baby Bianca for the snow, this delivery early in the new year promises renewal. Jane declares, "I knew, as I lay in the bed with new-born Bianca, that I would be saved" (243). Her prophecy is fulfilled.

Romantic passion completes the salvation birth initiates, fulfilling the partial redemption of *The Millstone*. The agent of Jane Gray's sexual salvation is James Otford, the husband of her cousin Lucy, Jane's alter ego. "Love has to be adulterous or forbidden, or it is not romantic," Drabble declares.[10] Seduced by Jane's newly-delivered vulnerability and by an Oedipal attraction to her uterine birth chamber, James completes Jane's liquefaction by the heat of his own passion, burning her in the image of the molten wax with which Psyche branded Cupid.[11]

Her frigid core melted by passion, Jane sinks into the deep waters of love and her own female nature. She symbolizes her sexual salvation by a series of water images and allusions to Victorian fictional floods of passion.[12] "Submitting herself helplessly to the current, abandoning herself to it" (41), Jane mirrors Maggie Tulliver, who also fell in love with her cousin Lucy's man and "drifted off down the river with him, abandoning herself to the water," and finally drowning in the flood. Jane is swept away by the force of her own desires, for, "since Freud, we guess dimly at our own passions, stripped of hope, abandoned forever to that relentless current" (163). After their blind suicidal dive into love, "the waters closed over their heads, and they lay there, submerged, the cold dry land of non-loving abandoned, . . . lost at the sound, at the syllable of the word love" (39). Shipwrecked in a sea of love, Jane is overwhelmed by passive passion: "I lay there, drowned was it, drowned or stranded, waiting for him, waiting to die and drown there, in the oceans of our flowing bodies, in the white sea of that strange familiar bed" (71). Although one of the things she had always most feared in love had been the wetness—as "arid, frightened, fighting like a child for the cold flat dry confines of a narrow bed," she resisted the flood of passion—now, after submerging her frigidity in orgasmic lovemaking with James, she lay there, drowned in a willing sea" (48). So Jane Gray's novel about her love affair, which forms the first part of *The Waterfall*, ends as it began, with the image of drowning, for, as Jane acknowledges, nowadays "we drown in the first chapter" (164).

All the water imagery that runs through the first part of the novel culminates in the first (figurative) waterfall which symbolizes the lovers' sexual union: "The cards fell, in an amazing careful rhythm, interleaving, dovetailing, one by one, joining and melting as they fell into one pack" (159). This cascade of cards, echoing the waterfalls of Victorian female fiction, also signifies Jane's sexual salvation, as she finally falls from her arid aerie into the depths of love, in her first sexual orgasm, until she is "drenched and drowned, down there at last in the water, not high in her lonely place" (160).

Water symbolism is intertwined with floral imagery in *The Waterfall* to signify love's power to nourish even the most arid spirit into fruition. The leafless unwatered twig which "still possessed, despite its barren decay, small faint green horseshoe scars on its brown stem that proved some hidden life" (43), symbolizes Jane herself, who bears "the scars and patched wounds of maternity" (175), which are evidence of regeneration for the dormant heroine also. For months Jane has neglected the plant, merely leaving it to heaven, just as she has passively abandoned herself to fate. But after being surprised herself by love from an empty heaven descending on her arid heart like a rain of grace, she waters the parched plant.[13]

Floral imagery symbolizes the redemptive power of love in *The Waterfall*, as James teaches Jane that "love could still rottenly, beautifully blossom" (90), even out of death. She is amazed to discover "the pure flower of love itself, blossoming out of God knows what rottenness, out of decay, from dead men's lives, growing out of my dead belly like a tulip" (89). Jane offers the fable of the blue rose to symbolize their romance, recounting:

> the tale of a princess in China who says she will marry only the man who brings her a blue rose. She rejects a rose of sapphire, and a rose dyed blue, and a porcelain painted rose, and accepts her lover who brings her an ordinary white rose picked from a hedge on the way, turning to her astonished court, saying to them, you are colour blind, this rose is the only blue rose that I have ever seen. (211)

The parable of the princess and the blue rose embodies perfectly the enchantment of their romance, for the magical bloom is really a garden-variety white rose, its beauty only in the eye of the beholder, who views it through the rose-coloured glasses of love.

Jane Gray employs parallel parables to symbolize the redemptive power of love. She envisions herself as the *princesse lointaine*, the sleeping beauty who is awakened from her death-like trance by love's kiss. James liberates Jane from her solipsistic prison, paradoxically, by enslaving her in an erotic bondage. Fauna as well as flora symbolize the regenerative power of love, for Jane views herself as the slaughtered albatross hanging about her husband's neck, and speculates on Malcolm's reaction to seeing her fly off on snowy unbroken wings. Although she seemed long dead through all her bandages, with her dead flesh bound like a mummy during her postpartum period, Jane is actually a Lazarus who is resurrected by her saviour. Imagining Malcolm's reaction to her revivification, she wonders, "What right had such a corpse to wake, and breathe and walk? How could he endure the sight of my ghostly resurrection?" (187).

James is Jane's god in her new religion of love, for she insists, "He changed me, he saved me, he changed me. . . . He redeemed me by knowing me" (245, 54). James is her creator, for "He had made her, in his own image," recalling Dickinson's Maker. "She was his offspring, as he, lying there between her legs, had been hers," for love is like birth, and Jane is a woman delivered, when she is born into happiness, echoing the birth that opens her tale (161). It is not a baby which is born this time, however, but an integrated adult. Jane lamented her lost soul in an image of alienation: "My mind hovered somewhere near, shut out, like a living soul trying to reenter its dead habitation" (123). Love recreates her by reuniting her spirit with her body. No longer transferring her sublimated blood to sheets of paper in the form of poetry, Jane is now living in her life instead of in her art. By giving body to her love, the word is made flesh.

James delivers Jane from her solitary confinement in her uterine birth chamber, both figuratively and literally, by drawing her out in an erotic pattern of spiralling circles, "delicate widening explorations of their islanded world" (76). After taking her to see the flower gardens at Hampton Court in the early spring, James drives Jane through the vaginal Blackwall Tunnel under the Thames into the open springtime countryside, and finally takes her on an erotic journey to the land of the midnight sun. Although she surrenders to the whole journey, Jane is afraid to emerge from their womb of love, for love "dies if it admits the outside world, or crumbles to dust at the breath of coarser air" (90). And indeed, James strains the umbilical cord too far, and their enchanted world of love shatters.[14] Drabble originally intended to end the novel, initially titled *A Moving Accident*, with the death of both lovers in this fatal car crash as a form of poetic justice or heavenly retribution for their incestuous passion.[15]

Their catastrophic car crash does constitute the climactic turning point of *The Waterfall*, dividing the novel into two parallel structures, the latter half mirroring all the themes and symbols of the former. The accident reduces James to a comatose condition reflecting Jane's earlier catatonic state so precisely that the pair appear alter egos and do share nearly identical names. James is reduced to a virtual corpse, bandaged like a mummy, cut off from reality and even his own psyche, just as Jane was at the outset of the novel.

James' moribund state embodies "the slow death of love, its slow lapsing into insensibility, its ultimate decease." As James lies dying, their love expires with him, for "How can love preserve itself in death? No hope, no hope of eternal preservation, of an ambered corpse, motionless in its glass coffin as he in his hospital bed" (214). The corpse cannot be resurrected this time, but rather collapses in the cold blast of scepticism: "She looked back on the past and saw it crumble to dust, preserved dust, mummified to this point by her sick persistence" (218-19).

The crash strips the blinkers of love from Jane's eyes. She recalls the fable of "the emperor's new clothes, discussed endlessly, stitch by stitch: and suddenly one looks in the light of undeceived day, and the man is naked, like other men, and wanting like them nothing but what all men want" (215). As the two alter ego cousins literally exchange identity, Jane adopts Lucy's sceptical attitude to James along with her name:[16] "I had gazed, in planetary obedience, at what I took to be the bright side of the moon, and I did not want Lucy, by a casual flick of her wrist, to tilt the heavens for me and show me the dark and craterous reverse" (191). In sexual love, "what seems to be a profound matter of the spirit is simply a passing matter of the body" (*NSHI* 287), says Drabble, and the difference appears to be merely a matter of point of view. Disenchanted now, Jane views the fabulous blue rose as "an ordinary white rose, picked from a hedgeful of ordinary indistinguishable blooms: and wilting now, crumpling and browning at the edges, subject to decay" (219).

The same images are used to symbolize love's death as its birth, but since the process is now reversed, the symbols are also. Even the seasonal parallel is reversed, as their love, born in the new year and blossoming in the spring, withers into decay as autumn descends.[17] Jane recalls that blood had been dripping from his nose and ears after the accident, making her realize "how liquid we are, inside our stiff bodies. But whereas Jane's liquefaction was a sign of revival, James' blood is an emblem of his demise. Similarly, love seems to drain away from her like water from a sieve, leaving her high and dry once again: "They had seemed to meet in the profound aspirations of their natures. but it had not been so: they had met in the shallow stretches of ordinary weakness" (219).

Disillusioned, Jane loses faith in their religion of love: "as non-existent an image they had pursued as God, as Santa Claus, as mermaids, as angels, as that non-existent image of eternity." She repudiates all the former symbols of their romance, "For what, after all, in God's name had they been playing at? Fast cars, card tricks, kisses, sighs, vows, the lot?" She realizes that their affair has been more artificial than fiction: "It had been some ridiculous imitation of a fictitious passion, some shoddy childish mock-up of what for others might have been reality" (215). Now that her love is bloodless again, Jane Gray sublimates her passion in poetry once more, living in her art, rather than in reality, since artifice, she concludes, is immortal, unlike love.

After this lapse of love, which is narrated appropriately in the objective third person, Jane recovers her faith in affection, recounting its revival in the intimate first person: "I identified myself with mistrust," she confesses, "and now I cannot articulate my suspicions. I have relegated them to that removed, third person. I identify myself with love, and I repudiate those nightmare doubts" (221). Jane relegates her scepticism, along with her false identity, to her alter ego, Lucy, and resolves to renew her devotion: "I would keep faith. I would refuse to let him die" (202).

The sleeping princess who was awakened by love's kiss now envisions James as the sleeping prince and herself as the faithful serving maid whose loving vigil effects his eventual recovery in the parallel fable:

> For seven long years I served for you,
> The bloody cloth I wrung for you,
> The glassy hill I climbed for you,
> Will you not wake and turn to me? (211)

Jane fulfills the fable rather self-consciously by washing James' bloody shirt in imitation of the maid, because she believes in the symbolic significance of such fables: "Why else had those stories been created, those tales of entranced lovers kept alive through the years by faith, those fables of sleepers and dreamers awoken finally by the intensity and endurance of desire?" (230).

Jane's faithful vigil by the deathbed of her vegetable love corresponds precisely to his watch by her childbed, and her devotion is similarly rewarded, for she observes that "He was responding to my faith" (223). His "lightening" is symbolized by the streak of green which Jane discovers in her basket woven of dry brown rushes, paralleling the plant which prophesied her own renewal, on the day that he first responds to her touch. She says, "I saw him revive, slowly, as he must have felt me revive for him at the beginning of the year" (238). As Jane's love revives, all the symbols of their romance are restored to their original significance. Even James' car, emblem of his virility and eventual destruction, is restored metaphorically by Jane, when she assembles a miniature model for her son Laurie. Joining the crucial pieces of the puzzle so that they articulate, causing the car to come to life, symbolizes Jane's success in reviving James by reuniting his mind and body, as he did hers previously.

As James recovers, so does their love. Jane employs water and vegetation imagery intertwined once again to symbolize the renewal of their romance. Parched with thirst, she recalls that "we saw love as the miraged oasis . . . blue water, green fronds and foliage breaking from the dry earth." But the oasis proves to be no mirage, for the image remained, the water was sweet and the leaves green to the touch. In the middle of the waste land, she finds an "undiscovered country, no shallow quickly-drained sour well, but miles of verdure, rivers, fishes, coloured birds . . . no ending but the illimitable, circular, inexhaustible sea" (223).

A "doomed romantic," Jane symbolizes their love in the Romantic image of a picturesque landscape, playing on the two concepts of romanticism:[18] "I have always believed that a passion adequately strong could wrench a whole nature from its course, and that all the romantic accoutrements of torn skies, uprooted trees, gaping earth and white torrential waters, would follow meekly such a natural disaster" (244). James is the revolution in the elements and Jane the disaster area, the landscape transformed by such an upheaval. Revolution engenders salvation, however, for "I spoke of violence and convulsions, but he made the new earth grow, he made it blossom" (245), she insists. By diverting the current of her fate from its headlong course toward death, James redirects Jane's destiny through the violence of his passion, into new channels of life: "I would flow in the course that he had made for me: there was no way of returning to the old confines, the old high banks through which I used to run" (246). In Victorian fiction, the price of love was death, Jane observes, but now love, even adulterous passion, leads to new life.

Goredale Scar is the culmination of all the Romantic landscape symbolism in *The Waterfall*. Recalling the maternal scars, emblems of regeneration, that score Jane's body, this final waterfall forms a female sexual symbol of fertility in a Freudian manner that Drabble explicates in *A Writer's Britain: Landscape in Literature*: "Any post-Freudian would of necessity see this landscape in terms of sexual imagery—the hollow cavern, the gushing water, the secrecy of the approach, the tufted trees" (129). Drabble's comment corresponds closely to Jane Gray's own description of "the roofless cave of the Scar itself, where huge curved echoing rock sides stretched up above us, and water leapt down through the sides of the cleft ... a wildness contained within a bodily limit" (252).

The lovers' pilgrimage to Goredale Scar forms an apotheosis to the novel, celebrating the continuing current of their romance, as well as James' recovery, just as the first waterfall symbolized Jane's salvation and the conception of their passion.[19] But the "feminine ending" (246) of a thrombic clot which forms such a "fitting conclusion to the sublimities of nature," provides a cynical postscript that redeems Jane's "romantic fallacy" (254). Romanticism has the last word in *The Waterfall*, nevertheless, for the resonance of Goredale Scar, echoed in the title of the novel, dominates the conclusion of the book as the natural culmination of all the water imagery which has run through the work. Climbing the waterfall, the lovers discover the wildflower called "Heart's Ease," an emblem that recapitulates all the water and vegetation imagery of the novel to symbolize love's power to inspire the spirit to blossom. Through symbolism, then, sublimity overwhelms cynicism to signify spiritual salvation through sexual passion.

NOTES

[1] Margaret Drabble, *The Waterfall* (London: Weidenfeld and Nicolson, 1969), 243, 192. Subsequent references to this edition will be documented within the text. *The Waterfall* was dramatized by Peter Duffell for BBC TV in 1980 as a four-part series, starring Robin Ellis, Lisa Harrow, and Caroline Mortimer.

[2] Drabble explains:

> Rosamund is a solipsist, and so is Jane. Jane is the dottiest, the nearest to madness, of all the characters. And she, through James, learns to go out and down the street and that kind of thing. I mean she has got in such a narrow world that she is more or less unable to face the outside world. Rosamund, through the baby, is forced to encounter the outside world. The idea is that once you're forced to make contact through your lover or your child, then it's all right somehow. The other people are there. They're not just part of the images of your own imagination. (*NSHI* 291)

[3] Drabble explains the unintentional origins of this interesting experimental narrative technique: "In writing *The Waterfall* I tried to begin in the third person. I intended to write the whole book in the third person about a love affair, and I found the language was undercutting itself the whole time, and I had to revert to the first person in order to speak more directly and tell a different kind of truth" (*TWF* 107).

Ellen Cronan Rose discusses the schizoid narrative method of *The Waterfall* in *Equivocal Figures*, 49-70. In *Critical Essays on Margaret Drabble*, ed. Ellen Cronan Rose (Boston: G.K. Hall, 1984), Joanne V. Creighton discusses the reader's response to this ambiguous narrative technique in "Reading Margaret Drabble's *The Waterfall*"; in "The Progress of a Letter: Truth, Feminism and *The Waterfall*," Eleanor Honig Skoller discusses Drabble's experimentation with narrative method as Jane Gray questions the possibility of representing the truth of female experience in traditional realist fiction (119-32).

[4] The typescript of *The Waterfall*, bearing the original title, *A Moving Accident*, is in the McFarlin Library at The University of Tulsa.

[5] In "Confessions of a Punster," in *More Words* (London: BBC, 1977), 44, Drabble says that "sinister dexterity" is her favourite pun.

⁶ Drabble states that "Gray's famous description of Goredale Scar [is] one of the most complete illustrations of the literary concept of the sublime" (*WB* 126). She insists, "Goredale Scar does exist and I went to it. It is an example of the sublime. The passions of Jane and James were meant to be an example of sublime, romantic passion" (*NSHI* 292).

⁷ In "Heroine in an Empty House," *The Times*, 21 May 1969, 12, Drabble told John Horder that "I have tried to face the pathological state of inactivity in *The Waterfall*. Also the fear of complete abandonment which sometimes goes hand in glove with extreme passivity." Drabble commented to Valerie Grosvenor Myer that she herself had a baby in circumstances very similar to Jane Gray's.

⁸ "For a woman, freedom begins in the womb," writes Drabble in "The Sexual Revolution," *The Manchester Guardian Weekly*, 12 October 1967, 9. Elaine Showalter, in *A Literature of Their Own: British Women Novelists from Brontë to Lessing* compares Jane Gray's delivery room to the uterine chamber in which Jane Eyre is imprisoned, adding, "For a Drabble heroine, a room of one's own is usually a place to have a baby" (336).

⁹ In "The Fiendish Curse," in *More Words* (45-48), Drabble discusses natural female symbols and the significance of blood. She laments "the shortage of female language" for *The Waterfall*, which she calls "the most female of all my books" (45). Drabble explains, "When I was writing my novel *The Waterfall* I ran into some very severe problems with the language which I tried to use to describe the experience of romantic passion" (*TWF* 107).

¹⁰ Drabble adds, "I felt a curious commitment to exploring the viability of romantic love . . . a complete madness which depends on two people being selfish at the expense of everyone else" (*NHI* 25).

¹¹ Roberta Rubenstein, in "*The Waterfall*: The Myth of Psyche, Romantic Tradition, and the Female Quest" (*GR* 139-57), explores Drabble's use of "myths and allegories of sacred and profane love," especially "the myth of Cupid and Psyche" (139).

¹² Showalter compares Drabble's use of "Victorian images of floods and cascades" (131) to George Eliot and Charlotte Brontë, two significant models referred to explicitly in *The Waterfall*.

¹³ Drabble says, "One of the images I like best is the plant

in *The Waterfall*" (*BMI* 64), because she believes in "watering the spirit" (*VGMI* 40).

[14] Myer writes, "Cars are driven by sexy, dangerous men, whirling women on journeys into illicit passion. Set on collision courses, these cars bring their own punishment in the form of crashes" (*PP* 135).

[15] Drabble acknowledges:

> When I wrote *The Waterfall*, which is about death and romantic love, I meant to kill the two main characters, because the end of romantic love is death. Then I realized I had a technical problem, that if you kill your half-narrator, how are you going to explain this away? And then, also, as I continued on with the book, I found that death was no resolution; they had to continue to live. So that book has a peculiar structure, in that it seems to be leading to death, and, in fact, they survive. . . . James is more or less killed and is resurrected: he dies the little death. (*VGMI* 4, 39)

Drabble's initial intention is reflected in the original title of *The Waterfall*, *A Moving Accident*, a Wordsworthian phrase that Rosamund Stacey discusses with Lydia Reynolds in *The Millstone*, 75.

[16] Drabble acknowledges: "The relationship between the two cousins in the book is actually very much more my relationship with a very close friend of mine: which I sort of transposed" (*NPI* 263).

[17] Drabble employs a similar seasonal parallel in her short story, "The Reunion," in *Winter Tales* 14 (London: Macmillan, 1968), 149-68, with the love affair budding in the spring, flowering in the summer and withering in the autumn—the parallel emphasized by a calendar, depicting the seasons, which overlooks the place where the lovers meet and part.

[18] In *The Waterfall*, Drabble plays on the relationship between the concepts "Romantic" and "romantic." "We are all post-Romantics now," she declares in her "Introduction" to her edition of Jane Austen's *Lady Susan, The Watsons, Sanditon* (Harmondsworth: Penguin, 1974), 29.

[19] Drabble comments intriguingly: "I went to see [Goredale Scar]. I'd nearly finished the novel when I went to see it. I went expressly in order to write the ending of the novel. I went with a friend of mine who in fact had got a bad leg, like James, so everything fit in very nicely" (*NSHI* 292).

Chapter Seven:

THROUGH *THE NEEDLE'S EYE*

The Needle's Eye (1972), written when Margaret Drabble's own marriage was coming to an end, is about a custody suit. But it is a divorce with a difference, for after winning the case, the heroine, Rose Vassiliou, takes her husband back—to the disgust of feminist critics who interpret her decision as a moral failure. Regarding "the defeatism of Rose's decision to return to her husband, Christopher, which women in particular, and Women's Liberation even more particularly, tend to see as some kind of sell-out,"[1] Monica Mannheimer judges, in the first published article on the book, that "*The Needle's Eye* is a sad and defeatist novel in which the possibility of genuine self-realization seems more remote than in any of Margaret Drabble's previous works."[2] Ellen Cronan Rose sums up the feminist critical view succinctly when she concludes, "Like Rose, Drabble has regressed" (*EF* 91).

As the title indicates, however, *The Needle's Eye* is not about liberation, but salvation. In "The Author Comments," her published response to Mannheimer's article, Drabble explains, "One of the themes I was trying to explore was the possibility of living, today, without faith, a religious life" (35). Reviewer Joyce Carol Oates was indeed prophetic when she predicted that *The Needle's Eye* dramatizes "a spiritual dilemma so profound that many readers—and writers—will not grasp it at all."[3] The dominant symbol of *The Needle's Eye*, which provides the title of the novel, embodies the major theme of the work: the relationship between financial success and spiritual salvation. As Drabble explains, "*The Needle's Eye* is a biblical title, referring to the phrase: 'It is easier for a camel to pass through the eye of a needle than for a rich man to enter the kingdom of heaven'" (*TWF* 93). The first novel in Drabble's mature social fiction of the seventies, and the author's own favourite (*BMI* 60), *The Needle's Eye* is not just about domesticity and romance, but money and morality in the modern world.[4]

In *The Needle's Eye*, Drabble debates two possible paths to salvation: through renunciation or possession of riches. The central conflict of the novel is between law and love—the negative method of sacrifice or the positive path of community. The key to Drabble's moral meaning is not so much in the surface vehicle of the action as in the underlying symbolism. *The Needle's Eye* approximates the complexity of allegory, as Drabble debates the opposing principles of nature and culture through a complicated network of imagery.

Love is symbolized by flowers, and law is signified by stone—the rock of renunciation on which salvation is founded. Floral images and Biblical and civil laws resound throughout the novel like refrains, as the flower of love is crushed beneath the double yoke of the law of God and the law of man.[5] Drabble uses her characters in this novel as allegorical figures to debate the conflicting themes. Her heroine, Rose, symbolized by flowers, represents nature, which is crushed by culture. Her hero, Simon, a lawyer, is signified by stone, suggesting the apostle Simon, called Peter.[6] Rose does become Simon's democratic deity when she forsakes her fortune in her quest for salvation. And Rose in turn builds her social religion on the rock of Simon's democratic dogma. To complete the triangle, Rose's impoverished husband, Christopher, whose name signifies the bearer of Christ, believes in the parable of the talents, whereas the heiress Rose is ruled by the law of the needle's eye.[7] Drabble uses the interwoven network of imagery to debate these opposing principles of possession and renunciation in her most allegorical novel yet.

The flower of nature in *The Needle's Eye* is Rose herself. As a child, Rose collects wildflowers, symbols of a childhood passed in harmony with nature in the gardens of her English country home. But Rose presses her wildflowers in a book, symbolizing the way her own nature becomes repressed by culture. Marking the end of her flower collection is the caterpillar accidentally crushed between its leaves—a humorous emblem of the existence of evil.

The real serpent in Rose's garden, however, is her puritanical nurse, who instills a sense of original sin in the young girl. Noreen crushes Rose's budding nature beneath the burden of Biblical law, just as Rose crushed the wildflowers in her book, for Noreen's laws were "all the cruel ones, like the camel and the needle, and to those that have it shall be given."[8]

The dictum "Strait is the gate" (332) forms the crux of Noreen's teaching, and in the motif of gateways that pervades the novel, the needle's eye is the straitest gate of all. Noreen teaches Rose that money is the root of all evil. The epiphanic experience of Rose's youth is a sermon about it's being easier for camels to get through needles' eyes than for rich people to get into the kingdom of heaven. Rose says, "it was like the Road to Damascus, a horribly heavenly light shone upon me" (74), for Rose is the heiress to a vast family fortune. Rose envies the poor in spirit, for they will inherit heaven, while the heritage of this poor little rich girl is not salvation, but damnation. Noreen is the angel who drives Rose out of the garden of Eden with a flaming sword, when her bitter revelation of the wickedness of riches puts a sudden end to the golden age of Rose's childhood innocence.

The sword with which Noreen drives Rose out of the garden is actually a razor blade, for Rose tries to cut at the very roots of Noreen's cruel laws, testing the truth of her dour revelation. By shedding her own blood in this ritualistic manner, Rose initiates herself into knowledge of evil: "So it had all seemed true. Razors cut, Christ was crucified, man was wicked, hell was open." Rose demands, "it being so, what can I do to be saved?" (329). Since her fortune is her fate, Rose is born with the burden of original sin. She declares, "I refuse to believe I was damned from birth," and so she effects "a personal revolution. It even had a little bloodshed, to prove it." She announces, "All alone, I arrest the course of nature. I arrest it. I divert the current" (104).

Convinced by this symbolic blood sacrifice of the truth of the laws "about the rich not getting into heaven, and the needle's eye, and unless you give all that you have to the poor ye shall not" (80), Rose decides to act on her revelation: "Rose thought about the camel and the needle's eye. What was the point of knowing what was right, if one didn't then do it?" So Rose takes a solemn vow: "I'll never possess anything, I said to myself, that I fear to lose" (75). She conceives a passion for renunciation, for only by divesting herself of her fortune can she pass through the eye of the needle.[9]

Rose renounces her heritage by marrying the poor Greek immigrant, Christopher Vassiliou: as a result, her capitalist father disinherits her, and her aristocratic mother disowns her. By marrying Christopher, Rose allies herself with the poor in spirit who will inherit heaven: "She had, after all, first wanted and meekly followed Christopher because he was one of the dispossessed—doubly so, financially and racially—and Noreen had taught her to despise possessions." But "few people would have been able to make the connection between Noreen, grim, evangelical, life-denying, pinched and priggish and retreating, and Christopher, beautiful, dirty, seedy Christopher" (79).

By freeing herself from the bondage of Biblical law, ironically, Rose falls into the bonds of civil law. To forestall her marriage, her father makes her a ward of court, serves an injunction on Christopher forbidding him to see her, and sentences Rose to eight months exile on the continent with a spinsterish chaperone until she comes of age. On the eve of exile, Rose finds her flower garden frozen:

> wandering aimlessly in a static frozen garden, knowing that the time would never pass until she should see him again, coming at one point to a standstill, transfixed, gazing at a flowering currant bush by the garage, each flower dripping red blood like a bleeding heart or a strawberry fruit pastille, she had turned to ice, it too, the bush, burning like a message, had frozen, each flower, each leaf, each twig instinct with eternity, a horrible hush, a horrible pause, a silence, a stopping of the blood in the middle of the evening. (333)

Law casts an evil spell on nature, freezing the flowers and halting time, just as it paralyzes Rose.

Although Rose crosses the Channel from her continental purgatory, like Leander swimming the Hellespont to his Hero, the chill of legal separation has frozen their passion to death. The dim prophetic pall of sky over the coffin-like white cliffs of Dover symbolizes the shroud of their murdered love. They marry nevertheless—"for better or worse. For worse, as it so happened." Rose acknowledges that "Christopher would have got life from a stone," but her frozen heart does not melt. Although they observe the letter of their marriage vows, the spirit is gone from their love: "they could do nothing to revoke the death of the spirit. The spirit bloweth whither it listeth"—just as Noreen said, for "it had died between them, it had been brutally murdered" (112).

There is no returning to the garden after their legal expulsion: "they had reached such depths now that the walls behind them—to that flat plateau of mutual co-existence, of occasionally sunny tolerance—were no longer scalable" (81).

Love, murdered by law, is handed over to the divorce courts for dissection. Rose envisions "love as some huge white deformed and not very lovely god, lying there beneath the questions and the formality, caught in a net of which points alone touched and confined him" (84).

Despite her divorce and disinheritance, Rose cannot escape her heritage completely, for thirty thousand pounds, put in trust to avoid supertax by her parsimonious father, mature when she does. In a frantic effort to free herself of this damning fortune, Rose donates her entire inheritance to Ujuhudiana, an impoverished African country, to rebuild a school which has been destroyed in a civil war in the capital, Gbolo. The donation goes up in smoke quite literally when the school is destroyed in a new outbreak of violence, killing over one hundred children.

Believing that "charity is for the sake of the giver, to save the soul of the giver, not the receiver," Rose has made a desperate attempt to purchase salvation. She acknowledges that her donation has been "a flamboyant, histrionic, disastrous, ruinous gesture" (77). Moreover, there is another huge sum due to mature in a few years, which she is powerless to prevent. Nor can she prevent her children inheriting the family fortune. Recognizing that she cannot escape her heritage, Rose acknowledges the truth of Noreen's bitter Biblical laws: "To them that have it shall be given," for riches increase and multiply.

After her philanthropic fiasco, Rose retreats from the danger of deeds, deciding that it is safer to seek salvation through faith rather than through works: "Better to do no very evident good than to do harm. . . . You can take this story as an explanation of why I've given up public causes—and why I think I ought to sit here at home and keep quiet and dig my own garden" (103). Rose reverts to utter passivity in an effort to recapture the innocuous state of her infancy.

Rose's real goal is to return to the garden of her childhood innocence, before Noreen poisoned paradise with a sense of original sin. As a child, Rose envisioned a land of "mystic and visionary loveliness, a thin aspiring castle on the brow of a green hill, a tower above the raging sea, a heavenly city" (107). As an adolescent, Rose finds her vision echoed in Christian's faith-created mirage of a heavenly city" in Bunyan's *Pilgrim's Progress* (329).[10] As an adult, Rose attempts to realize her ideal image of the city of God quite literally in North London.

Realizing that her school in Gbolo was a house built on sand, Rose determines to build her next house on a firmer foundation. She attempts to found a house of God in Middle Road: "she built up brick by brick the holy city of her childhood; the holy city in the shape of that patched subsiding house" (53). Her home becomes her sanctuary: "I created it for myself. Stone by stone and step by step. I carved it out, I created it by faith. I believed in it, and then very slowly, it began to exist. And now it exists. It's like God, it requires faith" (36).

Rose's heavenly house is built on the rock of renunciation. Poverty is paradise to this heiress, and the shabbiness of her furnishings measures her degree of righteousness: "There was some inexplicable grace, in living so. Useless it probably was, like living in a closed order. Irrelevant, unproductive. But, as a nun attaches significance to arbitrary vows, so she had attached it to this place that she inhabited" (148), for there, "her life had at last become. as she had so long willed it to be, innocuous" (50).

The house in Middle Road becomes a symbol of conflict between husband and wife, for, as Christopher prospers, he wishes to move to a more affluent neighbourhood where his children can benefit from his prosperity. But Rose refuses: "How can I move house? It's my whole being that's there" (258), she argues. Nevertheless, "She uneasily knew quite well that her position was false, whatever it was, and that she could only maintain it through certain kinds of cheating" (136), for she is actually a rich little poor girl merely playing the part of poverty. Her son Konstantin[11] calls her "a whited sepulchre" (161), and she acknowledges that, "living here in this little house, it's nothing but a mockery" (93). Although Rose tries to cultivate her garden in Middle Road, she cannot flourish in foreign soil.

The conflict in her origins is embodied in her name, Rose Vertue Bryanston, for Rose is torn between her mother's aristocratic, impoverished Vertue family and her father's bourgeois, capitalist Bryanston family. As the narrator observes, "What a ghastly mistake in evolution for man to have attached such significance to identity, when he is condemned for survival to partition" (261). More important, a moral conflict is represented by the name Rose, which links her with nature, and the name Vertue, which inspires "delusions of virtue" (312) in her breast. Into this fertile soil Noreen has planted the seed of discord by stimulating the virtuous side of Rose's nature at the expense of the natural side, teaching her that the path to salvation is through law, not love. Noreen finds an eager disciple in Rose, for, as the author says of her favourite heroine, "she is a girl who hungers and thirsts after righteousness" (*NSHI* 285).[12]

Law and love continue to war in Rose's heart, however, for, although she has renounced her heritage, her desire to cultivate her garden suggests her continuing urge to return to nature. After abandoning her wildflowers, the resurgence of this natural urge is represented by the floral birthday card, which, as a lonely adolescent at boarding school, Rose buys herself. As an adult, she stumbles on the card in a book: "there it was, the final blow, the lurking horror, as disagreeable as the caterpillar she had once pressed by accident in her flower book." But the flowery card contradicts the pessimistic passage it marks in Bunyan's *Grace Abounding to the Chief of Sinners*, for "the card, in marked contrast to the text, was cheerful and floral: it showed a bowl of flowers in a cottage window" (331).

Rose's quest for wildflowers has actually persisted, however: although deterred for a time by the indictment of the crushed caterpillar, Rose overcomes her squeamishness and continues her collection when she discovers a rare corncockle in Branston gardens. The gardener stimulates her search by saving rare blooms for her and teaching her the difference between flowers and weeds. But after the night of the frozen flowers, she has never returned home to continue her quest, even though Konstantin tempts her with news of rare bird's-nest orchids in the Branston woods.

Quixotically, Rose pursues her quest in Middle Road, where she searches for the London Rocket—a rare flower which symbolizes Rose herself, because it is a modest and unattractive little plant that grows on waste patches and is virtually indistinguishable from the common rocket, even though it is "the real thing" (218). Rose thinks she is ideally placed to discover this rare bloom in the waste land of Middle Road, but she never does, for she cannot discover her true nature when she is cut off from her real roots.

What Rose does discover is a bit of spurge, which recalls to her mind Rossetti's poem, "The Woodspurge." Rose recites:

"The woodspurge has a cup of three,/ After long grief and misery/ That is all that is left to me" (217). Rossetti's woodspurge, with its "three cups in one," inevitably suggests the Trinity, and the bit of greenery growing in a bomb site amidst a patch of weeds out of the sun implies Rose's righteous isolation in Middle Road. Religion is Rose's only consolation for her desertion of her true nature, for her real roots are at home in Branston gardens, not in the asphalt jungle of Middle Road.

Simon Camish, Drabble's first major male figure in her first novel with two central consciousnesses, is the character who looks through the eye of the needle that frames this modern portrait of a lady.[13] Simon relishes his Jamesian role as Rose's observer and confidant: "He watched her: she was a vision kindly bestowed" (299); "Gifts her words were, her confidences" (36).[14] As his name suggests, Simon is also a disciple who views Rose as a saint. Her antique dress inspires Simon's hagiography: "She looked, because of age and softness, authentic, as ancient frescoes look in churches, frescoes which in their very dimness offer a promise of truth that a more brilliant (however beautiful) restoration often denies" (17).

Simon is bound to Rose by complex ties, as these two central characters interact in this highly complicated novel. Although Simon and Rose have made opposite socio-economic journeys, their spiritual voyages are parallel. The same "spirit of desolation" inspired each of them, for Simon's mother and Rose's nurse are both cut from the same Calvinist cloth as Clara Maugham's mother. Mrs. Camish stunted Simon's young nature, just as Noreen crushed Rose, under the burden of Biblical laws, such as, "The fathers have eaten sour grapes, and the children's teeth are set on edge." The seminal experience of Simon's youth also occurs at church: "The psalm was the 137th Psalm, about the waters of Babylon, and its message was that the sins of the fathers shall be visited upon the children, and that the brains of the children of one's enemy should be dashed out upon the rocks." Simon fears that he can never escape from his hereditary doom, because he believes in the cruel laws of the Old Covenant: "The sour grapes, the crushing of grapes, and the battering of babies' soft skulls. Israel and Egypt, from generation unto generation" (23-24).

Simon's mother also hoped to evade this grim heritage:

"She had nourished dreams of escape herself, once she had looked forward to a brighter dawn" (118)—just like Clara Maugham's mother.[15] Frustrated in her own hopes, Mrs. Camish transfers her aspirations to her son, for mothers, Simon realizes, "bent on their sons the peculiar weight of their own thwarted ambitions. From generation unto generation" (24).

To evade this hereditary doom, Simon attempts to remake himself: "Oh Christ, it was exhausting, this living on the will, this denial of nature, this unnatural distortion," he complains. But in denying his nature, he merely stunts it, like Rose's crushed wildflowers, for "The distortions . . . rose sorrowfully, like plants in a cellar, deprived, but always rising. Plants in a cellar, laid away until the spring" (171-72).

Simon camouflages his working-class background under the protective coloration provided by the law. Just as Rose's emblem is the London Rocket, Simon's symbol is "the peppered moth, which had evolved a black species to survive in the industrial landscape. Biston betularia, the Manchester moth, its lighter brethren dying, its blackened survivors clinging grimly to the blackened walls and tree trunks" (271).

Simon escapes from his grim background by a mercenary marriage. The ostentatious prosperity of the Phillips family represents "the very opposite of his own cold, over-wrought, conscience-striken, guilt-ridden childhood, where every mouthful of food had been taken from his mother's very plate, or torn (figuratively) from her bleeding breast." Simon acknowledges that "He had fallen in love with a way of life," symbolized by "the heart-shaped cover on the lavatory seat—objects which made his mother's impoverished, sensitive heart shudder with alarm" (55-56). His fiancée's father celebrates the engagement by showing Simon his latest trivial toy: "The plastic pillow took on a symbolic significance: like a ring, it cemented the contract, it embodied his engagement to Julie, and was never more to be dissociated from that moment" (64).

Eventually, Simon wishes to renounce Mr. Phillips' self-made millions—generated by a hire-purchase mail-order business as distasteful as the crass capitalism of Rose's upstart industrialist father.[16] But "caught between reality and aspiration" (124), he is inescapably trapped by his duties and obligations: "his spirit would struggle feebly within the net that held it, and he would imagine some pure evasion, some massive rent through which he could emerge." But there is no escape: "he was caught. And his spirit would hunch its feathered bony shoulders, and grip its branch, and fold itself up and shrink within itself, until it could no longer brush against the net, until it could no longer entangle itself, painfully, in that surrounding circumstantial mesh" (126).

Frustrated in his desire for freedom, Simon clenches himself into a stony silence. If the heroine's natural emblem is the rose, the hero's symbol is the rock, for it consolidates Simon's sense of identity. He acknowledges, "It is precious to me, this dull and ordinary stone. It is always there. It is called resolution" (13).

Simon's spirit has petrified because he is rootless. He ponders the root of the word radical: "What does it have to do with roots, he wanted to know—a cutting of roots, a planting of old roots, a discovery of roots?" (24). Simon realizes how much he has lost by uprooting himself, for, like Rose, he cannot flourish when he is deracinated. The only emotion left in Simon's stony heart at the outset of the novel is nostalgia for his lost roots.

In the opening scene of *The Needle's Eye*, Simon is overwhelmed with nostalgia when he encounters a woman from this lost land: "He felt such violent waves of nostalgia possess him that he nearly spoke. He knew where she came from, this woman: it was a world from which he was forever exiled. But he knew it: he knew its domestic interiors, its pleasures, its horizons" (4).[17] Nostalgia is the first feeling that binds Simon to Rose, for he rediscovers his lost roots in Rose's house in Middle Road.

Following this seminal meeting, Simon visits his frozen garden: "A perpetual winter was what he expected: he would, he felt, experience no surprise should, one spring, the trees refuse to bud, and the flowers to blossom." But he discovers in the garden "a ghostly white crumpled bud of a rose . . . frozen into an everlasting flower, never to open, never to die, a witness, a signal, a heroic pledge." Recalling Rose's own agony in the garden, the rosebud symbolizes a promise of renewal for Simon.[18] He marvels at nature's generosity: "By what grace did these green hopes and gentle exhalations perpetually recur? He had done nothing to deserve so munificent a resurgence" (69-70). Despite the winter of his discontent, Rose renews Simon's nature by melting his stony heart, as the sun thaws the frozen earth in the spring.[19]

To celebrate the rebirth of spring, Rose and Simon visit the chickens and the armchair. Seeing this "vista of shabby amusements and moth-eaten satisfactions" through Rose's eyes redeems it for Simon. He acknowledges that "he loved Rose, in so far as he considered himself capable of love" (214). As a result of this resurrection of affection, "So great and innocent a peace possessed him that it seemed like a new contract, like the rainbow after the flood. He could feel it, on his bare hands and face. It lay upon him. It was like happiness" (219).

Simon resolves to emulate Rose by digging his own garden, both literally and figuratively. Stones rather than flowers flourish in his garden, but "Simon had a sudden apocalyptic vision, unsolicited, of the day when the world shall turn to grass once more, and the tender flowers will break and buckle the great paving stones" (123). He also takes his family to the Cornwall seashore for Easter, where he renews his relationship with nature and with his own offspring, from whom he has become estranged.

Simon's professional problem is that he "can't see the trees for the wood" (199), but Rose introduces him to the individual trees that compose the collective wood by leading him into her own forest at Branston. The dangling corpse of a stoat, strung up on a tree as a warning to trespassers, symbolizes the sign "Private Woods" on the gate. Rose counters this gruesome emblem of private property by inspiring in Simon a vision of a democratic paradise: "it was the wood in which the trees grew. May the forests of it cover the earth, he oh so hopelessly desired. Shake down the superfluity." Rose paints a picture of a heaven on earth for Simon: "It was as though one were to desire the kingdom of heaven. Where the rich may not enter, where greed may perish. Not of this world is the kingdom, but there is no other world" (200-01).

Simon admires Rose's personal revolution in pursuit of her ideal vision, because "He was no idealist, no visionary, no revolutionary" (199). Simon has sold his soul for money, while Rose has forfeited her fortune to purchase spiritual salvation. Rose redeems the democratic ideal for Simon when he sees her enter the gates of her own home as a paying guest on a Branston public day:

> What was the point of any virtue, any grace, if it was not of the common lot, there could be no beauty behind a gate marked Private, let them trample around on the

flowerbeds, all of them, any of them: there was a hymn they had sung at school, it came back to him often, it said, The grass is softer to my tread, because it rests unnumbered feet, sweeter to me the wild rose red, because she makes the whole world sweet. (301)

Rose becomes Simon's democratic deity, but she is soon to be toppled from her pedestal on the rock of Simon's resolution by Christopher's talents.

In the custody suit that forms the surface conflict of *The Needle's Eye*,[20] Simon defends Rose's rights: "He acquitted her, he credited her, he preferred to blame the man he did not know, the absent father" (179). As a good lawyer, however, Simon knows that there are two sides to every story, and the moment when he becomes Christopher's confidant marks the turning point of the novel. "It became clear to Simon that he would have to abandon, for ever, his hope, which had once been as strong as a certainty: his hope, that Christopher had married Rose for her money, simply, and would as simply, one day, forfeit her. Christopher, evidently, had no interest in the money at all. . . . What he was interested in was power, and motivation, and emotion, and love" (231-32).

The conflict between Christopher and Rose is not monetary, but moral. Whereas Rose's motivation is symbolized by the negative principle of the needle's eye, Christopher's is signified by the positive parable of the talents, for he believes that one should not bury one's natural gifts (or gold coins), but cause them to increase and multiply. As one of the dispossessed, Christopher appreciates roots, whereas the privileged heiress prefers deracination. So Rose's obsession with renunciation is in direct conflict with Christopher's passion for possession.

Christopher wants to rescue his children from Rose because he views her as "a crazed woman, denying her children for the thin glamour of an idea" (151). Christopher confides prophetically in Simon: "You've no idea how absolutely wicked and selfish people are when they get hold of this idea of being good. They destroy everything about them. They end up in a burning desert" (232-33).

Simon is a latter-day Solomon, forced to judge which parent's claim is greater.[21] "How dreadful it is, he thought suddenly, that children are born of two parents, that they are the property of two parents with equal claim, that they do not spring fully grown from the brain as Athene sprang from Zeus." In desperation over this insoluble conflict, Rose is tempted simply to sacrifice the children to their father to spare them from the axe: "Rose, the true mother perhaps, would leave the baby kicking there, in the chalk circle, unable to resist a rival claim" (261-62).

It is not the children who are split by the axe, however, but Rose's mind, which is divided between law and love. Rose believes that giving up her most cherished possessions, her children, is the logical conclusion of her vow of renunciation. Rose recalls, "If ye will not give up wife and mother and children to follow me," he said, unhelpfully, cruelly, "ye shall in nowise enter into the kingdom of heaven." She believes that sacrifice is essential for salvation: "It is sacrifices that God has always demanded. He demanded Isaac. On the hill-top, the innocent. He shall have my children" (263-64).

The mother struggles with the martyr, as Rose is tempted by a palpable vision of herself as a missionary in the burning desert of Ujuhudiana: "She contemplated the vision. It seemed real, it seemed solid, it breathed life. And then, to test it, she conjured up the image of her children. They too seemed real and living. Incompatible, incompatible." The conflict is intolerable: "She prayed for the angel that appeared to Jacob. Oh God, she prayed, release me, be merciful, send me an angel with a sword, tell me what I must do. Restore me, restore me, I cannot endure a moment longer" (263).

Despite her divided self, Rose recognizes the devilish nature of the temptation: "You realize, of course, what you've done, said Rose, mother of three children to that unpleasant martyr, that faithless missionary. You've simply constructed for yourself the most horrible renunciation your mind can conceive." Realizing that sacrifice is no salvation, Rose rejects the imaginary vision of martyrdom and returns to the reality of maternity: "the woman rose to her feet, white and wailing. In Rose's mind she wailed, like a soul in hell. On the bottom right-hand corner of the day of judgement she wept and wrung her hands, across the continents" (264-65). The mother has conquered the martyr at last, and Rose returns home to care for her children.

Christopher frustrates Rose's resolution, however, by kidnapping the children. He takes them to Branston via Grimes Graves, suggesting the purgatory before paradise. Rose, naturally, follows them there. Thus, Christopher reunites the entire family for the first time in the novel. Simon, relegated to the role of observer once again, witnesses Rose's reunion with her husband and children in the rose garden: "the meeting seemed to go on forever, in that exposed spot: or wave after wave of it occurred and reoccurred, as though time had broadened endlessly to describe it. . . . The high green hedges froze in a crest, about to break: the smell of trodden grass surged and rose and surged again" (300). Nature, which froze on the eve of exile, is redeemed by this renewal of relationship. The reunion marks the real resolution of *The Needle's Eye*—"so clearly had this gathering constituted itself as a finale, as a dénouement, as a conclusion" (305).

The "prodigal daughter" returned, Rose discovers that viewing the crusty old man through Christopher's eyes gives "her father's image a pale gleam of hope. . . . This attempt at insight startled Rose: she could not remember that she had ever seen him as a separate person before. . . . Really, thought Rose, whatever has come over me, I sit here forgiving them all, have I been wrong all this time, or is it that I have got tired of resentment?" She is even moved to forgive Christopher for the kidnapping: "ever since meeting him in the garden, she had been feeling (in the peace of victory) a slight forgiveness.... Rose looked at Christopher: really, she thought, in the end, one had just got to take him, and that's that. Her spirit, for the first time in years, moved to acceptance: she felt it embark for that final flight, she imagined it might one day rise and reach and settle in the clearer air" (304-23).

But Rose must still lay the ghost of Noreen and her own neurosis. Like Clara, Rose enters the forbidden room, infested still by the sinister fragrance of Eau de Nil. Finding the floral card in Bunyan's autobiography of anguish, she rereads the pessimistic passage and falls under its fatalistic spell once again: "It had all come about as Noreen had predicted: there had been no appeal from her darker pronouncements. And it being so ... what can I do to be saved?" (329).

Finally Rose recognizes that she has already been saved—by Christopher himself. Despite the rough-and-tumble of their life together, she realizes that never, since their first meeting, has she despaired or wished to die. Her motivation for marrying Christopher was not renunciation at all, but possession, for his vitality was a potent antidote to Noreen's poison. "What freakish providence had given her Christopher, so obsessed by the thought of possession that he refused to let her reject him? His desire to grab—herself, children, money, even parents-in-law—had proved too strong for her will to renounce" (333).[22] Recognizing that the positive parable of the talents is more powerful than the negative principle of the needle's eye, Rose finally exorcizes her evil demon, declaring, "To hell with Bunyan" (334).[23]

Rose returns from this revelation to her family. They celebrate their reunion by a return to nature, an excursion to the seashore, which appears as "a fabled land where children will cry no more, and adults will no more wrangle" (372). But of course the children whine and the adults bicker, because this is the real world of nature, not an imaginary vision of negation.

After winning the custody case with ease, following Christopher's Quixotic kidnapping caper, Rose takes her husband back into the family—a conclusion that outraged feminist critics.[24] "To most Drabble readers it is a disappointing alternative either to Rose's continued heroic solitude or to her loving union with Simon,"[25] writes one, and "When, at the end of the book, Rose returns to her overbearing husband who beats her, the reader is dismayed,"[26] declares another. Mannheimer concludes that Rose's "dominating motive is her mystical need for salvation through sacrifice" (34), but Drabble responds, "I would disagree with the idea that Rose is largely motivated by a religious sense of sacrifice. Indeed, she explicitly rejects the Old Testament notion of sacrifice as a temptation, and returns to her more humble attempt to live religiously." Drabble insists instead that, in reuniting her family, Rose is fulfilling "an image of love and community" (*AC* 37). So the resolution of *The Needle's Eye* is not a regression, but rather the logical conclusion of the entire development of the novel and indeed of all of Drabble's fiction.

Rose sees reunion as the only possible solution to this modern judgment of Solomon. She takes Christopher back purely "for the sake of charity and love," for true charity lies in loving community, not in facile philanthropy. "She had done it in the dry light of arid generosity, she had done it for others. Her duty, that was what she had done. For others. For him, for the children" (365). As Spacks says, Rose "reaches qualified moral success only by accepting impurity and compromise, abandoning some of her cherished divestitures."[27]

Reunion is not the primrose path to salvation, however, for Christopher is still a thorn in Rose's flesh. It is no accident that Drabble selects as the epigraph for *The Needle's Eye* W.B. Yeats's poem:

> The fascination of what's difficult
> Has dried the sap out of my veins, and rent
> Spontaneous joy and natural content
> Out of my heart.

In *The Needle's Eye*, as in *The Millstone*, Drabble shows that salvation stems from overcoming difficulty. She insists, "*The Needle's Eye* is not a defeatist or a depressing novel, because it shows people in a state of continual effort, rather than in a state of despair. . . . I do not find the spectacle of effort depressing. Perhaps there are people who believe that it is masochistic and neurotic deliberately to choose the difficult path, but that is certainly not the way I look at it" (*AC* 35-37).

Rose does regret the lost peace of her solipsistic isolation, for it possessed "a spiritual calm that it had been a crime to lose. And now she lived in dispute and in squalor, for the sake of charity and of love." But "she knew it had been narrow, her conception of grace, it had been solitary, it had admitted no others, it had been without community." She feels, however, that "She had ruined her own nature against her own judgment, for Christopher's sake, for the children's sake. She had sold for them her own soul . . . the price she had to pay was the price of her own living death, her own conscious dying, her own lapsing, surely, slowly, from grace, as heaven (where only those with souls may enter) was taken slowly from her, as its bright gleams faded" (365). As Ellen Cronan Rose writes, "The true measure of her moral achievement is that she can watch as 'heaven was taken from her, as its bright gleams faded,' and then step resolutely out into the light of common day."[28]

Rose knows now that the path to the true kingdom is through love, not law. So she struggles to stifle the spirit of neurosis inspired by Noreen, for it is "dark and crying and bloody, like a bat or an embryo." She strives to subdue the power of her repressive laws of renunciation: "the harsh clanging of her own voice, the sounding of righteous brass and the clanging of the symbols [sic] of her upright faith and demented ideologies, she would silence them all, she would learn to do so." Rose has chosen the bright realm of reality over the dark ideal of death: "The warm daylight of love she would aspire to, oh she would make it, though her nails were torn, her knees barked with hanging on" (366).

The dominance of Simon's point of view at the conclusion of *The Needle's Eye* may be responsible for influencing readers, for, like the feminist critics, Simon is not impartial in his judgment.[29] In his adoration of Rose, Simon resents her return to her husband. Moreover, he needs her saintly figure for his social religion. But ultimately, even Simon acknowledges Rose's transcendence, when he sees her "haloed there, a million shining in a bright and dazzling outline, a million in one. She walked ahead, encircled by brightness" (363). Illumined by the radiance of everyday reality, Rose is deified by her ordinary democracy.

The author makes her own view of her heroine clear in her final image, for the concluding symbol, not the open-ended action, provides the resolution to the thematic conflict in *The Needle's Eye*, as in so many of Drabble's novels. In a reprise of the gate motif, Drabble portrays her protagonist poised between the pair of stone lions which welcome the public to the Alexandra Palace. Rose prefers the domesticated, democratic British lion—"shabby, weathered, crudely cast in a cheap mould"—to the noble beasts—"elevated, distinguished, aristocratic, hand-carved, unique, with curled sneering lips and bared fangs" (295)—which frame the forbidding Branston Hall gates. "Mass-produced it had been, but it had weathered into identity. And this, she hoped, for every human soul" (369). Like the British lion, Rose chooses to wither into identity through the friction of affection and family life, rather than escape community and conflict through a specious solitary election. By placing her squarely between the social animals that frame the "palace of the people," Drabble makes it clear that Rose, poised on the threshold of the future, has passed through the needle's eye to her true salvation.

NOTES

[1] Margaret Drabble, "The Author Comments," *Dutch Quarterly Review of Anglo-American Letters*, 5 (1975), 35. Further references will be given in the text.

[2] Monica Lauritzen Mannheimer, "The Search for Identity in Margaret Drabble's *The Needle's Eye*," *Dutch Quarterly Review of Anglo-American Letters*, 5 (1975), 35.

[3] Joyce Carol Oates, "*The Needle's Eye*," *The New York Times Book Review*, 11 June 1972, p. 1.

[4] In "Money as a Subject for the Novelist," *The Times Literary Supplement*, 24 July 1969, pp. 792-93, Drabble discusses "the morality of wealth."

[5] In her acknowledgments to *The Needle's Eye*, Drabble refers to both of these sources of imagery: "I would like to thank all the lawyers who talked to me about this book, and also Hilary Dunkley who introduced me to the identification of flora." Drabble says she did considerable research into the legal profession in preparation for writing *The Needle's Eye* (*TWF* 83). Drabble's father, Judge John Frederick Drabble, was a lawyer and Queen's Counsel. Barbara Dixson, in "Patterned Figurative Language in *The Needle's Eye*" (*GR* 128-38), says, "A cursory count tallies no fewer than twenty-six direct Biblical references" (133).

[6] Drabble calls him "Simon, an apostle" (*BMI* 55). Jesus called the apostle Simon by the name Peter, meaning rock: "thou art Peter, and upon this rock I will build my church" (*Matthew*, 16:18). Dixson writes, "As plant imagery throughout *The Needle's Eye* resounds with Rose's name, so building imagery does with Simon's. Simon is the rock on whom to build" (*GR* 134).

[7] Arnold E. Davidson, in "Parables of Grace in Drabble's *The Needle's Eye*" (*GR* 66-74), says, "the book is, as its title implies, a parable—or more accurately, a series of parables" (66). Curiously, although Davidson discusses the parable of the needle's eye, he does not mention the parable of the talents. He concludes, "the novel can still end with an affirmation of hope and a parable of grace abounding in a seemingly graceless world" (74).

[8] Margaret Drabble, *The Needle's Eye* (London: Weidenfeld and Nicolson, 1972), 112. Subsequent references will be documented in the text.

[9] Rose may be modeled on Drabble's friend, the English

novelist Nell Dunn, an heiress who renounced her inheritance and who also lives on her own with her children in London. Drabble explains, "Rose doesn't want the larger responsibility that having the money would involve" (*DPI* 567).

[10] Drabble says that Bunyan made a great impression on her youth (*NSHI* 288).

[11] Konstantin, whose name means constancy, is constant in his love for Rose, even when the spirit temporarily deserts her. Konstantin was the Roman Emperor who made Christianity the official religion of the Roman Empire in the early fourth century. Thus, even Rose's son fits the novel's scheme of religious allegory.

[12] Drabble says that Rose is "a favourite of all my heroines. She is a very good woman, very modest, very unassuming, and very anxious to lead a good life" (*TWF* 86).

[13] Drabble comments: "I've never before written a book with two main characters" (*JCI* 6); "In *The Needle's Eye* I made my first attempt to write from the point of view of a man" (*TWF* 82); and "By *The Needle's Eye*, I found I could do what I'd always wanted, which was to write a third-person novel with the point of view spread between various characters" (*BMI* 60).

[14] Drabble comments: "The comparison I was thinking of was the James novel, *The Portrait of a Lady*, where she has the opportunities and does the wrong thing with them" (*DPI* 568); "When I was doing *The Needle's Eye*, I was very conscious of the one with the heiress, *The Wings of the Dove, The Golden Bowl* particularly—the question of how to, what to do with your money when you've got it" (*IRI* 336). There are also echoes of *Washington Square* and *The Princess Casamassima* in this Jamesian novel. In "Money as a Subject for the Novelist," Drabble writes, "the wealthy heiress is a common figure, and the exploitations she suffers and inflicts have been thoroughly documented, in Dickens, in Henry James."

[15] Drabble observes that "Simon is, in fact, from a similar kind of deprived background, culturally deprived background. . . . the same background as Clara. . . . he's entered the bright golden world and he's extremely miserable about it" (*VGMI* 16-17).

[16] In "Slipping into Debt," *The Guardian*, 12 August 1968, p. 7, Drabble laments the upsurge of hire-purchase and mail-order firms that entrap unwary customers and glut the courts with creditors.

[17] Drabble says that *The Needle's Eye* opens "with an event that actually happened to me" (*PFI* 118).

[18] The symbol of the rosebud in the garden recalls Chaucer's *Romaunt of the Rose*, based on Guillaume de Lorris' *Roman de la Rose*, which Drabble discusses in *A Writer's Britain: Landscape in Literature*, 106. Ellen Cronan Rose writes, "Rose represents the new covenant which will supersede the old, love which will make the law irrelevant. She becomes for Simon the mystical rose" (*EF* 80).

[19] Mary M. Lay comments on Drabble's use of seasons to symbolize characters' emotional states, in "Temporal Ordering in the Fiction of Margaret Drabble," *Critique*, 21, 3 (1979), 73-83.

[20] Mel Gussow says "*The Needle's Eye* began with a request from *The Guardian* for Drabble to write a short article on child custody for the women's page" (40).

[21] Drabble says *The Needle's Eye* "is constructed so that there is no answer: the two forces are equally balanced" (*VGMI* 4).

[22] Myer concludes that "Christopher, not Noreen, had been right about the use of riches," for "Christopher manages to reconcile God and Mammon" (*PP* 185-86). In a 1974 letter, Drabble commended Myer upon her "appreciation of Christopher's role, which most people (particularly militant feminists) have totally failed to grasp." In an unpublished article on literary references in Drabble's fiction, Myer says, "The thematic framework of *The Needle's Eye* comes from Saint Paul: 'Love is the fulfilling of the law' (*Romans*, 13:10)."

[23] Rose writes: "Imbued with Bunyan's sense that the self is worthless in respect to the transcendent Other, Rose had learned that the way to salvation is by renunciation. Her true spiritual progress, however, is the path of acceptance, which involves renouncing Bunyan and the ecstasy of self-abnegation" (*EF* 85).

[24] Drabble comments, "I wrote the whole of *The Needle's Eye* while Clive and I were still together. And I might not have made it and like I did if we had separated first. I might have allowed her her freedom. I wonder" (*NSHI* 277). In a 3 December 1974 letter to Monica Mannheimer, Drabble acknowledges, "If I were to write *The Needle's Eye* now, I would end it quite differently, but then, of course, it would have to be a different book right through."

[25] Norma Klein, "Real Novels about Real Women," *Ms.*, 1

(September 1972), pp. 61-72.

[26] Patricia Sharpe, "On First Looking into *The Realms of Gold*," *Michigan Quarterly Review*, 16 (1977), 228.

[27] Patricia Meyer Spacks, in her introduction to her edition of *Contemporary Women Novelists: A Collection of Critical Essays* (Englewood Cliffs: Prentice-Hall, 1977), 1-17, writes:

> In Drabble's *The Needle's Eye*, the central female character, Rose Vassiliou, has inaugurated her adult life by giving away, in one grand and futile gesture, her fortune. She wants to achieve moral purity by constructive relinquishment; in fact, at the novel's end, she reaches qualified moral success only by accepting impurity and compromise, abandoning some of her cherished divestitures. (16)

[28] "A Farewell to Renunciations," *Nation* 215 (1972), 380. Ellen Cronan Rose's view changes significantly by *Equivocal Figures* (1980).

[29] Drabble comments, "one of the reasons why I like *The Needle's Eye* is because you don't have to accept anybody's version of the truth in it" (*VGMI* 17). She explains, "two characters are presented to you as solid people, and you, the reader in the middle, can see them misunderstanding" (*JCI* 6).

Chapter Eight:

EXCAVATING *THE REALMS OF GOLD*

In *The Realms of Gold* (1975), Drabble excavates her greatest goldmine ever to reveal rich lodes of themes and images. American feminist critics have mined this novel as a gynaecological goldfield, interpreting its core variously as a uterine metaphor, a "gynocentric" vision, and an ancient female myth.[1] But *The Realms of Gold* is a profound work, not merely a "profoundly feminine" one, because in it Drabble dares to ask the overwhelming question. If the existential question is to be answered in the affirmative, she shows that it is first essential to discover the realms of gold. In her next novel, *The Ice Age* (1977), the female protagonist contemplates "a golden laurel wreath in a remote Iron Curtain museum," and wonders why "she had turned from gold and chosen the leaden casket."[2] The characters in *The Realms of Gold* must also choose between gold and lead or life and death.

Gold is buried deep beneath the surface, and the tool the author uses to excavate it is symbolism. The major symbol of the novel is the realms of gold of the title, quoted from Keats's sonnet, "On First Looking into Chapman's Homer," which celebrates the treasures of the past: "Much have I travell'd in the realms of gold."[3] This vision of a golden realm in the past provides the major symbol of the spiritual quest for an ideal world which forms the true subject of this contemporary female odyssey. "The themes of *The Realms of Gold* are about the past, the present, the future" (*VGMI* 21), Drabble explains, for, in order to pave the road into the future, it is necessary to excavate the gold from the past. The heroine, Frances Wingate née Ollerenshaw, an archaeologist, digs for literal golden realms of the world's past and searches for figurative golden worlds in her personal past.

Frances is free to choose gold or lead, survival or suicide, for both exist as surely as the Pacific, but only a spirit as adventurous as Cortez can discover the golden realm. The difficulty is to know where to search, for, in *Jerusalem the Golden*, the fable of the "Golden Windows" revealed how elusive the golden vision may be. Whereas Clara Maugham searched for her terrestrial paradise in crass goals of future social success, Frances Wingate learns to excavate her cultural heritage from the past for the treasures required to furnish the future.[4] Once the golden artifacts are exhumed, the crucial question for the character (and the critic) is to interpret them correctly.

Archaeology is the major metaphor Drabble employs to excavate the realms of gold, and it generates multi-layered strata of themes and symbols from the womb of Mother Earth.[5] Frances Wingate is the perfect person to dig for gold, for, even gold in colour, she is "the golden girl" herself.[6] She has lost the golden realm of her childhood in Eel Cottage, her grandparents' Midlands home. Its nursery garden was her infant Eden: "For Frances, at first, it was like paradise, like the original garden" (91). In her adolescence, however, it became a paradise lost, although "it wasn't exactly an angel with a flaming sword that had expelled her," but rather "the sins of sex" which left a "rust-coloured guilty stain" (93).

Thrust thus rudely out of the garden of childhood innocence by the serpent of sex, Frances, like Clara, seeks an adult golden realm of worldly success. All of the successful Ollerenshaws "had struggled out by their wits and climbed perilously up from the flat load, up the beanstalk of the grammar school, to the golden world above" (257). Frances does unearth a literal golden realm in the treasures of Tizouk, the ancient Phoenician trading centre she excavates from beneath the Sahara desert. But ultimately, Frances discovers, like Clara, that worldly success is not gold, but gilt, and by the outset of the novel, she despairs of discovering in the past the gold required to ransom the present. The glitter has gone from the golden casket of professional success, revealing the leaden coffin of personal despair beneath the gilded façade.

By the beginning of the book, even the golden girl herself has become somewhat tarnished. At the outset of the narrative, Frances is in the midst of a mid-life identity crisis, as she wonders what the future holds for her, now that her maternal function is over: "The past had been so full: overfull. What of the future? What on earth could it still hold for her?" (11). The octopus that opens the novel[7] symbolizes the choice between suicide and survival, because "the female of the species died, invariably, after giving birth. . . . Unlike the octopus, she seemed resolved on a course of defying nature. Maybe that was why she felt so bad?" (5-6). Frances is even more horrified, however, by the spectacle of the male octopus surviving in a perspex box into which he retreats from contact, just as she escapes from intimacy into her hygienic hotel rooms.

The depressive attack that opens the novel is instigated by the associations of this port city where Frances inexplicably ended the happiest years of her life by parting some months previously with her lover, Karel Schmidt, the only man she has ever loved—although she still carries his false teeth, like a saint's relic, in her brassiere, warding off would-be lovers. For Frances, romantic love is "the last resort, the last deliverance, for those who could not aspire to the holy love of God. She was not well balanced enough for the holy love of God, she had not the spiritual capacity for it, though she had spiritual concepts from time to time. No, passion had been the only hope for her" (19). Moreover, Karel "had been something of a salvationist, he had wished to save her, with evangelical passion, and she was afraid of disappointing him, and simultaneously rather afraid of being saved" (10). So Frances has sacrificed the personal salvation of love to her professional quest for a golden realm. "A future without him stretched like the desert, dry and hot" (68), for her spirit feels arid, lacking the salvation that springs from Karel's profound nature and the depths of his love. Frances sees herself "suffering in the upper mountain reaches of her being, while his nature lay deep and opaque, levelled to base level, without the jagged cataracts of the self, deep, persistent, continuous, deep like the river meeting the sea" (67).

Frances' depression runs even deeper than personal desolation, however, for "the Midlands sickness," as she terms it, is a family affliction, as well as a regional blight. Suicide runs in the Ollerenshaw family, and Frances also has a theory of inherited depression and environmental heredity:[8] "there must be something positively poisoning the whole of South Yorkshire and the Midlands, or they wouldn't all be so bloody miserable up there, and live in such appalling conditions" (85-86). Frances is also convinced that her depression has a deep spiritual significance. She despairs at the human condition, which is symbolized by the image of an empty crater, signifying the void in which she finds herself: "The effort of comprehension was beyond her. In the middle of nowhere, high up, a solitary lunatic, in her dry crater. The world was drying out, and everything she touched would die" (48).

Frances' nadir proves pivotal, however, when her lecture on Tizouk, the ancient Phoenician trading post she resurrected from beneath the arid Sahara sands, reminds her of her creative power: "she had not even pillaged the dead, on the contrary she had made them live again," as, quickening the dead and resurrecting edifices, "digging in the cold dawn, her city rising from its burial in the sand" (25), she reverses the process of death and burial. Tizouk is truly the creation of her imagination, because "She knew with such conviction that it was like a revelation—the evidence was all there, it was simply that she alone had produced the correct interpretation of it. . . . I must be mad, she thought to herself. I imagine a city, and it exists. If I hadn't imagined it, it wouldn't have existed. All her life, things had been like that." Recognizing her divining power, she wonders what she should now create:

> What next should she imagine? What terrifying enormity should she next conjure forth? Should she dig again in the desert and uncover gold? Should she plant down her foot and let water spring from the dry land? Should she wave her arm and let the rocks blossom? She had been as arid as a rock, but she had learned to flow. Or should she conceive of desolation? Defoliate forests? Slaughter innocent children and bury them in little jars with Punic inscriptions? (26).

This recollection of her creative power inspires her to anticipate another revelation: "It was there, something was waiting, something must be waiting. But she must imagine it well. She must get it right. She had too much force to be able to afford even minor errors." So Frances embarks on a new quest for another realm of gold.

The first place Frances searches for the golden realm is in her professional excavation of the past. Drabble employs the metaphor of archaeology, framed by history and geology, the professions of the three major characters of the novel, to span the evolution of the world from the primal slime to the final cinder. All those scientific excavations of the past discover lead as well as gold, however, as Frances realizes: "The pursuit of archaeology, she said to herself, like the pursuit of history, is for such as myself and Karel a fruitless attempt to prove the possibility of the future through the past. We seek a Utopia in the past, a possible if not an ideal society. We seek golden worlds from which we are banished, they recede infinitely, for there never was a golden world, there was never anything but toil and subsistence, cruelty and dullness" (107-08).

Even in her Tizouk triumph, Frances excavates not only golden treasures, but also buried urns full of the bones of sacrificed children: she protests, "we unearth horrors, and justify them. Child sacrifice we label benevolent birth control, a dull and endless struggle against nature we label communion with the earth" (108). Frances despairs of discovering the realms of gold in her professional pursuit, wondering "why she had become an archaeologist and what on earth it was that she was trying to prove about the past. . . . What is it for, the past, one's own or the world's. To what end question it so closely" (107-08).

Historian Karel Schmidt personifies a charnel-house view of the past: as a survivor of the Nazi holocaust, he carries in his bones a communal memory of the worst crime of history, embodying a view of the earth as a mass grave. As an expert on eighteenth-century agriculture, he also unearths a leaden rather than a golden age in "the whole story of enclosures, of labourers' wages, of rural poverty, of Captain Swing and peasants' revolts" (107).

"As a geologist, [David Ollerenshaw] took a long view of time: even longer than Frances Wingate, archaeologist, and very much longer than Karel Schmidt, historian" (167).[9] The geologist also unearths not only gold, but lead: fossils in the rocks paint a post-Darwinian picture of the earth as an ancient graveyard. David, unlike Frances and Karel, however, is not disturbed by this vision of death, for, as a geologist in love with rocks, he prefers the inhuman to the human. He does not entertain "the slightest sense of man as a necessary part of creation, as in any way a significant part. Man's life, as the Bible says, is grass, a mere breath: so was the whole history of mankind" (166). His favourite geological phenomenon is the volcanic crater, symbol of the void. As he stands on the lip of a crater, he regrets its quiescence, for David would have liked a large cataclysm—just like his cousin, Janet Bird née Ollerenshaw, who also "would have welcomed a cataclysm, a volcano, a fire, an outbreak of war, anything to break the unremitting nothingness of her existence" (117). Janet pours molten wax from the crater of a candle over a sign of the zodiac in an ashtray, symbolizing the destruction of the world in a volcanic eruption.[10] David's dream is to witness the end of the world:

> He thought, not for the first time, that it would be his idea of heaven to sit on an observation platform somewhere and watch the earth change—watch mountains heave and fold, seas shrink, rivers wear down their valleys, continents drift and collide, forests dry into deserts and deserts burgeon into forests. The process, the constant flux, enthralled him. Man's life span was too short to be interesting: he wanted to see all the slow great events, right to the final cinder, the black hole. (166)

Since scientific investigation of the past unearths a leaden rather than a golden realm, Frances determines to search for her golden vision in her personal past, rather than in her professional career. The benign lump in her breast—crystallizing the stone of grief that grows in her heart when her message of love elicits no response from Karel—saves her, ironically, by driving her back into the bosom of her family. She determines to seek new connections in kinship: "she'd always been expecting to get Karel back, since their parting she had lived in a kind of nothingness, a kind of limbo. She would have to come to terms with the future. She would have to make new connections" (69).

So Frances, like all of Drabble's heroines, goes home again. She is determined to investigate her theory of the Midlands sickness and the Ollerenshaw family depression: "She felt that she would like to know where she began and the family ended" (87). Although she fears that "One cannot escape one's destiny" (72), the doom bred into one's bones, she hopes to exorcize the dark demon by confronting her destiny, rather than attempting to escape her doom. Failing to reveal her ideal in the Sahara desert, she searches for it in the Midland marshes. She makes a pilgrimage to her childhood Eden at Eel Cottage, the one still point in her turning world. It contains "an electro-cardiogram of her childhood, a map of her past" (101), which she hopes will provide a blueprint for charting the future.[11] She digs up her family roots in its nursery garden to harvest the sustenance needed to nourish her family for the future. But her homecoming is a grave disappointment, for, anticipating "some untouched corner of Britain, a rustic paradise," she discovers instead that there is literally no country left.

She repairs to the most important place in her childhood, the teeming ditch behind the Eel, for this fertile groove spawned the evolution of the Ollerenshaw family fortunes by inspiring her father's scientific success, thus raising the family from the low-lying fenlands to the highlands of success, where Frances is ultimately stranded high and dry in her arid aerie. But Frances' excavation of the origin of her species reveals that the golden age of rural England has been transformed into an industrial wasteland by the modern ice age of property development: "A thick oily scum covered the water: bits of paper, fag ends, Coca Cola bottles, an old tyre, a chunk of polystyrene and a car seat floated in it. Bubbles, not from fish or newts, but from some invisible putrescence rose to the surface" (102).

Frances excavates, not a golden age, but a field of stones in her personal past. She has a nightmare vision of a field full of people harvesting rocks instead of crops. Of course, they are merely clearing a new playing field for their school, but Frances is disturbed by her misinterpretation: "Why then had she seen something quite different? For what she had seen had been an image of forced labour, of barrenness, of futility, of toil, of women and children stooping for survival, harvesting nothing but stones" (106). The stones she sees being harvested match the stone of grief growing in her own breast. Her vision of the past is also a form of inherited memory, for "Generations of her ancestors had gathered stones in those fields" (108). Frances, like Janet Bird, Clara Maugham, and Margaret Drabble herself, is the child of stony ground: "Stony ground, stony ground, tolled the bells for Janet Bird" (117). Frances' misinterpretation stems from her own restricted viewpoint, for her flat native fenlands furnish no perspective; as Janet Bird says, "I will lift up mine eyes unto the hills: from whence cometh my help. There were of course no hills round here, and therefore no help" (115).

Frances' next horrific vision is inspired by an eel stang in the local museum, when she misreads the label, calling the black pronged fork a useful instrument for "trapping" eels, as an implement for "turning" eels—a singularly futile activity.[12] "She had had a vision, she had to admit it herself, of old men pointlessly turning over eels in ditches in meaningless labour, just as those women and children in the field had appeared to her at first sight as an allegory of pointless rural toil. We dig, we plant, we reap, we dig again, and barely we survive." She interprets her sinister vision as an ominous portent: "A man with an eel stang, like Wordsworth's leech gatherer, stood around portentously in her mind, aimlessly searching the ditches for eels to turn. He meant something to her, she had not conjured him for nothing, she had not misread that notice for nothing. What did he personify, that ancient labourer? She looked in horror at his black pronged fork, and turned away. She turned back to modernity and her bedroom's efficient plumbing" (106). The source of this personal misinterpretation of her own past, like the scientists' professional misinterpretation of the world's past, is her own jaundiced viewpoint which colours her vision, transforming gold to lead in a reverse alchemy.

The field of stones that Frances unearths in Tockley is no better than the valley of bones she excavated in Tizouk. The leaden vision she sees in the past makes her despair of discovering a realm of gold for the future: "what hopes should one have of any future? Should one merely regress to a field full of stones, one's own safe place? What about sex, what about salvation? The eels go back to the same beds, the swallows fly south in the summer. And she had gone back for a weekend to the flat Midlands. What had she found there? What held her like a stone round her neck, like a stone in her chest, heavy, solid, inert? A field of stones, a valley of bones" (174).

Failing to unearth sustenance for the future from her family roots in the past, Frances returns to her professional pursuit of treasure from the world's past when she attends a conference in Africa on gold in the Sahara. But, as she flies over the desert, its aridity seems to symbolize her personal desolation and professional despair: "The endless sand flowed under them. Work was all that was left, with Karel gone and the children growing. But somehow, when one was good at it, it lost its charm. Why bother? What did it matter, one archaeologist more or less?" The vision of futility inspired by the eel stang is embodied for Frances in the sonnet she quotes from Shelley on the futility of all human endeavour: "My name is Ozymandias, King of Kings. Look on my works ye mighty and despair. The lone and level sands stretch far away" (206-07).

Frances' lowest point proves to be a turning point once again, however, for her excavation of her own golden realm in England begins in Africa, where the Adran Minister for

Culture teaches Frances about the need to find stones from the past for founding the future: "We are in possession of a future and a past beyond our imagination. We must discover our own rich cultural heritage, stone by stone, and we must build a rich future" (223). This professional illumination is complemented by a personal revelation when Frances discovers a distant relation at the conference in David Ollerenshaw. This coincidence prompts an anthropologist to paint a picture of kinship which shows that the family tree is the tree of life: "Spirelli, expert in family structures, drew them some diagrams of marriage patterns in Western Europe, and constructed for them a family tree, and proved to them that everybody was related to just about everybody, at remarkably few removes" (239). Inspired by this vision of connection, Frances resolves to return home to be reunited with her family and her lover: "She would make no more cities, she would make love."

Frances' resolve is reinforced when the family tree sheds a pile of leaves in her lap: leafing through a sheaf of green telegrams from her relations, Frances finds "skeletons stacked up in the cupboard, and now about to rattle out and spill all their dusty bones over the front pages of the Sunday papers" (246), as reporters rattle the family skeletons loudly enough to be heard all the way to Africa. The discovery of the corpse of Frances' Great Aunt Constance Ollerenshaw—with her stomach full of cardboard from the box of "Black Magic" that Janet Bird left as an offering to propitiate the old witch[13]—proves that one could carry disassociation to extremes. The news prompts Frances to realize, "If one could discover a dead Constance and a living David within the space of twenty-four hours, what might not the future hold of contact and complication? . . . Perhaps they would all gather together, in some terrible Midlands twilight" (251). Recognizing, finally, like all of Drabble's heroines, that "Blood is thicker than water" (264), Frances returns home to take responsibility for her family; now she "saw herself as an adult, her parents declining feebly to the grave. The matriarch, arranging funerals" (266).

Frances ultimately unearths her golden realm, not in the golden emporium she excavates in exotic Tizouk, but in the golden age of England she discovers in humble Tockley, where her leaden vision, symbolized by the dour Eel Cottage, is countered by her golden vision, embodied in the enchanting

Mays Cottage. Although her first pilgrimage revealed a field of stones, her second homecoming does discover a realm of gold, for, in excavating her family origins, she unearths an ancestral heritage, a spiritual mother, and a buried self, as well as a golden age of England. "It was not quite as spectacular a rediscovery and reclamation as Tizouk, but it offered many private satisfactions. It even proved, in its own way, to be of historical, if not of archaeological interest" (325). Searching for the proverbial family skeletons in Con's cupboards, Frances finds a family of nineteenth-century Ollerenshaw shoes buried in a wall, an interesting footnote to the family history, proving that even in the heart of the industrial depression the Ollerenshaws became prosperous. So Frances is not a freak or sport after all, she realizes, but the natural product of her ancestry.

Mays Cottage, suggesting a puzzle to be penetrated, furnishes further evidence of the Ollerenshaw family history in old documents: "Nearly as indecipherable as hieroglyphics, nearly as sparse in their information as Phoenician shopping lists, they contained a past, a history" (277). Frances deciphers the secret source of Con's reclusiveness in letters that reveal a lost love and a dead child, inspiring Frances to acknowledge the importance of community and affection and prompting her to resolve to marry her lover and unite their families.

By identifying her true descent through mementos of her aunt in Mays Cottage—just as Clara Maugham found hers in souvenirs from her mother May's youth—Frances discovers a kindred spirit which completes her quest for a spiritual mother. Through identifying with Con, Frances defines her deepest identity. She discovers not only a spiritual mother in her aunt, but also a benevolent Mother Nature in the garden of Mays Cottage, which is "The Real Thing" for Frances:[14] "It had none of the rural bleakness of Eel Cottage, none of that open struggle. Nature had gently enfolded it" (276). Whereas the Eel, a 1779 labourers' cottage named for the phallic eels of the fens, is forbidding, the Mays, suggesting femininity, is inviting. Drabble describes it in female, anthropomorphic, even uterine, terms: "From an overturned stone pot struggling clematis straggled dry and wild like an old woman's hair. A few purple flowers of honesty huddled and blossomed in the dark secret wetness." Even in decay, the vegetation surrounding Mays Cottage suggests the rebirth of nature in the spring: a rotten hawthorn tree "still budded and blossomed, even though undeterred by death, the leaves still breaking from it in its grave" (259)— suggesting the continual cycle of renewal.

In unearthing Mother Nature, Frances also excavates the golden age of England: "Oh so different, so beautifully different from the parched red mud of Adra, from the glaring altitudes of rocky, weathered Tizouk. England. A bird sang in a tree" (274). As Constance is laid to rest in the English earth, even Karel, fruit of history's mass grave, resurrects a vision of England's golden age that redeems the vision of the leaden coffin:

> Karel, raising his eyes from the too open earth, and staring at the middle distance where the cows browsed, peacefully, as though in another age, reflected on his own passion for the rural England he saw so rarely, his haven, his place of exile, his unknown land, his subject, his livelihood: and on Frances, who came from this land. The eighteenth-century cows munched on undisturbed, in their golden age, by the still waters, by the bending willows, in the autumn light. (308)

Frances' second pilgrimage is as positive as the first was negative, each cycle of her quest forming half of a complete picture of existence as an amalgam of gold and lead. Life and death are the warp and woof that are interwoven to create the richly-textured tapestry of this imaginative artistic work. While Frances follows the golden thread, her nephew Stephen Ollerenshaw chooses the dark thread, which he cuts short with fatal shears. The discovery of Con's corpse, which elicits Frances' illumination of life, inspires Stephen's revelation of death: "The revelation was one of extreme simplicity. It came to him like a light from heaven. It was better to be dead than alive." A personification of the death wish, Stephen is horrified by all the frailties that flesh is heir to: "Being alive was sordid, degrading, sickly, unimaginable.... Whereas if one left now, if one leapt now, unsubdued into the flames, one would be freed, one would have conquered flesh and death, one would have departed whole, intact, undestroyed" (317-18). Stephen's suicide is symbolized by the figure of Empedocles on Etna—the ancient Greek philosopher who leaped into the fiery crater of the volcano in order to prove his immortality—an emblem that unites all the images of David's volcano, Janet's cataclysm, and Frances' crater to symbolize the void. Like Empedocles, Stephen is engulfed by "the red crater, made one with nature, transformed to black ash" in a London crematorium, purified by the refining fire to pure spirit. "Death and love. How dreadfully they contradict all culture, all process, all human effort" (320), Frances concludes.

But even Stephen's death is not totally negative, for, like the fated hero of Greek tragedy, Stephen is the scapegoat of the novel,[16] because his self-sacrifice exorcizes the family demon, as Frances finally realizes: "She taught herself, over the years, to see his death as a healing of some kind, the end of a long illness, a sacrifice. Taken from them for their better health. Her own children, certainly mercifully, showed no inheritance of the more unwelcome Ollerenshaw traits. Stephen had taken it all away with him" (321). By tying together all the dark threads that have run through the novel, Stephen, the scapegoat, redeems them: by sacrificing his own child's life out of love, to save her from decay, he redeems the small bones of the slaughtered children in the Sahara.

Whereas Stephen selects the leaden coffin, Frances chooses the golden casket: "With a certain admirable determination, he had faced his own nature, and the terms of life and death and seen what to do. He had had the revelation she had always been denied, which she had glimpsed so often in the distance. It was a revelation that she did not want at all. She would continue to live, herself. He had spared her, and taken it all upon himself" (321). While Stephen selects suicide, Frances, like all of Drabble's heroines, chooses survival: following Stephen's funeral, she turns from the fiery crater back to "culture, process and effort. They were wedded to them, after all" (320).

Frances can choose to live because she rediscovers the love that nourishes life. Reunited with her lover, the salvationist Karel, she thanks God for her survival and for Karel's salvation. "Death brings us together" (202), as one character observes, and indeed, "Frances' reunion with Karel, though achieved in ill-health, and cemented by death and tears, proved permanent. Their separation had been an aberration" (323). So death generates new life and love: "Karel in bed had turned to Frances and wept, as she had wept for Stephen, and it all seemed a part of the same fate. A fate which had spared them, and left them with so much, with each other. What could one do, what sense could one make of it? One could only give thanks" (322).

The second source of salvation for Frances springs from the roots she resurrects from the past to foster the future. Her ancestral English heritage is embodied in her inheritance of Mays Cottage, where she and Karel unite their offspring: "they slept together amongst the cobwebs, making good lost months and years, in a terrifying, a safe, a giddy, a precarious, a secure and all-excluding secluded conclusion, as final in its own way as Stephen's had been: as final, as ruthless, and it seemed, as natural" (324). Frances maintains her roots in her family by digging her garden in Mays Cottage both literally and figuratively and by continuing her connection with her cousins. She preserves the past, "like a talisman, a seed, a pledge of the unimaginable spring" (57), along with Karel's teeth and her desert relics, sowing them with her own roots, where they nourish the new life of the next generation.

Frances' positive perspective and Stephen's negative nature together form the two halves of a complete whole—the comic and tragic masks of this Janus-faced work. Their diverse interpretations of the past and opposite responses to the present stem from their intrinsically different natures. Frances, the golden girl, "the blessed and the lucky, the winner at cards, the finder of gold" (278), discovers a golden vision where Stephen sees a leaden one: "Like a medieval contemplative, he dedicated himself to mortality, decay, the corruption of flesh, disease. The end of all things" (317). Even after revisiting Karel's tortured roots in the Jewish cemetery in Prague, Frances is suddenly surprised by joy:

> His dead mother and brother and sister and father and dead Stephen dust and ashes rising from a crematorium chimney, were all part of a salvation so unexpected, that she lay there with him, perishing and fading it was true, but who cared, who cared, if one can salvage one moment from the sentence of death let us do so, let us catch at it, for we owe it to the dead, to the others, and it is all the living and the lucky can do for the dead, all they can do, given the chance, is to rejoice. (322)

Whereas Stephen, David, and Janet wish to immerse life in the volcano, Frances wants to draw life out of the void by resurrecting the dead and redeeming the past. In her personal and professional excavation of the apocalyptic tombstones and golden treasures of Poland, Frances transforms the leaden coffin into a golden casket: "overcome with joy she lay awake and thought of the gold baroque of Prague, and Kafka the mad Jew, and of those perilous grave stones, grave stones, her profession, her trade, her living, on account of which (account, account) she lay here with Karel in this double bed" (322). Through the alchemy of love, Frances and Karel redeem the personal memory of the holocaust and the professional discovery of dry bones, transforming the leaden vision into a golden realm.

Ultimately *The Realms of Gold* celebrates the comic vision which overcomes the tragic viewpoint by comprehending it in an all-inclusive perspective symbolized by the ancient ironic figurine with its "comic look, as of one who appreciates the twists of fate" (241). Comedy is the complete cycle that encompasses the tragic partial cycle in a continual circle of regeneration.[17] The comic vision in *The Realms of Gold* is symbolized by flora and fauna.[18] Even at the nadir of her despair, Frances is encouraged by the bizarre vegetation that symbolizes "that there was hope, that there were more manifestations than man's miserable limited mind could dream of, that not even she, all-thoughtful, never-resting, never-rested, could either create or destroy by her own misery the variety of the earth's creation" (16). Frances and Karel discover hundreds of frogs in a round erect drainage pipe at a crossroads—clearly a phallic symbol of fertility—after which they "lay down on the mud and made love, which was, after all, the purpose of their expedition" (18). Frances also sees a comic vision of the creation in the newts in her beloved ditch: "They were surely a sign to her, a blessing. They floated there, green grey, pink bellied, frill backed, survivors from a world of pre-history, born before the Romans arrived, before the bits of bronze-age pot sank in the swamp, remembering in their tiny bones the great bones of the stenosaurus, a symbol of God's undying contract with the earth" (92). Discovering "a whole unnecessary and teeming world of creation" in this fertile groove, "wondering what God had bothered to make it all for, and pondering on the origin of species," Frances realizes that "God had done it all for fun, for joy, for excitement in creation, for variety, for delight. Why seek to justify? There it all was."[19] Together, the phallic symbol of the frogs in the cistern and the uterine symbol of the fecund ditch—uniting Eel and Mays, male and female principles—draw new life out of the void, transforming the tomb into the womb of creation, as Frances finally recognizes.

This celebration of recreation concludes, appropriately, with marriage, the traditional "happy ending" (324) of comedy.[20] The union of Frances and Karel is celebrated in a suitable symbol, the lump of pale yellow silica glass that David discovered in the desert and presents to them as a wedding gift: "scooped, pitted, smoothly irregular, carved and weathered by the desert wind, apparently translucent but finally opaque, it had seemed an appropriate gift" (326). Like the stone lions at the conclusion of *The Needle's Eye*, the desert glass symbolizes the way that existence weathers individuality into identity, just as Frances has been weathered "by sun and sand, like an ancient monument" (82). *The Realms of Gold* concludes with a fitting symbol of the creation, the block of smoky quartz that Frances discovers in David's amazingly elegant apartment: "it was dense within, streaked by refraction, like a petrified forest. Human nature is truly impenetrable, she said to herself" (326). In this ambiguous final symbol, the author does not try to solve the mystery of life, but rather to celebrate the infinite variety of the creation by recreating a vision of a realm of gold.[21]

NOTES

[1] Carey Kaplan, "A Vision of Power in Margaret Drabble's *The Realms of Gold*," *Journal of Women's Studies in Literature*, 1 (Summer 1979), 233-42, writes, "the central image of this profoundly feminine novel [is] the empty womb, potentially full of life, waiting to quicken, but very likely to stay empty unless the right fertilizing agents are found" (237). Rose states, "Drabble's vision in this novel is gynocentric" (*EF* 95). Judy Little, "Humour and the Female Quest: Margaret Drabble's *The Realms of Gold*," *Regionalism and the Female Imagination*, 4, 44-52, writes, "the novel uses much imagery which has been traditionally associated with the Demeter-Persephone myth" (44). Drabble says that "the American response was very largely feminist. . . . it sold extremely well in America, but it sold for the wrong reasons, in my view" (*VGMI* 21).

[2] Margaret Drabble, *The Ice Age* (London: Weidenfeld and Nicolson, 1977), 117.

[3] Drabble explains, "The 'realms of gold' for Frances are her own equivalent of reading poetry, the discovery of

professional satisfaction. In fact, the theme of gold runs through the book. By this time I was very, very conscious of plotting my symbolism and putting the images in the right place and it was all highly deliberate. So gold is exactly what she finds when, as an archaeologist, she digs in the Sahara" (*TWF* 86-87).

Patricia Sharpe, "On First Looking into *The Realms of Gold*," *Michigan Quarterly Review*, 16 (1977), 225-31, writes: "Thus *The Realms of Gold* reenacts the drama of discovery found in Keats's poem from which its title comes" (231). Margaret Rowe, "The Uses of the Past in Margaret Drabble's *The Realms of Gold*" (*GR* 158-67), writes: "In the title, Drabble underscores the thematic and structural prominence of the past in *The Realms of Gold*, for in drawing on Keats's "On First Looking into Chapman's Homer," the author provides gloss as well as designation for her novel" (158). Pamela Bromberg, "Romantic Revisionism in Margaret Drabble's *The Realms of Gold*" (*GR* 48-65), writes, "The novel's argument with Romanticism begins in its title, taken from Keats' early sonnet, 'On First Looking into Chapman's Homer,' and emblematic of the Romantic belief in the recovery of an inner paradise through the poetic imagination" (48).

[4] This concept is discussed in my essay, "Margaret Drabble's Golden Vision" (*GR*, 3-17). Drabble explains, "Frances Wingate, the heroine, has to go back to her roots" (*VGMI* 21). In *Shadows of the Past in Contemporary British Fiction* (London: Macmillan, 1984), David Leon Higdon demonstrates how *The Realms of Gold* involves "coming to terms with the past, both personally and culturally."

[5] John Updike, "Drabbling in the Mud," *The New Yorker*, 51 (12 January 1976), 88, writes: "Archaeology brings a wealth of metaphors and incidental illuminations to the book, and in a sense informs its very structure; we have less a plot than a lode of prose and description, through which, as he reads, the reader digs down toward some underlying message about kinship, ancestry, vitality, and life's meaning."

[6] Margaret Drabble, *The Realms of Gold* (London: Weidenfeld and Nicolson, 1975), 35. Further references to this edition will be documented within the text. Drabble comments, "She is very much a creation conscious of the developments of feminism and the Women's Movement in Britain in the 1960s and 1970s. . . . So Frances Wingate, I

decided, should have a happy life and a fortunate career." Drabble says the name Wingate "obviously has something to do with winning through and entering through the triumphal gate. It is a success name. . . . Wingate clearly had for me a symbolic significance. . . . I had also given the hero and the heroine sexually ambiguous names. . . . I think that again must have been on some level intentional, that Frances has many masculine qualities and Karel has many female qualities, and that in my view is why they arrive at a very happy marriage at the end of the book" (*TWF* 85, 96).

[7] Drabble explains, "I use the image of the octopus to open *The Realms of Gold* because I kept looking for an image that would be both amusing and bizarre and significant" (*VGMI* 33).

[8] Drabble predicted, "I'll try and tackle hereditary depressions that run through three generations of a family. It would fit in very nicely with my interest in predestination and fate and whether you can escape your destiny" (*NSHI* 288-89). Of her maternal family, she says, "it's as though there's an ancestral ghost haunting the family" (*BMI* 56).

[9] Drabble explains:

> My original plan was to make all three characters equally prominent and to write the book in three sections, slightly intercut, but I found this impossible because Frances Wingate insisted on occupying most of the plot. . . . I took a correspondence course in geology at O-level . . . and I learned about rocks and crystals and volcanoes. . . . I had to cut out twenty thousand words of my book. David Ollerenshaw in the original version is a much more prominent presence. (*TWF* 84-85)

The original typescript of *The Realms of Gold* in the McFarlin Library at The University of Tulsa shows evidence of this revision.

[10] The author interpolates, "I had a fine leap, from Janet staring at the small crater in her melted wax candle, to David staring into the crater of a small volcano" (*RG* 163). Cynthia Davis, "Unfolding Form: Narrative Approach and Theme in *The Realms of Gold*," *Modern Language Quarterly*, 40 (1979), 390-402, comments on Drabble's use of this symbolic device as a method for structuring her narrative.

[11] Drabble explains, "The only place in my family that has been constant in my lifetime is what was my grandparents'

house (my aunt now lives there) which is in Lincolnshire. I used a bit of it in *The Realms of Gold*. It's partly Eel Cottage" (*DPI* 572).

[12] The dust cover of the original edition of *The Realms of Gold* portrays a black forked eel stang framing the face of a woman.

[13] "*The Realms of Gold* was inspired by stories that Drabble read about 'old ladies dying alone in cottages', in particular one woman who starved to death and was discovered to have 'eaten the family bible'" (*MGI* 41).

[14] Rose concludes: "To the extent that Frances's search for a mother returns her to nature, the 'maternal matrix of being,' *The Realms of Gold* is a 'gyn/ecological' book" (*EF* 107).

[15] Drabble discusses "The Golden Age" of England in *A Writer's Britain*, 247-77. Roger Sale, reviewing *The Realms of Gold* in *The Hudson Review*, 28 (1975-76), 628, declares that in this novel Drabble recreates "the private history of an England, that, if only in this beautiful novel, is becoming a realm of gold."

[16] Drabble explains, "I think that, artistically, it was right that this character should die: he is the scapegoat of the novel, and he dies. . . . one of the reasons also why I allowed him to die was that the man to whom the book is dedicated [Francis Hope] died while the book was being written, and I thought, well, death is death, and there is death, and we can't avoid it forever" (*VGMI* 38-39).

[17] Drabble comments, "my novel ended in comedy rather than in tragedy," acknowledging that it is "the only one of my books that I would describe as a comedy" (*TWF* 61).

[18] Drabble observes, "suddenly there it was, a lot of imagery of nature: the natural world of species, the flora and fauna, the fact that Frances' father studied newts. It all just seemed to fit very nicely. Once you've got a starting image, the thing just naturally goes on" (*BMI* 51).

[19] Drabble comments, "there is a very considerable evolutionary interest in this book, and I find it quite extraordinary that the image of the bank should be there in Darwin and there in my own work without any possibility that I myself could have made that particular connection" (*TWF* 95).

[20] Drabble comments, "I felt at the end that I was creating my own happy ending, a Jane Austen ending, a happy marriage, but that it would undoubtedly arouse a great deal of opposition. And it did" (*TWF* 16). Ellen Cronan Rose con-

cludes: "Anthea Zeman calls *The Realms of Gold* 'a defiantly, blatantly optimistic novel from a professed pessimist. It is an aberration. The age of gold is succeeded by *The Ice Age*" (*EF* 110). Drabble explains, "I'd also thought of integrating the plot by making [David] marry Janet Bird at the end, you see. They were also going to have had an affair in the past, and that would have integrated the structure: the plot would have stuck together if I'd made that happen" (*VGMI* 37).

[21] Kaplan concludes: "the act of creation, the god-like act in this novel, is precisely this courageous dive into the abyss—of personality, of one's family, of history—and the coming back to tell the tale, recreating in the process a book, a child, a city, a life, a past" (241-42).

Chapter Nine:

BRITAIN'S COLD WAR WITH A NEW ICE AGE

The Ice Age (1977) is considered by many Drabble's best book because, in this dramatization of the decline and fall of the British economy, she broadens her scope to encompass financial, political, and cultural concerns.[1] In this study of the traditionally masculine subjects of real estate and high finance, Drabble also extends her technical dexterity to include a combined male and female central consciousness in Anthony Keating, her first male protagonist, and Alison Murray, his mistress.[2]

Britain's power failure is more than a mere energy crisis, however, and in this novel Drabble portrays a nation that is not only economically but also spiritually bankrupt. The author takes the temperature of the times accurately in *The Ice Age*, but while the realistic surface detail reflects the desperate financial climate of the country, the artistic imagery reveals the glacial spiritual atmosphere of the nation. Drabble employs a complex allegorical scheme of natural and architectural images of glaciers and prisons to symbolize the way that property speculation is freezing and imprisoning England both as a land and as a people. As the new dark ages overshadow the land, Drabble questions whether the spirit of Britain can survive.

Drabble begins her allegory of Britain's decline by personifying the nation as a giant, quoting Milton's *Areopagitica* (1644) as the first epigraph of *The Ice Age*: "Methinks I see in my mind a noble and puissant Nation rousing herself like a strong man after sleep, and shaking her invincible locks."[3] By following Milton's heroic image with Wordsworth's sonnet, "London, 1802," Drabble makes it clear that the same patriotic spirit is once again required to revive the moribund colossus:

> Milton! Thou shouldst be living at this hour:
> England hath need of thee.... We are selfish men:
> Oh! Raise us up, return to us again;
> And give us manners, virtue, freedom, power.

The British giant is clearly being bled by a severe economic recession. Drabble employs the image of the inconstant moon as a symbol of the fluctuation of fickle fortune: "Three-quarters full and on the wane. Soon, the bright and savage sickle. The soft, unshapely shape, the unfinished circle swam in the clear sky. What has she to do with profit and loss? Something, perhaps. She too waxes and wanes" (85). The savage sickle of the grim reaper of economic depression has cut the British giant down and left it bleeding to death. *The Property Investment Review* is riddled with "such mortal words as deathpangs, moratoria, fatal bleeding" (45), as the British people watch "the unedifying spectacle of the death-throes of greed in their once so-privileged nation" (67). Anthony Keating is "mesmerized by the bleeding and draining and seeping away of profits in bank charges and interest, paralyzed by prospects of disaster," represented for him personally by "the flagging pulse of the Imperial Delight Property Company" (82-83).

While Drabble certainly puts her finger on the flagging financial pulse of the country, she also puts her ear to the moral heart of the nation. Drabble makes it clear through the person of classics scholar Linton Hancox that the British giant is suffering from a cultural as well as an economic malaise. "The golden age of solid education which Linton evoked" (75) has been snowed under by the modern ice age. Classics, that ancient sanctuary of culture, is now "an empty shrine, a pillaged tomb," and the Muse herself is silent, perhaps dead. Nowadays classics is "a pond, out of which the water had slowly drained, leaving Linton stranded, beached, useless" (77). Linton himself is atrophied, like Daphne, who was metamorphosed into a tree to escape the pursuing Apollo, god of intellect and art: "There is no blood left in me, thought Linton Hancox. I am a dry husk, dry as parchment. There is no blood in my veins, but some strange woody sap. Xylem or phloem. A protective spirit has mercifully turned me into a tree, to spare me the rape of the mind" (226).

A stoat scurrying from under his headlights to refuge in the forest symbolizes to Linton the death of civilization and a regression to a primitive state of barbarism: "Would it matter," he wonders, as he meditates on a return to the jungle law of the survival of the fittest, "if the new dark ages rolled over the face of Europe?" (226). In the "dark days" of this "terrible year," the sun no longer shines on Britain, "the nation on whose empire the sun had never set" (97). As darkness covers the earth, Britain is once again approaching her "darkest hour," a phrase that recalls the blitz and the Battle of Britain. *The Ice Age* does demonstrate "the blitz spirit" (*VGMI* 20), Drabble insists, that spirit of defiance and sardonic humour with which embattled Britain is wont to face disaster, for this novel shows Britain fighting another bitter battle: a cold war with a new ice age.[4]

The golden age that Drabble unearthed in her previous novel has clearly been frozen over by a second age of ice which is freezing the British giant to death. Drabble symbolizes this concept in the novel's central image: "A huge icy fist, with large cold fingers, was squeezing and chilling the people of Britain, that great and puissant nation, slowing down their blood, locking them into immobility, fixing them in a solid stasis, like fish in a frozen river" (65). The title symbol of the ice age dominates the entire novel as an extended metaphor characterizing "the state of the nation" (68) in images of "cold, ice, imprisonment, stasis" (*TWF* 90), symbolizing the spiritual paralysis of Britain.[5]

Drabble intertwines natural imagery of landscape and meteorology with images of flora and fauna, as apocalyptic storms herald the doom of the nation in this "cataclysmic book" (*VGMI* 39). Drabble describes "gusts of anguish that shook the country" (67), as Arctic winds of austerity sweep affluence away. These winds of change that sweep through Britain are a spiritual as well as an economic scourge, for they blow from "the black wastes, where the winds of hell perpetually howled" (165), home of the damned. "The new darkness" (171) signifies "The end of the world" (45), and the lightning that illuminates the land like a lurid revelation suggests the last judgment.

These apocalyptic storms herald the onslaught of the second ice age. The novel opens in sombre November, and the glacier gradually encroaches as the novel progresses, freezing the landscape in a figurative frost:

> The sky was hard and iron grey, and a thick frost, the thickest Anthony had ever seen, had appeared; the yard and drive and lawn were white as with snow, and the trees encased in a thick crystalline fur, a jewelled coating as though they had been dipped into some strange chemical, as though some mysterious transformation had changed their very substance. It was beautiful, but sinister. (118)

The frost transforms the countryside into "another kingdom," suggesting death's other kingdom, since cold symbolizes death and comes from the north, traditional home of the devil. At the midnight of the year, the frost gives way to snow, "a thin, fine powder, a white cold dust" (188), that falls on Christmas Eve, covering the dying country like a shroud, symbolizing the spiritual paralysis of the people, as it does in James Joyce's "The Dead."

Drabble portrays the effect of this glacial atmosphere on Britain symbolically by showing how the ice age transforms the countryside into a wasteland of dying vegetation: "bare stalks and withered plants, mudspattered, hung desolately onto a dirty life, tattered, bent, spent, spattered" (119). The fate of Britain in the new ice age is symbolized by the old elm that has stood for generations as a landmark at the entrance to High Rook House, the hero's historic country estate. The lightning that ushered in the ice age has felled the big tree, causing it to fall across the entrance to the house, cutting it off from the outside world. By cutting off the power, the felling of the elm allows the ice age to invade this symbol of British history, so that the hero is forced by the encroaching chill to burn the tree as firewood: Anthony "crouched in the ancient hearth, staring at the grey wood ash, the crumbled knotty joints, the charred fissured shining black stumps" (236), that were once the proud limbs of the grand old tree. Like the wych-elm that symbolizes England in Forster's *Howards End*, the fate of Anthony's elm also embodies the fate of Britain, as he meditates upon the shattered tree: "England. It would never shake to the roots surely" (178). But it does, in the modern ice age.

The ice age kills fauna as well as flora. The critical condition of the legendary British lion also embodies "the state of the nation," for the once powerful king of the beasts is now on its last legs: "England was a safe, shabby, mangey old lion now: anyone could tweak her tail." Drabble portrays "England, sliding, sinking, shabby, dirty, lazy, inefficient, dangerous, in its death throes, worn out, clapped out, occasionally lashing out" (96-97), as upstart powers bait the impotent beast.

The moribund emblem of the British lion is supplemented by the multiple corpses of man's best friend, for the pages of this novel are littered with dead dogs. The wounded Alsatian that crosses Alison Murray's path upon her return to England appears to her as the personification of death itself, for its bloody flank, ripped by an automobile, looks literally like "the red flank of death" (177). As the Alsatian plods to its death, like a wolf to its lair, Alison realizes that no wilderness refuge awaits it, but only a wasteland of concrete. Reaching her own sanctuary at High Rook House, Alison finds her homecoming marred by a second grim emblem, as she stumbles over the rigid corpse of a pet dog, another victim of the modern ice age. When Anthony Keating shoots an Alsatian near the end of the novel, we know that the ice age has invaded even the heart of the hero.

The novel opens portentously with the death of a bird, as a cock pheasant flying overhead drops dead of a heart attack at the very feet of the hero. Anthony Keating, who had not died of his heart attack, naturally identifies with the pheasant, for his own weak heart is compared repeatedly to "a baby or a bird, a delicate creature that must not be shocked or offended" (12). Like the legendary lion and the old elm, the eagle, alluded to in Drabble's opening epigraph from Milton's *Areopagitica*, is a patriotic symbol of the spirit of Britain:

> Methinks I see her as an eagle muing her mighty youth, and kindling her undazl'd eyes at the full midday beam: purging and unscaling her long abused sight at the fountain it self of heavenly radiance; while the whole noise of timorous and flocking birds, with those also that love the twilight, flutter about, amaz'd at what she means, and in their envious gabble would prognosticate a year of sects and schisms.

The quotation suggests that Drabble too hopes that blind Britain will recover its vision.

If the eagle symbolizes the heroic spirit of England, then the flocks of gabbling birds are the nation's parasites. These inferior fowl recall the rooks, archetypal emblems of villainy, that pervade *The Ice Age*. Anthony's noble aspirations are punctuated by "the mocking cries of bleak rooks" (75), provoking him to shoot these raucous hecklers who are driving him crazy with their sarcastic cackle. The rooks, for whom High Rook House is named, suggest that Anthony himself has been "rooked" in buying this historic monument, just as he has been swindled by his partners over the Riverside deal. But the nation's parasites are rooked themselves, when the big elm in the lane that had for generations housed the rooks falls, dislodging them at last. Drabble points out in the branches of the fallen tree "the skeletal remains of the nests of the rowdy stiff-legged rooks, which they patched up from year to year: next year they would have to find a new property. After centuries" (178)—like the parasites of fallen Britain.

The ice age proves fatal not only to wild and domestic animals, but also to the social animal, man himself. A plague of violence stalks the land in the new dark ages, for Britain in the mid-seventies has become a "dangerous, violent place . . . where each step could mean death" (158). Deaths punctuate the pages of *The Ice Age*, from the murder of Max Friedmann in the explosion of an IRA bomb in London at the beginning of the novel, to the assassination of the British consul in the explosion of violence in Walachia at the end of the book. The characters who are not dead are either diseased or disabled: the bomb that killed Max Friedmann also shattered the limb of his wife Kitty, necessitating the amputation of her foot. If the Friedmanns are victims, like the eight million Jews, of man's inhumanity to man, then Alison's daughter Molly is an example of "the tragic instances of God's inhumanity to man" (110), for Molly was born with cerebral palsy, one of "the wretched and maimed of the earth" (101). Other characters develop diseases that are physical symbols of spiritual corrosion: Alison's sister Rosemary develops a malignant lump in her breast (the result, Alison thinks, of sibling jealousy) and has to have her breast amputated. Throughout the novel, Alison herself is bleeding profusely with "dark-red clots of blood," symbolizing the female fate; she thinks it would be "poetic justice" (158) if she too contracted cancer or some serious ailment like Anthony, as a physical manifestation of the mental anxiety she has shared with him during this "terrible year" (11). The main example of Drabble's use of medical malaise to embody the fatal effect of the ice age on humanity is, of course, the "weak heart" of her hero.

All of the characters in the novel are said to be freezing to death, either literally or figuratively, as we learn that many old folk died of cold in the glacial climate of contemporary Britain. Those who are not dead or diseased are disabled in another way, by being incarcerated in prison. They are equally the victims of the ice age, for, although not frozen to death physically, they are frozen spiritually—souls on ice.

The question is, what is the cause of this fatal glacier? *The Ice Age* is more than just topical reportage on England's economic recession, for in this novel Drabble examines the causes as well as the effects of the new ice age. Private property is the source of the "freeze and squeeze" (65) that is chilling Britain spiritually as well as financially. "Property speculation had become a kind of gold rush" (116) during the sixties, but the boom has gone bust, and by the mid-seventies, "politicians were declaring open war on property developers, denouncing them as the scourge of Britain" (71). In *The Ice Age*, Drabble investigates "the problems of a mixed economy, state capitalism, the profit motive, corporate ownership, personal incentives" (46), speculating about what will happen "if capitalism and inflation continue to govern the land" (247).[6]

In *The Ice Age*, Drabble portrays property development destroying Britain in two ways, both as a land and as a people. The basic opposition between nature and culture is presented as a dual conflict between property and country and between property and humanity, with the first conflict symbolized by natural imagery and the second embodied in architectural images. Drabble also dramatizes this opposition by personifying the land and people of Britain in the persons of her male and female protagonists. Anthony Keating personifies the British character perfectly, for he is almost a caricature of the English gentleman, "standing for old-world British chivalric imperialism" (*JTI* 175). Recently, however, Anthony has undergone a metamorphosis from traditional gentleman to contemporary speculator—Victorian man gone mod. Drabble dramatizes the plight of Britain in the fluctuating fortunes of her hero, for "he, like the nation, was living beyond his means, on borrowed time and borrowed money" (182). Anthony's mistress, Alison Murray, embodies Britain as a land, the beautiful English countryside that Anthony and his partners in greed exploit for economic profit. In modern times the people have become alienated from the land, just as Anthony and Alison are separated by geography and by a schizoid narrative technique as rigid as the iron curtain itself—as well as by Anthony's enforced abstinence, which divides the lovers as surely as prison separates their comic counterparts, Len Wincobank and Maureen Kirby.

Alison's face, which is "as typically English as the English rose" (39), symbolizes the face of the land, for Alison, like England, is growing old and must face the fact of deterioration and the consequent question of identity. For Alison, as for England, "beauty had for years been identity. She had no other. How could she ever make another, for the second half of her necessary life?" (99). Britain faces the same mid-life identity crisis as Alison: "The country was growing old. Like herself. The scars on the hillside were the wrinkles round her own eyes: irremovable. How could one learn to grow old? Neither a country nor a person can stay young forever" (173).

Travelling through England, Alison sees the landscape, scarred by mine pits and slag heaps, as the ravaged face of a woman weeping over her violation, for the land "wept black, dank, perpetual tears." She recognizes the rape of the fair country, realizing how the old profiteers gouged the riches out of the womb of Mother Earth, leaving it barren: "was it true that the English had ransacked their riches for two centuries, had spent like lords, and were now bankrupt, living in the ruins of their own past grandiose excesses?" (173). On returning to High Rook House, Alison berates Anthony for "what people like you have done to the face, to the very face of the country" (183).

But to the contemporary property speculators, "this waste land had spelt not muck but money" (174), for they view the ravaged countryside as a plaything to be dissected and reassembled: developers "enjoyed collecting sites and fitting them together like expensive jigsaw puzzles" (51), as Anthony Keating's "I.D. Property Company negotiated for the other parts of the jigsaw" (33). Such vivisection has bled the British giant to death.

"Property is theft" (219), declares one character, quoting Pierre Proudhon's dictum, but Drabble suggests, rather, that property is prison. In *The Ice Age*, Drabble portrays the concept of property imprisoning nature symbolically, through images of walls and fences. She recalls "the enclosure of the Commons," pictures "the beaches of the Riviera, parcelled out and cordoned off and sold" (69), visualizes "the miles of coast, as yet unenclosed, not yet roped and staked and parcelled," and wonders, "What next? The roping, the selling, the plundering?" (224). Anthony loves his obsolete gasometer, emblem of his new career as speculator, for it "enmeshed the skies" (203). Anthony also likes stone walls: "He liked the way they marched across the contours, and up the steep slopes. He liked their grey whitenesses, their persistence, their human scale, their mathematical parcelling out of the infinite. They squared it off and captured it, as his gasometer had caught and enmeshed the sky" (152-53). The old elderberry tree in the courtyard of The Imperial Delight Property Company is uprooted, exemplifying "the end of an age"—to be replaced by little trees fenced off in wire cages, another emblem of the imprisoning of nature by property. But "Anthony somehow felt that they would lack the charm of the cobbled yard and the secret elderberry, that the grass would be covered in dog shit, that the trees would be vandalized and killed off even inside their chicken wire protection" (31).

The parallel opposition between property and humanity is symbolized by images of architecture and dramatized by the fortunes of the hero. Anthony meditates on the significance of historical monuments:

> Ozymandias, King of Kings. Look on my works, ye mighty. Well, he hadn't been far wrong, Ozymandias, he had lost his kingdom, perhaps, but at least part of his monument remained. By their monuments ye shall know them. By the Pyramids, the Parthenon, by Chartres and St Peter's, by St Pancras Station and the Eiffel Tower, by the Post Office Tower and the Chrysler Building. All large buildings express both piety and pride: how could they not? Man's own achievement, they point to the skies. His own gasometer had enmeshed the skies. They witness at once man's sufficiency and his insufficiency. (203)

Ironically, however, Shelley's sonnet demonstrates that such hubristic (and phallic) monuments to man's desire to dominate nature are symbols, not of success, but of the failure of all human endeavour.[7]

Anthony's own personal monuments symbolize British social history, and his company, frivolously called "The Imperial Delight Property Company," after the old sweet factory which it displaced, is referred to by the abbreviation "I.D."—suggesting in a humorous manner both the individual's and society's desperate search for identity through symbolic monuments. Anthony grew up under the shadow of Crawford Cathedral, which dominates the landscape with its gothic tower—"a fine example, if not the finest, of eleventh and twelfth century architecture in Britain" (202). But Anthony is converted from traditional Christianity to the contemporary religion of property speculation by the visionary zealot Len Wincobank and consequently replaces his medieval monument with a modern one which also inspires him with a religious ecstasy: "A derelict gasometer, radiant with significance. One could see it from miles away, right across the Thames from some directions. It lifted the heart. Up soared the heart like a bird in the chest, up through its light and airy metal shell, to the changing, so much before unnoticed, sky" (33).[8]

Modern monuments, "built to the glory of commerce," rather than the glory of God, are the most hubristic. Architects are truly the enemy of the people in *The Ice Age*, for they put buildings before people. They build constructing structures that imprison their inhabitants: "what did it matter if they went mad like animals too constantly displayed in their cages in the zoo?" (52). Contemporary architecture is brutal and dehumanizing: "windowless buildings were rearing themselves up, buildings with arrow slits like medieval fortresses, conserving heat, repelling invaders" (171). Developers, like self-made millionaire Len Wincobank (suggesting beat the bank), are guilty of a sin against society, "raping the city centres of Britain and making millions" (27), as Northam Centre, "a monument to Wincobank," illustrates.[9] Alison's nightmare experience, when she returns to England from behind the Iron Curtain, only to find herself stranded on a traffic island amidst a wilderness of underpasses, flyovers, and roundabouts, designed to accommodate machines, but inaccessible to people—"walled in by high elephantine walls" in "an environmental offence as bad as a slag heap" (175)—is vividly highlighted by the gruesome emblem of the doomed Alsatian. Ultimately, however, Ozymandias' pronouncement is validated, for "Centre Point stood as empty as Crawford Cathedral, an anachronism before it had even been occupied" (203), abandoned in the property freeze, like white elephants or hairy mammoths fossilized by the ice age.

Drabble portrays these grotesque obelisks stranded in a surrealistic landscape and luridly lit by lightning in an apocalyptic atmosphere that forebodes the last judgment:

> The steep hillsides and valleys [were] laid bare by the flashes of the lightning. The white blocks arose on the distant slopes like marble statues, like the pillars of Stonehenge, like resurrected souls, standing palely, elegantly, lifting their heads against the noisy wrath of the elements. . . . The reclaimed hills, lit a lurid green, rose up to the sky's edge. The dark satanic smoke had gone forever, and Sheffield lay purified by the apocalyptic flames of a new Jerusalem. The white sisters stood, bearing witness to the shining urban dream of the sixties and early seventies. How forlornly they

might stand there in the new darkness, who could say. (171)

The author's apocalyptic allegory suggests implicitly her moral disapproval of such irresponsible property development.

After destroying the urban centres, the villains of the piece desert the sinking ship, escaping the rat-race of the city for the underdeveloped countryside in a desperate attempt to return to nature. Anthony Keating's purchase of High Rook House with money made from rooking others is highly ironic, as even Alison appreciates: "I do think it's a bit awful of you, Anthony, to knock other places down, and that nice Mr. Boot from the sweet factory, and drive them out, and put up all those great blocks, and then come and sit up here in this—this Pevsner Ancient Monument" (183).

High Rook House, a Jacobean stately home on the Yorkshire moors and a symbol of English history, embodies Anthony's desire for historical regression. Anthony's most recent personal monument, this stately home is his latest replacement for the gothic cathedral, supplanting the gasometer. Here in the English countryside Anthony "had built his own cathedral, bought his own close. His pond, his beck, his trees, his rooks, his house" (199). This new sanctuary represents Anthony's attempt to find a fortress to fend off the encroaching glacier—"seeking every Englishman's dream: his own plot, his own castle" (70). Although an Englishman's home is his castle and the initials of High Rook House, "HRH," do signify His Royal Highness, Anthony has no real right to this aristocratic ancestral seat, as the sarcastic cries of the mocking rooks remind him. Eventually the ice age invades even High Rook House, isolating Anthony as surely as Len Wincobank in his nearby penitentiary on the Yorkshire moors, so that Anthony's "fortress, so dearly purchased, was to him not unlike a prison" (71).

Prisons are the primary architectural symbol in *The Ice Age* of the way that property development imprisons people.[10] Most of the characters in the novel are in prison either literally or metaphorically. Alison thinks of "Jane, in prison: of Len Wincobank, in prison: of poor Anthony, imprisoned with Molly in his remote eyrie" (164). Property developers are the villains of the piece in *The Ice Age*, and they are punished for their sins against society by being incarcerated in prisons as hostile to humanity as their own brutal structures. Corrupt city architect Tom Callendar and arch-speculator Len Wincobank are imprisoned together in a frigid jail on the Yorkshire moors, while the baby trees they tend are protected in hothouses by people who put trees before men—just as the developers put buildings before people.

Much of *The Ice Age* is staged behind the Iron Curtain in an obscure totalitarian state called Walachia, suggesting walls. Walachia is itself a prison, for both Jane Murray and Anthony Keating are imprisoned there in Krusograd jail, and even Alison feels caged in her prison-like room in the Krusograd hotel. But the iron curtain of a second ice age has fallen over Britain too, so that Anthony could echo Hamlet in declaring, "England's a prison." The author inquires rhetorically, "Where was the new bright classless enterprising future of Great Britain?" and replies, "In jail with Len Wincobank" (261).

The characters who are not in actual jails are in metaphorical prisons of their own psychological alienation—like Humphrey Clegg, with his locked "Bluebeard's Cupboard" full of women's clothing and his secret penchant for transvestitism: "He had been imprisoned by this misfortune in a jail from which there would be no release" (260). Jane Murray's literal imprisonment in Krusograd jail is not as rigid as the prison of her own alienation, represented by her refusal to eat or speak. Nor is Alison's imprisoning room in the Krusograd hotel any more confining than the psychological prison of her own emotional frigidity: "I am held in some cold grip. Let me out, she prayed, let me go" (195). She hopes that she may thaw back home in England, but she is irremediably frozen by the ice age. Alison is also trapped in the biological prison of her maternal role, for, as the mother of a disabled child, she will never be free—as Drabble emphasizes in the concluding statement of the novel. Molly is herself a prisoner of God, who has confined her in a physical handicap from which she cannot escape.

Certain characters deliberately choose imprisonment, either literal or metaphorical, because of their fear of freedom, preferring solitary confinement to the terrifying responsibility of choice. "Freedom is a mixed blessing," comments Anthony, for "there's something rather consoling about the lack of options" (294). And "There is only the tiniest area, thought Alison, in which one can stay peacefully, without hurting, without being hurt. The smallest space, the smallest cell" (249). Anthony laments that "no guardian angel would put him quietly away in a cell" (228), freeing him of the burden of deciding his own future.

But Anthony's guardian angel does in fact transport him to that very cell through a curious metamorphosis. The moment of grace during Anthony and Alison's brief pastoral idyll proves to be the proverbial calm before the storm: "Time paused: they heard its heart stop, they heard its breath held, they heard the lapse of thudding and rustling and pumping and beating." As they listen to the sound of silence, "It seemed to them both that some secret was about to be revealed, was perhaps even there with them: the secret of living without ambition, agitation, hope" (250). This eternal moment proves to be a time machine that transports Anthony into another dimension in which the secret of life will be revealed to him. Although many reviewers criticized the conclusion of the novel as unsuitable, this metaphorical state, distinguished by a shift to the historical present, seems a fitting conclusion to the extended allegory of *The Ice Age*.

It is appropriate that Anthony should be literally incarcerated at the conclusion of *The Ice Age*, for he has been in a figurative prison throughout the entire novel. First, a property speculator, he has been "caught in a trap of his own making" (15). He has also been a prisoner of his own weak heart, which has sentenced him to an enforced abstinence as strict as that which Len Wincobank endures in Scratby Open Prison. He has already been effectively "imprisoned in High Rook House" (42), where he is literally isolated in solitary confinement. There he becomes obsessed with images of prisons, including his memory of the claustrophobic experience of being locked in a lavatory—"shut up in a small square box without a window . . . with no prospect of deliverance" (41). At the conclusion of *The Ice Age*, Anthony realizes that "those long winter days alone at High Rook House were a warning and a preparation" (295) for his final incarceration.

Anthony's imprisonment is appropriate nationally as well as individually, for the British populace he personifies has been imprisoned throughout the novel in a spiritual paralysis. Anthony is a scapegoat figure, like Oedipus, for Britain today, like Sophocles' Thebes, is polluted and must be purified. Anthony becomes fascinated by the sacrifice of Antigone, for "Antigone had gone out and died for a completely meaningless code"—just as Anthony himself is "prepared to represent

Queen and Country with the polite and honourable codes of the English public school" (285). A latter-day Paul Pennyfeather or Tony Last, Anthony even begins to identify with Saint Anthony the martyr.

Anthony's solitary confinement in Krusograd prison suggests the cell of the self, a metaphorical womb in which the embryonic spirit is reborn. On his way to the jail, he realizes, "I do not know how man can do without God," and he is stopped in the middle of the road by the thought, "like Paul on the way to Damascus" (267). Like Boethius before him, Anthony writes a book in prison about "the nature of God and the possibility of religious faith. . . . If God did not appoint this trial for me, then how could it be that I should be asked to endure it, he asks. He cannot bring himself to believe in the random malice of the fates, those three grey sisters. He is determined, alone, to justify the ways of God to man" (295-96)—like Milton in *Paradise Lost*.[11]

The Ice Age concludes with a Miltonic leap of faith, for at the very end of the novel, Anthony has a vision of God, symbolized by a rare bird that he believes is "a messenger from God, an angel, a promise. . . . his heart rises, he experiences hope. He experiences joy" (297). The rare bird, significantly a "wall creeper," symbolizes in its free flight over the prison walls the freedom of the spirit, for it is neither fettered by fences nor bound by a rib cage.[12]

Images of birds in flight frame the spiritual allegory of *The Ice Age*: the novel begins with the death of a pheasant and ends with the flight of a wall creeper, and in between it asks, "Is there providence in the fall of a sparrow?"[13] The fall of the pheasant is redeemed by the final ascent of the rare bird, recalling Milton's hoodwinked eagle, whose eyes are opened to the heavenly radiance at last, and the British giant, who finally arises from his long slumber. Thus, the concluding symbol of *The Ice Age* suggests the spiritual rebirth of Anthony Keating and new hope for the future of the spirit of Britain.

Near the end of *The Ice Age*, Anthony has a vision of Britain's revival:

> He saw, as he sat there, some apparition, of this great and powerful nation, a country lying there surrounded by the grey seas, the land green and grey, well worn, long inhabited, not in chains, not in thrall, but a land passing through some strange metamorphosis, through

the intense creative lethargy of profound self-contemplation, not idle, not defeated, but waiting still, assembling defences against the noxious oily tides of fatigue and contempt that washed insistently against her shores. An aerial view, a helicopter view of this precious isle came into his head, and he saw the seas washing forever, or more or less forever, round the white and yellow and pink and grey sands and pebbles of the beaches, this semi-precious stone set in a leaden sea, our heritage, the miles of coast, as yet unenclosed, not yet roped and staked and parcelled. What next? The roping, the selling, the plundering? The view shimmered, fragmented, dissolved like a cloud. The silence lasted. (224)

The echoes of Milton's heroic vision of the recovery of Britain and of Shakespeare's rhapsodic eulogy on the glory of England in this eloquent central passage of *The Ice Age* suggest that the author has faith that Britain may recover from its vivisection at the hands of speculators, that the spirit of Britain may be revived, and that the ice age may yet melt into another golden age.[14]

NOTES

[1] Mel Gussow, in "Margaret Drabble: A Double Life," *New York Times Book Review*, 9 October 1977, p. 41, writes of *The Ice Age*: "The book, her most ambitious to date, has a cinematic sweep and an extraordinary timeliness. It is a conscious effort on her part to lose the label—undeserved—of 'woman's writer.' 'I was fed up with women—slightly,' she said, explaining that she wanted to write about a man as a central figure."

[2] Drabble comments: "I experiment with point of view and the author interjecting . . . most of the story is recorded from about six different points of view, through the eyes of six different characters, but there's an occasional authorial interjection" (*VGMI* 29). She also observes, "it was time to write, if I could, from the point of view of a man. This was the first time I had attempted this. It was a challenge to me, and I felt that if I did not do it now I never would" (*TWF* 88).

[3] Margaret Drabble, *The Ice Age* (London: Weidenfeld and Nicolson, 1977). Further references to this edition will be given in the text.

[4] In "Once Again, the Dark," *New York Times*, 6 January

1974, p. 15, Drabble writes, "Britain is filled with a wartime spirit of panic." The lack of Christmas lights in Britain are reminiscent of the blitz blackouts and suggest that Britain is entering a new dark age with the new year.

[5] Drabble told Gussow that her title is "shorthand for economic depression—everything frozen, including wages. It is not a permanent state. With luck, it could thaw a bit." Keith Wilson, "Jim, Jake and the Years Between: The Will to Stasis in the Contemporary British Novel," *ARIEL*, 13 (January, 1982), 66, writes: "*The Ice Age* can offer only visions of contemporary decline and willed retreat, a late-seventies stasis that is given visual rendering in the dust-jacket illustration for *The Ice Age* that shows tortured eyes staring out from the blue depths of an ice cube."

[6] Drabble says that her research for *The Ice Age* was inspired by reading Oliver Marriott's book, *The Property Boom* (*TWF* 89).

[7] Rose concludes that "the central male enterprise in *The Ice Age* is the assertion of the superiority of culture over nature . . . the imposition of order on chaos, the domination of nature, the victory of the male over the female principle." She judges that Alison provides a "feminist critique" of Anthony's "phallocentric vision" (*EF* 113-116). Elaine Tuttle Hansen, "The Uses of Imagination: Margaret Drabble's *The Ice Age*" (*CEMD* 151-68), contrasts male and female uses of imagination.

[8] James Gindin, "Three Recent British Novels and an American Response," *Michigan Quarterly Review*, 27 (1978), 230-33, writes that "historical metaphors are comically qualified or carefully particularized" in *The Ice Age*, and images of "England changing from allegiance to cathedral spires to allegiance to gasometers are repeated throughout the novel, as if we all leap from one grand vertical obeisance or apocalypse to another."

[9] Drabble comments on the model for Wincobank: "I travelled around England with this property speculator in his golden Rolls-Royce which was all he had left from his money—he had lost the lot—and we looked at the buildings that he had created" (*TWF* 89).

[10] Drabble comments, "By this time I was very conscious of symbolism and a lot of it takes place in prison. There are a lot of prisons in this book. Three characters are in real prisons and there are many spiritual imprisonments as well

within the book" (*TWF* 90).

[11] Korenman concludes "The 'Liberation' of Margaret Drabble," *Critique*, 21 (1979), 61-72, thus:

> The uneven tone suggests that Drabble herself may be unsure how fully she endorses Anthony's turning to God. Like the fairytale marriages at the end of *The Realms of Gold*, Anthony's religious awakening and the contrived circumstances under which it occurs may testify primarily to Margaret Drabble's reluctance to allow her vision of meaninglessness to prevail. (71)

[12] Drabble comments on the conclusion of *The Ice Age*:

> I feel that in all my novels there's this gesture towards faith and towards belief in God, because I hope that God is there . . . in the novel I've just finished, again it seemed at various points that it was leading towards death: and the character who's had a heart attack on page one, and various possible disasters loomed before me, and, in fact, I had to reject them. It ends . . . not too badly, but because, again, this feeling of optimism had reasserted itself. It's a very cataclysmic book. In fact, I'm afraid to say that on the last page he has a vision of God. (*VGMI* 38)

[13] Ellen Cronan Rose applies this quotation to *The Ice Age* in "Paradise Lost," *National Review*, 29 (23 December 1977), 1504.

[14] Drabble comments, "For quite a long time I thought I would have a reasonably happy or peaceful ending and then it just didn't seem very plausible" (*BMI* 49). She explains:

> I intended to redeem this overwhelming gloom by some kind of vision of Britain rising out of its chains and, in fact, I've used the quotation from Milton about Britain stirring in its chains, and rising up. But when I got to the passage, and I knew where it had to come, my characters were sitting in a night club and everything was very bad, and one character, my main character, had to have this vision of Britain, an aerial vision of recovery, and I couldn't get it. I couldn't resolve the problem I'd set myself, which was to have some kind of uplift, optimism, resolution. I think I finally solved it, but I was stuck with that paralysis for far, far longer than I liked, and I think that was reflecting not art, but life. (*VGMI* 4-5)

I discuss this image as part of a literary tradition in "The Aerial View of Modern Britain: The Airplane as a Vehicle for Idealism and Satire," *ARIEL*, 15 (Summer, 1984), 17-33.

Chapter Ten:

THE EXCREMENTAL VISION AND THE AERIAL VIEW OF *THE MIDDLE GROUND*

Drabble took a glacial view of the climate of contemporary culture in *The Ice Age*, but in *The Middle Ground* (1980), the ice has melted into "the mud of existence" (*VGMI* 37), in the author's words. As its title suggests, the subject of the last of Drabble's social novels of the seventies is middle age: "If it is a mid-life crisis, such as everyone suffers, what on earth is on the other side of it?" wonders her journalist heroine, Kate Armstrong.[1] Through a complex narrative technique of multiple viewpoints, Drabble also portrays the identity crisis of contemporary society, for her four major characters, all members of the professional middle class, provide a panoramic picture of society as a whole. The middle ground is also the present, that stumbling block between the past and the future—"The middle years, caught between children and parents, free of neither: the past stretches back too densely, it is too thickly populated, the future has not yet thinned out" (165).[2]

Reviewers criticized Drabble's cross-section of contemporary society as "endless and pointless trivia, which may be the stuffing of life but isn't the stuff of art,"[3] and as "a snapshot, not a painting. A snapshot reproduces the flesh—a great painting also portrays the spirit."[4] One reviewer complained that "it is impossible to find any pattern in this carpet,"[5] and another objected that "there is more background than foreground in *The Middle Ground*."[6] The clues to Drabble's underlying design lie not in the background or foreground, however, but in the underground level of her art. Several recent critics have searched in Drabble's complex narrative method for the organizing principle of *The Middle Ground*, but in vain, for the key to the spirit beneath the ample flesh of Drabble's "big baggy monster" (*VGMI* 37) is in the substructure of symbolism.[7]

In *The Middle Ground*, symbolism becomes a social tool for probing the festering sores of society: since Drabble portrays contemporary society as a cesspool, her primary symbol is, appropriately, a sewer.[8] "The title is significant" (*TWF* 115), Drabble insists, for the middle ground itself is a sewage embankment—a green spine that forms the backbone of society, just like the proverbial railway tracks, dividing urban from rural and suburb from slum. The life of the Fletcher family revolves around the sewage bank, for Kate's father is employed in the Blackridge Works, like his father and grandfather before him. A dedicated sanitary engineer, Walter Fletcher entertains "a lively interest in the science of drainage, sewage and pollution," writing impassioned letters to the *Sewage Workers' Gazette* about "the overloading of drains with new-fangled tampons and contraceptives and indestructible detergents, about fluorization and the dangers of waterborne viruses" (11-12), and delivering rhetorical speeches, "conjuring up the Dickensian horrors of the polluted Thames" in the days when "cholera was king in London" (106). He is delighted when an Irishman claims to have planted a bomb in the sewage works, which would "spread disease and destruction for many miles around," for the incident proves that "sewage plants were vital organs" (195).

"Perhaps so close an infantile connection with sewage would be bound to have some effect on the psyche" (118), Kate reflects, for the shame of the sewer sticks to her brother Peter, driving him into neurosis, obesity, and possibly homosexuality, since his peers enjoy rubbing his nose in it, taunting him with the name "Stinky Fletcher" and chanting:

> Pete, Pete
> What does he eat
> A nice thick sandwich
> Buttered with shit. (17)

Her father's daughter, Kate, conversely, is fascinated by the sewer, unlike her squeamish mother: "The sewage bank she deplored as a horrible reminder of the district's grim functional gracelessness, though to Kate it was its most interesting feature" (15). Kate makes the stigma of the sewer work for her when she discovers that "There was nothing, literally nothing, that couldn't be turned into a joke. In fact, the more horrible and discreditable the subject matter, the better the joke." She develops a clever technique for turning the shame to her own ends: "She instigated a playground game called Confessions (her profitable flair for journalism was evident this early) which consisted of forcing everyone present to recount the most embarrassing experience of the last twenty-four hours. The girls loved it, and the game became immensely popular, though Kate usually won, simply by being more truthful than everyone else" (18-19). Drabble adds, "This, of course, is her technique to this day," for Kate's system in the "Badness Stakes" remains her method as a professional journalist who writes pieces on sewage and dog shit, as well as specifically female "dirt," like menstruation, contraception, and abortion.[9] "She started to write new-wave women's pieces some time before they became fashionable, sharing her pregnancies and indignation with a shocked and enthralled public" (31).

A scavenger by nature, with "an unerring eye for the crap" (25), Kate becomes a muckraker by profession, winning fame by writing about the very sewage system that spawned her confessional technique. She actually descends into the sewer to research her piece on sanitation, going "down through a man-hole in the middle of Piccadilly, climbing down a greasy ladder to the underworld" (104). These "notes from underground" are a metaphor for the journalist's profession, which involves investigating the secret underside of society and transforming the experience into literature: "the sewage works, out they all came, translated into art. It was like a kind of magic, turning shit into gold" (19). Processing sewage also symbolizes the curious artistic alchemy of the social novelist, as Drabble transforms fact into fiction.

While the sewer is clearly a metaphor for the dark underbelly of society which the journalist must expose, it is also a personal metaphor for the heroine's buried subterranean self, the dark tunnels, the mysterious network of the psyche. As a child, Kate's favourite activity was sniffing the forbidden smell of sewage from the underworld she exploits as a journalist: "There had been something magical about the dark race of water and the powerful odour of London. She had lain there and thought of the mysterious networks of drains and pipes and tubes and gulleys and sewers linking the underground city" (103). When Kate goes home again during her mid-life crisis, she just follows her nose directly to her old stamping ground on the sewage embankment, where "recollections just beyond the reach of memory gathered in the distance, took shape as she approached." The smell of sewage stimulates waves of nostalgia, triggering remembrance of things past: "She'd heard of Proust's madeleine. How typical of her, to have chosen a sewage bank for such stirrings, instead of a nice little cake and a nice cup of tea" (105). The odour spirits her back to her past: "She shivered, as the sensation of childhood overpoweringly returned, the sense of her small guilty child's body, covertly sniffing its own strange drug" (103). The grill on the man-hole cover becomes Kate's window on the past: "Was this what she had come for, was this the window, the grill through which she could escape the prison of the present into the past, where the dark spirits swam in the fast-moving flood?"

The sewage system is the centre of an extended network of imagery which is intertwined with a complex technique of characterization and narration. Drabble fractures the central consciousness of this novel into multiple viewpoints which provide a jigsaw puzzle picture of today's fragmented world: Ted Stennett, the medical researcher for the World Health Organization, states the scientific view of the world; Hugo Mainwaring, Middle East correspondent, provides the political perspective on the international situation; Evelyn Stennett, a social worker in Britain's welfare state, conveys the social view of "London Today"; and Kate Armstrong, the journalist, offers the feminist view of "Women Today." The images with which these characters view their several segments of society are interwoven with the central network of sewer imagery to convey an excremental vision of the contemporary world, as the sewer breeds bacteria which are borne by insects and rats, spreading disease throughout society. Drabble draws her images of decay from a varied background of literary quotations, paintings, dreams, and nature imagery to convey a devastating vision of the decadence of contemporary society.

The centre of this kaleidoscopic consciousness is Kate Armstrong, whose function as focus is symbolized by several metaphors. A journalist by profession, Kate is both a suitable voice for such a journalistic novel and a fitting spokeswoman for the author, who is also a journalist by her own account.[10] Kate is currently composing a documentary, another appropriate metaphor for this documentary novel in which the author uses her protagonist as a telescope for examining a typical cross-section of society. Just as Kate cannot locate a pattern in the data, so Drabble offers detail but withholds the revelation of the underlying pattern—a narrative method characterized by this misquotation from Wordsworth's *Prelude*:

>   The hemisphere
> Of magic fiction, verse of mine perhaps
> May never tread; but scarcely Spenser's self
> Could have more tranquil visions in his youth,
> More bright appearances could scarcely see.... (189)

Drabble substitutes "see" for "create"—a metaphor for this narrative which offers observation rather than creation.[11]

"The Silver Saucer and the Transparent Apple" is another metaphor for Kate's visionary role, for the heroine of the fable can see the whole world when she spins the transparent apple in the silver saucer, just as Kate's figurative crystal ball reflects a vision of a world awry: "I had this strange sensation, as if the world had in fact slipped, and I'd fallen off it. Lost my footing. I can't explain, as though it had all tilted away from where I thought it was, and had slid away. This picture kept coming into my head, of a great dark globe rolling through the darkness at a strange angle. Though how could a globe be at an angle? A giddy feeling, as though I'd fallen off into space. The ground gone from under me" (229). Kate's sensation of being off balance in a world that is off kilter is humorously symbolized by her "Achilles heel" on the fashionable but unstable high-heeled boots that make it so difficult for her to keep upright on the middle ground: "She trod firmly on her loosening heel, driving the nails back to their homes. Sanity and madness. Well, certainly, sanity is a precarious state, a thin ridge, a tightrope. How ever do most of us keep upright? Like tightrope walkers, by not looking to either side, I suppose, like horses in blinkers. I should never have looked" (119). As a journalist too, Kate is trying desperately to keep her balance sitting on the feminist fence, like the author, who comments: "Between these two, the Scylla and Charybdis of feminism and womanhood, one is walking a tight rope. I think in my novel *The Middle Ground*, my heroine is standing on a very, very small patch of middle ground which isn't really a middle ground at all; it is a rope and if you move either way you fall off" (*TWF* 115). "Sea Change" (171),[12] a statue of a sexy mermaid sitting on a dolphin, is another symbol of Kate's delicate balance, for the statue is so unbalanced that it makes Kate feel seasick; "I sometimes think that if so many people weren't leaning on me, from different directions, I might fall over" (234), she complains.[13]

Looking in her metaphorical crystal ball, Kate sees excrement in every walk of life, and the word "shit" recurs as a *leitmotif* throughout *The Middle Ground*, for Kate encounters shit, both literal and figurative, everywhere she goes. As a journalist, she writes impassioned pieces on the problem of dog shit, and as a feminist, she is struck by a contemporary women's novel's formulation of woman's life as "shit and string beans." The phrase prompts odious comparisons: "her own father had indeed spent his life dealing with shit, real shit, whereas women only have to deal with nice clean yellow milky baby shit" (51). The implication is that everyone is a sewage worker, like Kate's father, at least figuratively speaking. "Eating shit" is another metaphor for Kate, the muckraker journalist who is often forced to eat her own words. Kate identifies with an old schoolmate: "Sally had been a classic case, one of those women who revert to eating their own shit in middle age in complete collapse" (118).

All of this excrement breeds parasites in the sewer, for insects infest *The Middle Ground*. The novel opens with Kate examining her salad for ladybirds, after inadvertently eating one in her spinach during ladybird plague year. As a child in the Fletcher's bug-infested outdoor lavatory, Kate was haunted by nightmare visions of insects: "She dreamed of them walking on her face. Once Peter, in less protective mood, had cruelly told her a story about a girl who fell into a bog and had her eyes stitched up by spiders" (116). Parasites flourish in the sewer of contemporary society; observing the drunken Hunt, Kate visualizes him as an insect: "Grasshopper shanks. Like a dried up insect, he was. A pickled cockroach." He reminds her of a nursery song about grasshoppers who "earned no money and paid no rent," but merely "fiddled a song called Rillaby Ree" (237). Kate realizes that the parasites like Hunt will inherit the earth, while the kings of the beasts, like noble Evelyn, aristocratic Hugo, powerful Ted, and angelic Kate herself, become extinct. Ted contemplates the survival of the fittest, concluding that parasites are fitter to survive in the sewer of contemporary society than the king of the beasts: "The lords of creation. But on their way out, like most of the large and the lovely. The real survivors were tsetse flies and mosquitoes, insecticide-resistant cockroaches, waterborne meningitis viruses swimming their way through the heavily treated waters of London" (170).

Ted Stennett, the medical researcher into the disease-bearing mosquito, provides the scientific view of a world riddled with disease, as these parasites breed bacteria in the sewer of society, spreading sickness throughout the world. Ted has an "apocalyptic vision of the end of the world, of a world united not by brotherhood or multi-national combines or oil crises, but by illness. A new pandemic, brought about by increasing air travel, increasingly resistant strains of mosquito and rat, brand-new illness from new tissue cultures. Increasing communion and technical sophistication engendering increasing disease" (33). Ted views this predicted plague as a moral judgment on a sick society: "The notion of international disaster excites him, clearly he thinks we deserve it, and that the wrath of God is due to fall once more." Disease is a metaphor for social ills: "Sensibilities were inflamed, catching insults where none were intended; an ideological epidemic had swept through Britain, perhaps through the world. The raw membrane caught every passing disease. Swollen organs of indignation impeded natural functioning on every side" (95).[14]

Hugo Mainwaring, the Middle East war correspondent, provides the political perspective on the international situation. Honorably *hors de combat* after his injury, Hugo attempts to write his Middle East book, or, failing that, to write an autobiographical novel—like everyone else, including the author. Hugo himself, typing his book with one finger, is "a fine figure of impotence. Diminishing powers, leading to silence" (145). He reflects that "modern consciousness is so burdened with its own past that it has worked itself into a state of paralysis, which I myself might all too aptly symbolise" (165). Hugo's difficulty with his novel-within-the-novel about Kate is a metaphor for the author's difficulty in expressing truth through art, for Hugo judges that "Life was too bizarre for fiction these days" (155). His conclusion that "Modern life is in some mysterious way too fragmented to be comprehensible" (165) is exemplified by the fiasco of Kate's attempt at an international evening of dinner and theatre for Mujid, her Iraqi guest. The play, a futuristic drama about the collapse of civilisation, is significantly inscrutable, and the company, composed of a typical cross-section of international society, proves during the dinner following the drama that "the ideologies of the late twentieth century mingled but did not mix," for the group produces merely a "mini-Babel."

Evelyn Stennett, welfare worker, provides the social perspective, which is equally excremental: "She saw more of failure than of success. The welfare state itself, and all the caring professions, seemed to be plunging into a dark swamp of uncertainty, self-questioning, economic crisis." Kate has compared contemporary society to a sore festering with buried dirt—wondering, "Would it fester fatally, a gangrene of the spirit?" (97). Similarly, Evelyn meditates on a glob of spittle, recalling "the saints who had sucked the abscesses of the sick, and embraced the lepers, imagining that in so doing they sucked the bleeding wounds of Christ." She realizes that she "had always been tempted by such masochistic displays. And indeed, what was she up to herself but rubbing her nose in the dirt?" (121).

"London Today," seen through Evelyn's eyes, is a crazy jumble, clearly decaying. Abandoned craters in the road reveal subterranean pipes, suggesting the sewer underlying the city. London's decadence is symbolized by the gruesome names of rock groups—"The Necrophiliacs, Sore Throat, The Scum"—and the pop posters that assault the eye with lurid images: "a huge eye floating in a saucer, a giant target-striped tit, a doll in a coffin, a three-toned snake, a witch on a broomstick" (120). The growing violence of London is reflected in the warlike images the youth create, as they go into battle each day along their own streets, "dressed in battle dress, adorned with plate armour of badges on their bosoms and clinking chain mail of staples and safety pins and paper clips" (121). A newspaper story about a man who bought rats from a sewage worker to shove through the letter box in the house of his ex-mistress seems symptomatic of the decadence of contemporary society.

Kate also provides a worm's-eye view of the city, "wondering what Mujid made of London Today, and trying to see it through his eyes" (92). Her Iraqi guest provides a focal technique, for he is "like an extra conscience and a pedagogue rolled into one" (74)—a Jiminy Cricket character. Kate is acutely aware of "the embarrassment of seeing Britain through censorious foreign eyes" (78), as she observes the grotesque mélange of graffiti and garbage, posters and punks, emblems of decadent civic society.[15]

As a feminist journalist,[16] compiling a documentary called "Women at the Crossroads," Kate provides the feminist view of "Women Today," which proves to be as excremental as the scientific, political, and social views. The documentary, nick-named "W.C." by the producer, Gabriel Denham,[17] reveals that the women's liberation movement has become bogged down by female conservatism and male reaction, symbolized throughout by the recurring image of the veil, traditional emblem of female repression. Kate's personal experience corroborates this professional perspective, for as a wife she maintains that she was treated "like a shit," and indeed, at her lowest ebb, a large Alsatian pisses on her, stigmatizing her professional dejection and personal desolation.

As protagonist of *The Middle Ground*, Kate represents woman's function in society in every possible role: as daughter, sister, wife, mother, mistress, and professional woman. Each role is symbolized by significant imagery, and in every case, the diagnosis is excremental. The distastefulness of Kate's role as daughter is suggested by the poisonous name of her deadly childhood home, Laburnum House, and symbolized by the sewer which is both her window on the past and the umbilical cord that attached her to her paranoid father and agoraphobic mother: "she had loved these two terrible people, in the dawn of time, in the dark before dawn, in the underground she had loved them. And nothing in her conscious self, in her daylight self, had been able to love. . . . No blood flowed from one to the other, the cord was cut, she withered and grew dry" (104). Evelyn's own role as daughter is embodied in the sinister symbol of a luminous but lethal lamb: "The lamb had been a little household god, symbol of a nice safe middleclass childhood. Though, of course, it had subsequently been discovered that these benign little darlings were full of lethal radioactivity, and they had been made extinct" (137).

Woman's role as sister is equally poisonous, as illustrated by Kate's sibling relationship with her brother Peter and symbolized by "Alenoushka and her Brother." In this fable, an orphaned brother and sister set out to walk through the wide world together, but Ivanoushka disobeys Alenoushka. He drinks from the print of a lamb's foot and is instantly transformed into a lamb and slaughtered, and his sister is drowned (143-44). Kate connects this sinister fable with Peter's anonymous letter of abuse, for this lamb too has turned lethal and sends his sister hate mail constructed out of her own newspaper column.[18] Kate compares Peter's method to "stewing an octopus in its own ink. Or a kid in its mother's milk" (231): by piecing his letters out of her own pieces on homosexuality, Peter is forcing her to eat her own words, or, to use Drabble's metaphor, to eat shit—appropriate for the muckraker journalist. Kate reflects, "Eating shit. No doubt it all had something to do with the anal phase, whatever that was. And pot training. Wasn't homosexuality supposed to have something to do with all that too? Was Peter a latent homosexual?" (118).[19]

Woman's role as lover, as seen in Kate's affair with Ted Stennett, is equally fated, for the plague of contemporary society has spread to romance as well, and even love is dying: "Love had ceased to be a journey, an adventure, an essay of hope. It had become an infection, a ritual, a drama with a bloody last act" in which both actors "could foresee the final carnage" (168). The death of love is symbolized by a mysterious disappearing painting called "Psyche Locked out of the Palace of Cupid," in which Psyche, desolated at the loss of love, clearly represents Kate, who has been abandoned by Ted. Kate wishes that Psyche would realize that "The castle of love was a prison, a fortress, a tomb," and would recognize "the open sea shining with invitation, and radiant, far out, the paths of the sea" (199).

Even woman's role as mother has been contaminated by the same poison that has killed romance. The malaise of maternity is symbolized by the image of a deformed foetus, which reflects the distorted passion that engendered it. The birth defect, *spina bifida*, producing "a wretched baby with no bowel control and a spine split like a kipper and a head like a pumpkin" (68-69), signifies an inner sickness that has to be cut out, like a cancer, leaving Kate sterilized and obscurely crippled. Kate is assailed by grotesque nightmare images of "dead babies, lying on a butcher's slab, like skinned rabbits" (61), symbolizing the slaughter of maternal love in the modern world. Another character describes a vivid vision of a decomposing infant: "I saw this dead baby, lying half in and half out of the water. On the water line. It was almost a skeleton. Rags of skin and flesh. Like a little drifting cape, going up and down in the water. But it wasn't a baby. It was only a cat. It had a little grinning head, with teeth" (40).

Crippled creatures, symbolizing contemporary corruption, riddle *The Middle Ground*, as Kate is continually halted by emblems of death in her path: "She nearly trod on a very dead bird, lying in the middle of the wide pavement. And passed the huge bole of a lopped tree, sprouting with thousands, literally thousands of tiny transparent toadstools, born of the damp" (70). She encounters a pigeon on her front walk, "one of those dark-grey, streaky, scruffy, glazed-eyed things with missing claws, hobbling on pink stumps, crawling with lice and meningitis" (76). Kate sees all these "pigeons, dogs, dead babies, washed-up babies rotting on the seashore" (77) as evil omens.

The very characters of *The Middle Ground* symbolize the decadence of contemporary culture, for virtually all of them are diseased or maimed: Hugo Mainwaring, the prize specimen in Kate Armstrong's menagerie of lame ducks, has lost half of his right arm in Eritrea, "buggering around drunkenly with a stray grenade" (14);[20] Kate herself is spiritually crippled, although "It wasn't an arm she'd lost, but a baby" (14); Evelyn's accident temporarily blinds her, leaving her staring into darkness with wide open but sightless eyes; Kate's husband Stuart is suffering from "a lingering malaise which was tentatively identified as glandular fever" (192); after a mistake in the anaesthetic during an operation to remove a lump in his neck, Hugo's bright young son David suffers permanent brain damage which reduces him to a mere vegetable and his mother to a demented creature obsessed with revenge;[21] the young son of Kate's Eastern friend, Beatrice Mourre, has been killed by a sniper's bullet in Beirut, like Jessie Parker's son who is killed in Belfast; and the unbalanced Mrs. Sondersheim, hostage in a WHO siege, is killed accidentally in a police shootout. While most of these characters are victims of grotesque accident, some of the mutilation is deliberately self-inflicted: when Hugo confesses his relief at his own mutilation to the surgeon who amputates his damaged arm, the doctor recounts a story of a man who deliberately amputated his own leg, commenting, "Very strange people are, the ways they devise of mutilating themselves" (15), and indeed many of the characters in *The Middle Ground* do demonstrate "a perverse instinct for self-destruction" (30).

The major symbol of self-mutilating humanity is the crippled god who governs this sick society in the following poem quoted from Emily Dickinson:

> Those—dying then,
> Knew where they went—
> They went to God's Right Hand
> That Hand is amputated now
> And God cannot be found—

> The abdication of Belief
> Makes the Behaviour small—
> Better an ignis fatuus
> Than no illume at all— (223)

Evelyn meditates on the poem: "A fatuous flame. A small ghostly light, a marshy phosphorescence. Misleading the night traveller, betraying him, leading him to a lonely grave. A pink plastic hand. A burning man. What a lot of very nasty images" (224). This amputee deity presides over a decaying world governed not by logic or love but by crass casualty. "The concept of the accidental" (149) is the ruling principle of *The Middle Ground* (as well as *The Ice Age*), revealing an underlying darker pattern: "Maybe the false events (an exploding grenade, a botched operation) will turn out to be the true ones after all" (163). Like Anthony Keating, the characters long for "A peace of mind free from all vicissitude, which cannot be undone by death or time, by falling bricks, by random snipers, by lumps in the neck, by crashing cars" (149).

The crescendo of catastrophes that constitutes *The Middle Ground* climaxes in Evelyn's domestic disaster, which marks the turning point of the novel: "All in all, the accident turned out quite well," for it transforms Evelyn's son into an affectionate child, unleashes a flood of goodwill from Evelyn's friends, symbolized by gifts of flowers, and inspires Evelyn with "a renewed assurance that her work was, after all, despite all, worthwhile. Why expect results, progress, success, a better society? All we can do is to join the ranks of the caring rather than the uncaring. All we can do in this world is to care for one another, in the society we have. It seemed enough, it seemed a great blessing" (216).

Evelyn's recovery signals the revival of all the characters: Hugo embarks for Baghdad to renew his work as a Middle East correspondent, and we learn "the truth about his accident, which had in fact resulted from the one true act of bravery in his life, and which therefore had not been random, pointless, purposeless at all" (228); Ted resumes his activities by "looking at a research project on new resistant strains of mosquito" in India, and by contemplating "the possibility of a golden world with golden Chloe" (167-68); Kate's recovery is symbolized by a reprise of the Alenoushka fable: "The little sister is resurrected, dug up, dragged from the river, the stone that weighted her dissolves, she rises up" (218). Kate too realizes that she loves her work, for the sheer rich human diversity of it, despite the despair of discovering patterns beneath the plethora of data: "No wonder a pattern is slow to emerge from such a thick clutter of cross-references, from such trivia, from such serious but hidden connections" (165).

The true pivot of *The Middle Ground* is not a physical action but a motion of the spirit from pessimism to optimism, which is symbolized by Kate's aerial view of London from the lofty perspective of Evelyn's hospital room, when the sky clears after the storm:[22]

> From the twelfth-floor window London stretched away, St Paul's in the distance, and the towers of the City, and beneath them, nearby, the little network of streets, backyards, cul-de-sacs, canals, warehouses, curves and chimneys, railways, little factories tucked into odd corners; unplanned, higgledy-piggledy, hardly a corner wasted, intricate, enmeshed, patched and pieced together, the old and the new side by side, overlapping, jumbled, always decaying, yet always renewed; London, how could one ever be tired of it? How could one stumble dully through its streets, or waste time sitting in a heap staring at a wall? When there it lay, its old intensity restored, shining with invitation, all its shabby grime lost in perspective, imperceptible from this dizzy height, its connections clear, its pathways revealed. The city, the kingdom. The aerial view. (218)

By exchanging her worm's-eye view of London for a bird's-eye view, Kate achieves the aerial perspective that Anthony Keating could not quite rise to in *The Ice Age*. The redemptive overtones of Kate's view of London as the City of God, the Kingdom of Heaven, suggest a vision of salvation for society which redeems the hellish chill of *The Ice Age* and the grim quagmire of *The Middle Ground*. Point of view is all, for perspective discovers the divine pattern beneath the distracting detail, revealing the truth about change: change involves not only death and decay, but also rebirth and renewal, in a continual cycle of destruction and reconstruction.[23]

Following this pivotal epiphany, Kate decides to have a party to celebrate change, including Evelyn's recovery, Hugo's embarkation, Mark's homecoming, Mujid's marriage, and Kate's own revival. Now Kate sees change as a force for good as well as ill: "The world is changing, thought Kate, and all the nice people will inherit it" (240). The party celebrates the fact that the characters have all survived their mid-life crises and are now ready to embark on the future with new optimism. The burial of the past is symbolized by

Kate's ritual purification of her home in preparation for the communal celebration, "as they scrubbed and parcelled and incinerated, sneezing in the disturbed dust, black-fingered, heroically cleansing the Augean stables" (227). As she drains the filthy fluid from the rain-filled bin of pre-strike garbage, "Out poured the most astonishing thick black liquid, the rotting sediment of ages: down into the drain it went, smelling of the Black Death." Thus she relegates the poison to the sewer, the proper place for plagues, just as she relegates the skeletons to the past, along with all the "unlived lives, roads not taken, roads blocked, children not born, ghosts and shadows" (232).

Drabble discovers the antidote to the poison of contemporary society in the domestic life of the home, where "love, joy and peace" form a counterpoint to Meister Eckhardt's "vision of desolation" (224). "Domesticity and its dark charm" is symbolized by fish heads, and the real thing for Kate is found in "the cult of the everyday," celebrated in her favourite portraits by Dutch painter Peter de Hooch of a housewife cleaning a fish and a mother and daughter peeling apples (147). Although Kate realizes that "there was more to life than backyards and fish heads and apple peel" (199), she chooses to "stay here, amidst the fish heads" (227). "Hugo, watching her, thought that sublime was indeed the word, for at such moments something in Kate seemed to shimmer just beneath or above the surface, *sub limen*, [sic] a breaking light, and she had this knack, this gift, for catching a little of it and bringing it, but just, but just within range, like an astral halo flickering on the sight, calling from him a corresponding gleam: a bright person, an angel in the house, among the crumbs and dustbins and fish heads" (233). Kate enjoys her sublime domestic role as "Kate the Good Angel, the Proxy Mum" (195), orchestrating the themes and variations of her busy household: "Here am I, busy Kate, comic Kate, conducting my own little modern domestic symphony, isn't it delightful?" (80), as she declares at the outset with self-mocking pride.

The flowers Kate buys for her party symbolize her felicitous vision of domestic harmony as the medication for a sick society, just as Clarissa Dalloway's flowers for her postwar party celebrate the rapture of personal life, despite harrowing visions of horror seen by neurasthenic Septimus Smith.[24] The cut blooms, while bright and beautiful, are fragile and perishable too, however, and so Kate buys a tree which will outlive her, like her own son Mark, now a grown man who chauffeurs his mother home in triumph with her arms full of flowers.[25]   Kate's flourishing green bay tree is an ambiguous symbol, for its triumphant associations with the laurel wreaths used to crown victors, emperors, and poets, symbolizing hope for the younger generation, are tempered by Hunt, who drinks a libation to Mark, praying, "May you flourish, not exactly like the green bay tree as I have done, but in a more godly manner." But when Kate inquires anxiously whether his allusion to Psalm 37—"I have seen the wicked in great power, spreading himself like a green bay tree"—is a bad omen, Hunt replies, "No, just a small sign that our common culture is perishing" (245).[26]

Kate's party celebrates international accord, as well as domestic harmony, with a reunion of all the characters in a grand finale that mingles nations, races, and religions, as well as generations and sexes, in a communion that succeeds where Kate's artificial "theatrical" effort failed. This multicultural harmony is symbolized by "a pair of little emerald-green slippers, embroidered with pearls and sequins and golden stitching, a pair of Arabian slippers" (246), which Mujid gives Kate, instead of the educational tome on the integration of modern Iraq that she expects. Significantly, Kate finally doffs her boots with the broken heel and dons her new "slippers from the Arabian nights," which are like magical seven-league boots giving her the power to o'erleap "the barriers of sex, race and age" through imagination and affection.[27]

As Kate dresses for her party, the author says, "Let us leave her there in an attitude of indecision, confronted by choice. Not, of course, a very serious choice, unless you wish to read it symbolically" (247). What it symbolizes, of course, is Kate's choice of optimism in facing the future: "Anything is possible, it is all undecided. Everything or nothing. It is all in the future, excitement fills her, excitement, joy, anticipation, apprehension. Something will happen. The water glints in the distance" (248). Kate, like Psyche, has recovered from her past desolation at the death of love and is ready at last to embark on the future with new hope. The novel can hardly be said to conclude, for it ends, as it began, *in medias res*, but the difference is that now the Janus-faced heroine is looking forward to the future, not back to the past, as she stands poised on the brink of embarkation.

There is a pattern underlying the detail after all, if one can stand tall enough to see "the aerial view of human love, where all connections are made known, where all roads connect" (218). The pattern Drabble discerns beneath the dither of data is the domestic circle of a star and satellites, as she portrays Kate "looking around her family circle, feeling as she sat there a sense of immense calm, strength, centrality, as though she were indeed the centre of a circle . . . a circle and moving spheres" (246).[28] The excremental underground view of social discord is ultimately answered by the celestial aerial view of human relations as a harmonious pattern echoing the music of the spheres.

NOTES

[1] Margaret Drabble, *The Middle Ground* (London: Weidenfeld and Nicolson, 1980), 9-10. Subsequent references will be given in the text.

[2] Drabble explains the significance of the title:

> *The Middle Ground* is a title which came to me after infinite trouble. . . . It is about being caught in the middle of life and not being extreme on either side, being stuck in the middle between parents and children, unable to move in any direction because so much is leaning on you. It is about the woman in the middle of the family, on the middle ground, in her middle age, stuck, unable to progress into the future because her children need her, her parents need her, and she feels that she has been in the same place for a very, very long time. (*TWF* 93)

[3] John Lucas, "Endlessly," *The New Statesman*, 11 July 1980, p. 55.

[4] Barbara Amiel, "Relentless Torment of Urban Souls," *MacLean's*, 93 (29 September 1980), 56.

[5] Francis King, *Spectator*, 5 July 1980, p. 22.

[6] Victoria Glendinning, "The New Matriarchy Reaches Middle Age," *Sunday Times*, 29 June 1980.

[7] Articles on *The Middle Ground* tend to focus on narrative technique. Ellen Cronan Rose, "Drabble's *The Middle Ground*: 'Mid-Life' Narrative Strategies," *Critique*, 23 (Spring 1982), 69-82, writes: "Drabble challenges the idea embodied in her novels by male characters, that art ought to impose a kind of

order on the chaos of experience. . . . she seems in quest of a truer mimesis, seeking narrative structures which are open rather than closed" (80). Lynn Veach Sadler, "'The Society We Have': The Search for Meaning in Drabble's *The Middle Ground*," *Critique*, 23 (Spring 1982), 83-93, asks, "What is the reader to do with a writer who stops rather than ends but who, on the way to stopping, leaves her audience amused and bewildered by this soap-opera/radio-serial list of questions meant to set us up for the next book in the Drabble canon?" (84). Pamela S. Bromberg, "Narrative in Drabble's *The Middle Ground*: Relativity versus Teleology," *Contemporary Literature*, 24, 4 (1983), 463-79, judges that "*The Middle Ground* is an antinovel, Drabble's bold attempt to hammer out a new realism consonant with late twentieth-century relativism" (465-66). Mary J. Elkins, "Alenoushka's Return: Motifs and Movement in *The Middle Ground*" (*CEMD* 169-80), writes, "to find where the search for order, meaning and pattern leads, we must look to the novel as a whole, to its structure and development." Another article on the subject is Roberta Rubenstein's "From Detritus to Discovery: Margaret Drabble's *The Middle Ground*," *Journal of Narrative Technique*, 1984.

[8] The sewer is a central motif in Victor Hugo's *Les Miserables*, and Dickens uses imagery of refuse in *Our Mutual Friend*. Drabble discusses sewage and sanitation in Dickens' London and in Dickens' novels, calling Dickens "the great poet of pollution" (*WB* 208-09).

[9] Drabble has published articles on menstruation in "The Fiendish Curse," *More Words* (London: BBC, 1977), 45-48, on contraception in "The Sexual Revolution," *Manchester Guardian Weekly*, 12 October 1967, p. 9, and on rape in "Thinking About Rape," *New York Times*, 21 January 1979.

[10] Drabble observed, "I think there's a lot of the journalist working away in me as well, that just wants to go nosing around in other people's affairs and finding out what is going on" (*VGMI* 38). She wrote to Valerie Grosvenor Myer, 19 December 1979, with reference to *The Middle Ground*: "I have a good plan (I hope) for a new novel, which will be very different and long and precious, and not at all journalistic."

[11] The quotation from Wordsworth's *Prelude* is from Book VI, 11, 87-91. Ted misquotes Wordsworth's 1800 poem to his sister Dorothy, "On the Naming of Places" (190). The narrator comments, "Neither of them ever found out how significantly they had misquoted Wordsworth" (192).

[12] Drabble may be alluding to Lois Gould's novel, *A Sea-Change* (1978).

[13] Drabble comments, "My last novel *The Middle Ground* gave me immense problems, in that I was trying to write about my response to the Feminist Movement and trying to write honestly about it and about the pressures from two sides towards the center" (*TWF* 116).

[14] In a 1 November 1988 letter to Nora Stovel, in response to reading the proofs of *Margaret Drabble: Symbolic Moralist*, Drabble commented: I particularly liked the chapter on *The Middle Ground*, which made it sound more coherent than it seemed while writing, and made me feel happier about the book in retrospect—particularly since it made it clear to me that Ted's vision of a great pandemic was clearly AIDS, which hadn't then surfaced, and which has not alas yet united the world, though it might yet, I suppose. . . ."

[15] Drabble comments on the model for Mujid: "While I was writing [*The Ice Age*], I had a Lebanese friend staying with me who was a lecturer at the University of Beirut. . . . It was talking to him that made me feel I ought to put England's problems into some larger context" (BMI 49).

[16] Drabble observes, "I retreated in my new novel *The Middle Ground* and wrote again about a woman, a woman journalist with a lot of problems about feminism" (*TWF* 90). She says Kate is "an analogy for the novelist who is fed up with the feminist critics" (*DCCI* 75). The model for Kate may be Drabble's acquaintance, London journalist Katherine Whitehorn.

[17] Drabble comments, "in my new novel *The Middle Ground* we see again Clara's lover, Gabriel, who reappears in a short scene towards the end as a television director. He is not very nice any more. He has become very selfish, opinionated, fashionable, shallow" (*TWF* 94).

[18] Peter's anonymous hate mail may suggest the writing of Drabble's own sibling, novelist A.S. Byatt, who has been waging an underground war with her sister in her fiction: her first novel, *The Game* (1967), seems a reply to Drabble's first novel, *A Summer Bird-Cage* (1963), also about two sisters, and *The Virgin in the Garden* (1978) contains an unflattering portrait of Drabble.

[19] Drabble comments on Arnold Bennett's stammer: "there is an analogy with over-rigorous pot-training, which Arnold like all his generation probably suffered from, and which is

thought to produce many of the Victorian-Wesleyan qualities of thrift, neurotic cleanliness, bowel fixation, interest in figures and statistics and hypochondria" (*AB* 33).

[20] Drabble comments, "I created this woman with a strong arm, and to my horror discovered that I had also created in the main male character a man with a missing arm. . . . I needed it for many symbolic and plot reasons" (*TWF* 96-97). Drabble originally called the two major male characters Hugo and Hugh, suggesting alter egos; although Drabble changed the name Hugh to Ted, the copy-editor did not catch all the instances in the first edition.

[21] David's accident may reflect the accidental death of A.S. Byatt's son in 1972. *The Virgin in the Garden* is dedicated to him, and a mother in the novel loses a son in a similar accident.

[22] In "The Industrial Scene," Drabble writes of Dickens' London: "The overall impression, despite the sordid detail and the social rage, is of intense exhilaration, of wonder at life's infinite variety, and at the infinite variety of the London scene" (*WB* 213).

[23] Drabble comments:

> What I'm perpetually trying to work out is the relationship between coincidence and plan. And, in fact, I have this deep conviction that if you were to get high enough up over the world, you would see things that look like coincidences are, in fact, part of a pattern. This sounds very mystical and ridiculous, but I don't think it is. I think that I, in particular, and maybe certain other people have a need to perceive this pattern in coincidence. It may be that psychologically we're so afraid of the unpredictable, of the idea of chaos and disorder, that we wish to see order. (*BMI* 62)

[24] Drabble observes, "The book, in fact, ends up with a literary joke, a Mrs. Dalloway-type party" (*DCCI* 75), and "It ends with a conscious quotation of Virginia Woolf" (*TWF* 116). Kate's aerial view of the city echoes Clarissa Dalloway's rhapsody on London.

[25] Drabble comments on the relationship between art and life:

> She is a woman leading a very busy life in London with her family of children, very similar children to my own. In fact for the first time I put a straight description of one of my own children in this book. There is a scene

at the end of the novel—facts and fiction are very interesting, the relationship between the two is very interesting—where the heroine Kate Armstrong goes to buy some flowers for a party. She can't drive and her son who can drive drives her to the flower shop and she buys the flowers. When the book was published, I gave a party for my book to celebrate its publication and I said to my son, "Will you please drive me up to the flower shop?" And I bought these flowers. It was exactly as though I had entered into the world of my own book. . . . (*TWF* 90-91)

[26] Gail Efrig, "*The Middle Ground*" (*GR* 178-85), writes:

The tree is a bay, and there can be little doubt that it stands for England. On a gold medal cast for Queen Elizabeth I in 1588, to celebrate the defeat of the Armada, the queen's goldsmith modelled the island planted with a large bay tree at its center. *Non ipsa pericula tangunt*: No dangers touch her, says the motto; the bay is eternal. And it is significant that in this book the final symbol is . . . green, glossy, flourishing; a small sensation, the bay tree lives and breathes. More than a promise or a hope, it is life itself. (184)

[27] The dust cover blurb says, "*The Middle Ground* is a brilliant and witty novel about communication and non-communication across the barriers of sex, race and age, and it ends on a note of guarded optimism."

[28] Drabble comments on her conclusion: "She is sitting with her family before the party and she feels herself, for a moment of harmony, to be at the centre of the whole universe. This is her centre and she knows it for a moment. But only for a moment" (*TWF* 116). She observes, "I end the novel on a complete question mark. . . . I left my character at the end of *The Middle Ground* about to give a party but uncertain what the future holds. This is very much my own feeling about the novel as a form, the woman's novel as a form, and about the future of women" (*TWF* 17).

Chapter Eleven:

QUESTING *THE RADIANT WAY*

The Radiant Way (1987) marks Drabble's first return to fiction after a hiatus of seven years, the longest ever in her creative career. The ostensible reason for this hiatus was the five-year contract Drabble accepted in 1980 to reedit *The Oxford Companion to English Literature* (1985), a momentous task which rendered her a formidable figure on the literary landscape. Drabble's critical work in reediting the *OCEL* has had a significant influence in developing her technical command in her creative writing also. *The Radiant Way* clearly reflects this influence, for Drabble interweaves many narrative threads into a rich tapestry of contemporary life in this latest novel, as she leads her considerable cast of characters through a complex chronology and an elaborate urban labyrinth beset by numerous literary models and monuments.

Another reason for this unprecedented hiatus, however, may involve the hostile critical reception of *The Middle Ground* (1980), which reviewers labelled superficial and shapeless. Drabble explained, "I did [the *OCEL*] partly because I didn't particularly want to write fiction at that time. I felt I'd come to the end of a certain style or kind of novel."[1] She actually acknowledged that "*The Middle Ground* was a mistake, an organic mistake, but an inevitable one,"[2] and predicted that her next novel would be very different from her last: "I have a good plan for a new novel, which will be very different and long and precious, and not at all journalistic."[3]

The Radiant Way is indeed a more impressive work than *The Middle Ground*, although it differs in quality rather than in kind. *The Radiant Way* does not diverge from so much as extend and refine the journalistic panorama of London life portrayed in *The Middle Ground* to paint a kaleidoscopic portrait of the political, economic, and social reality of Britain as a whole. Far more skillfully controlled than her previous novel, *The Radiant Way* has been applauded by reviewers as an impressive portrayal of the state of the nation.

Reviewers have compared Drabble to Dickens and *The Radiant Way* to *Middlemarch*, labelling Drabble both "Queen" and "Ambassadress" of literary London.[4] One critic called Drabble "the chronicler of contemporary Britain, the novelist people will turn to in a hundred years from now to find out what things were like, the person who will have done for late twentieth-century London what Dickens did for Victorian London, what Balzac did for Paris."[5] Certainly *The Radiant Way* deserves these accolades for its sweeping scope and probing depth.

The Radiant Way is a compelling psychological study of intriguing individuals, however, as well as an impressive socio-political documentary. The novel traces the intertwined narratives of three women: Liz Headland, psychiatrist, Alix Bowen, literature teacher at a women's prison, and Esther Bauer, art historian, as well as Liz's sister Shirley Harper, Northam housewife—each representing various facets of intellectual and social life. Each protagonist also trails elaborate webs of families and friends, patients and pupils, in order to convey a panoramic public and personal view of contemporary Britain. As Margaret Atwood observes, "we aren't dealing just with people's personal or psychological lives, we're dealing also with the political and social dimensions of their lives as well."[6]

The Radiant Way is a modern tragicomedy of manners in which Drabble examines every aspect of the political, economic, and social life of Britain over the last three decades, considering everything from the Open University to the miners' strike: "National Service, Jury Service, Men, Women, Manual Work, Fear, Picket Lines, the Royal Family, Social Class, Adult Education."[7] Drabble's narrative is equally comprehensive in chronological terms, as it chronicles the eighties in Britain, contrasting them with the seventies. Flashbacks return us to the fifties, when the three friends first meet at Cambridge, and strands them in the "Thatcher wasteland" of the present, where they stand on the threshold of the future.[8]

Despite this comprehensive scope and dense detail, some readers have complained that "nothing happens" in what Drabble's narrator terms "this non-story, this non-sequence of non-events" (301). However, the important events in Drabble's novels are the invisible ones, which can only be signified by symbols, not realized by external events, for

Drabble's transcendent vision of a possible future cannot be realized on the narrative level, but only symbolized on the ideal plane. The turning point of each of Drabble's novels could be called a movement of the spirit from negation to affirmation, from paralyzing pessimism to guarded optimism. Just as Kate Armstrong finally transcends the impasse of a personal and public midlife crisis in a mystical moment of vision in *The Middle Ground*, so the protagonists of *The Radiant Way* ultimately overcome the quagmire of the contemporary to achieve an epiphany of a possible future.

Drabble insists that she is constantly searching for an "underlying meaning" because she is convinced that "a pattern will emerge," revealing the grand design behind the apparent chaos (*BMI* 63-65). Similarly, in *The Radiant Way*, Liz, the individualist, and Alix, the socialist (two sides of the author), debate the existence of patterns connecting individuals: Alix "aspired to a more comprehensive vision. She aspired to make connections" because "she had a sense that such interlockings were part of a vaster network, that there was a pattern, if only one could discern it." Like Drabble herself, Alix is convinced that "We are all but a part of a whole which has its own, its distinct, its other meaning: we are not ourselves, we are crossroads, meeting places, points on a curve, we cannot exist independently for we are nothing but signs, conjunctions, aggregations" (72-73). In all of Drabble's fiction, this vision of a grand design is conveyed by the underlying symbolism which informs the complex characterization and convoluted plot of Drabble's novels. The purpose of this discussion will be to discover the deeply-embedded symbols which can reveal those secrets buried in the dark past that have the power to illuminate the radiant way into the future.

But discovering the redeeming design beneath the depressing detail is harder than ever in this latest novel, for *The Radiant Way*, despite its aureate title, portrays Drabble's darkest vision ever. Where the vision of *The Middle Ground* was squalid and even excremental—its personal and national midlife crises symbolized appropriately by the central symbol of sewage—the vision of contemporary life in *The Radiant Way* is indeed demonic. Since the vision in this latest novel is so very dark, seeing any underlying pattern that might redeem the surface horror is more difficult than ever for the characters and even the author, as well as for the reader. Drabble struggled throughout the winter of 1984-85 to begin her new novel in a nightmare of literary paralysis, until she finally had the brilliant idea of beginning her new book precisely where her former one left off, with her protagonist preparing for a party.[9]

Appropriately, Drabble opens *The Radiant Way* with a New Year's Eve party commemorating the end of one decade and heralding the beginning of a new. The nation has reached a paralyzing impasse, and the characters are desperate for a new start. Liz Headleand, like a witch with "preturnatural power," conjures these people up from all walks of life to make them dance to her tune (8), but this *valse macabre* turns out to be a "dance of death" (326). Liz is confident that "these ghosts would materialize" to congregate at the ritual witching hour, holding hands in a ring and singing *Auld Lang Syne* to the ominous booming of Big Ben—"in the hope of a miracle, in the hope of a midnight transformation, in the hope of a new self, a new life, a new, redeemed decade" (1). Preparing for her party with one eye on her digital clock (a more modern symbol of Father Time), Liz contemplates a Christmas gift from her eldest stepson Jonathan: "a tiny, cut-glass snowdrop vase which holds a posy of cold hothouse snowdrops, white and green, delicately streaked, fragile, hopeful, a promise of futurity" (5) —symbolizing the characters' hope for salvation.

New Year's Eve is a significant date for Liz, for as a child, she had elected New Year's Eve to "represent the Nothingness [a key term in this novel] which was her own life" (4), and now she is astonished to discover that she is "a partygiver as well as a party-goer" (5). This New Year's Eve party is not the celebration of the "modern marriage" that Liz expects, however, but rather the "farewell party," the "grand finale" (43) which her husband Charles intends, for it is at the "magic moment" (35) of midnight that Liz's pessimistic ephiphany occurs. Ivan "the Terrible" Warner proves true to his last as well as his first name, when he warns Liz that Charles is about to leave her, the plebian pewter princess, for Henrietta Latchett, the sterling *Debrett* debutante.

This ironic betrayal plunges the optimistic opening of both novel and decade into a maelstrom of defeat and despair. Liz is precipitated into a midlife crisis where all of her comfortable assumptions are undercut: "Where to go from here? Where but onwards?" (145), she courageously concludes. But the question is how? "Almost cheerfully, she assented to her own stubborn proposition, her own long-held proposition, that effort will be rewarded. So it had been before: so it might be again. A continuing contemplation of the unpleasant will generate enlightenment, information, knowledge: and knowledge will restore health and life. So it had been, so it would be. She would continue" (145). This faith in the efficacy of effort constitutes the thesis of the novel and of Drabble's entire *oeuvre*.[10] "There is a goal to this journey, there will be an arrival, Liz Headland believes. It is only by refusing to move onwards that we truly die" (15). Drabble's novel provides a chart for this spiritual journey through the wasteland of the present, as the characters quest the secret hidden in the past that will illuminate the radiant way into the future.

A study of the pathology of the modern malaise, *The Radiant Way* chronicles the potency of evil in both private and public life. The novel is studded with examples of public evil, as Drabble tirelessly catalogues lists of political, economic, and social catastrophes—from inflation to recession, from the miners' strike to school closures, from privatization to rationalization—as the disastrous situation escalates towards Orwell's prophesied dystopia of 1984. One reviewer complained that *The Radiant Way* is too "pessimistic, diffuse and anecdotal." But, as Drabble's narrator observes, "There was, perhaps, a thread linking this rambling, discursive, allusive, exclusive, jumbled topographical discourse" (217). That thread underlying the dither of detail is, as always in Drabble's novels, the seam of symbolism which leads us to the monstrous truth in the middle of the maze. The reviewer is correct in this following comment:

> Where her vision does come into focus is in its iconographic fusion of squalor, decay, wounds, evil, sex, death and madness—seen as part of 1980s life but also belonging to a darker mystical world. *The Radiant Way* is less like the familiar, warm baggy panoramic novel of the nineteenth century and more like the paintings of the Neapolitan School mentioned in the book: a large, allegorical canvas scrupulously filled with writhing bodies and conveying, in a highly sophisticated frame of reference, images of horror and messages of dire import.[11]

This apocalyptic imagery of evil comes to a head in the psychotic paintings that illumine the walls of Jilly Fox's squat: "Daggers, pierced hearts, severed heads, dripping blood, gaping wounds, severed limbs, floating eyes. . . . A rat gnawed a human foot. A monkey drank a jar of blood. A breast floated on a plate. A tooth was held aloft by pincers. A starfish flamed in the sky" (326). To this grotesque *mélange* Jilly has added her own peculiar contribution, a cockatrice: "a strange little monster, half-hatched from an egg: a twining serpent with a beaked cock's head, a red cock's comb" (326). The cockatrice, or basilisk, with its lethal look, is a fabulous reptile hatched by a serpent from a cock's egg, a divided creature with a cock's head and serpent's body. This psychotic vision presages Jilly's own decapitation: like the cockatrice, Jilly's head will be divided from her body by the "Horror of Harrow Road" (203).

The "HARROW HORROR'S HEADLESS HOAX" (207) is the link connecting the public realm with the private. These harrowing decapitations which connect the characters of the novel and typify the modern malaise also provide the nexus of the novel's complex network of imagery. Literal and legendary severed heads abound in *The Radiant Way*, including the "Gorgon and the Medusa and Géricault and Demigorgon and Salome and the Bessi of Thrace" (347), as well as actual severed heads. Eight grotesque victims have been discovered in bizarre circumstances in eighteen months: "all of them female, most of them black, and the last three ostentatiously decapitated: one found in the service lift of the Bellenden flats, one on the canal bank, one in Kensal Green cemetery, one in a derelict house under the motorway arch, one in a Carnival float, one in a dumped car" (208). The latest ludicrous victim was found "sitting in a waste lot in the driver's seat of a wheel-less Notting Hill Carnival float, headless, neatly wearing a safety belt with her head by her side on the passenger's seat" (203). But the identity of this Jack the Ripper reincarnated remains unknown. The major public mystery around which *The Radiant Way* is structured, the decapitations signify the insanity of modern society. The fact that the victims are all female and headless suggests sexual repression and psychotic sadism. The motif of decapitation may suggest that women are divided, especially in the eyes of their male beholders, into head or rationality and torso or sexuality—like the cockatrice.

The severed head motif is underlined by Esther, scholar of religious art of the Italian Renaissance, who dreams, prophetically, of stumbling upon a severed head on the towpath beside the canal bank near the Harrow Road, where, unknown to Esther, another severed head has actually been found. The "dream-severed head" (249), ostensibly that of John the Baptist (209), but in fact that of Esther's Satanic lover Claudio Volpe, begs her to save him (205). This dream, one of numerous nightmares in the narrative, leads Esther to a vision of absolute evil which lies at the heart of the novel:

> Esther sat by the canal, reading Dante's *Purgatory*, and thinking of Hugh Capet, who became king of France: *Figlio fu'io d'un beccaio di Parigi.* Son was I of a butcher of Paris. A good man, the father of evil. From good sprang forth evil. She sat in Kensal Green Cemetery and read Zola's *La Bête Humaine*. She dreamed, twice more, of the severed head. *Io fui radice della mala pianta.* I was the root of the evil tree. (244)

The severed head motif is at the centre of a network of monstrous imagery, including fabulous beasts, such as the cockatrice or basilisk, which are a conflation of two creatures.[12] *La Bête Humaine*, the novel which Drabble remarked influenced *The Radiant Way* most profoundly, is the true subject of this novel—the human beast, divided between mind and body, angel and devil, as symbolized by the monsters of mythology. The motif of metamorphosis is paramount in this novel, as apparently innocuous individuals are transfigured into hideous monsters in a Dr. Jekyll and Mr. Hyde transformation.

Werewolves, another divided creature, with the head of the wolf and the body of a man, also prowl the pages of *The Radiant Way*. The metamorphosis of Liz and Edgar Lintot epitomizes "the hideous transformation which overcomes the partners of a bad marriage, who grow fangs and horns and sprout black monstrous wolfish hair, who claw and cling and bite and suck" (13). Images of the werewolf, a creature with "the upper body of a man, the lower limbs of an animal" (252) emanate primarily from Esther's passionately platonic lover, the satanic anthropologist Claudio Volpe (meaning wolf in Italian), who is defined by Esther as "a werewolf" (346) and by another character as "the devil" (350). Volpe declares absurdly, in a formal lecture at the Montano di Salvo Institute in Italy, that he encountered in the mountainous Greek-Bulgarian border region a werewolf which led him to a young woman who proved to be a witch—as demonstrated by the two supernumerary sets of nipples beneath her naked breasts (253). Ironically, the audience interprets the bizarre lecture of this satanic structuralist as a "deconstructive attack on diachronic methodology" (254).

There is even a suggestion that the devilish Claudio has possessed the soul of the innocuous-looking serial-murderer, P. Whitmore—certainly an ideal candidate for the role of ventroloquist's dummy (372). Indeed, the death of Claudio and the capture of Whitmore are closely juxtaposed. When Esther commits euthanasia on the malingering potted plant (a gift from Claudio), by placing it out on the porch to die of cold, her upstairs neighbour, P. Whitmore—"the monster under [her] roof" (368)—addresses his first and only words to her, ironically protesting, "You'll kill the poor thing if you leave it out there" (345).

The climax of the plot and the apex of the apocalyptic imagery occur at the decapitation of Jilly Fox. Building up to this gruesome climax, the surreal landscape imagery escalates, as Esther's wanderings through the urban maze of Harrow Road unveil "A landscape of nightmare, an extreme, end-of-the-world, dreamlike parody of urban nemesis" (244), filled with surrealistic images, including a mad midget, a lifesize dummy of a hanged man, and the bizarre façade of the Apocalypse Hotel: "Giant graffiti marched and sprawled, machinery rusted, padlocked gates labelled 'Reception' and 'Welcome' led to nowhere" (244). Liz and Esther interpret the sight of the canal filled with "thousands of small dead fishes, belly upward in the sun" as "a sign of the end of the world," for "this is where the apocalypse would announce itself." Esther declares prophetically, "That's why I stay here. To be in on the act. *Il trionfo della morte*. The final scene" (245). And she is.

Nature goes into mourning in preparation for the tragic ending, casting a funereal pall over the world as it approaches the winter solstice, "the darkest hour of the longest darkest night of the year" (282). Alix, with her Cambridge degree in English, recalls Donne's "Ode Upon St Lucy's Day": "Tis the year's midnight, and it is the day's" (266). Mourners at a funeral sing appropriately, "The day Thou gavest, Lord, is ended, The darkness falls at Thy behest" (317).

The personal and public situations darken likewise, as both characters and nation approach the target-date for Orwell's dystopia, nervously wishing each other a "Happy 1984": "I prophesy it will be a grim year," warns one character, "but not quite in the way Orwell predicted" (291). And it is. Deaths proliferate: Fred Bowen and Deborah Manning die, Rita Ablewhite is left by a stroke in a living death, and Dirk Davis is shot to death by masked gunmen on live video. Disasters spread: the miners go on strike, Brian Bowen's lectureship is terminated, and Alix is filled with despair for the future of Britain:

> It's all hopeless, hopeless. Sandbags against the tidal wave. Patching up holes in the dyke before the deluge. Little boys, with their thumbs frozen. And drowning, drowning. . . . I don't believe in anything. I believe its all hopeless. Hopeless. It's all over. There's no way back, and no way forward that we can go. We're washed up. (360)

Alix concludes that "There is no hope, in the present social system, of putting anything right" (392). Even Liz acknowledges that there is "Nothing at all" (355)—a recurring refrain. Shirley learns respect for the mystery of their mother's depression, when she recognizes "how bleakly and boldly she has stared over the years into the heart of nothingness. For it is trivial, it is all trivial . . . it is nothing, all of it nothing." Shirley has her own vision of the void: "Coldness, nothingness, grips Shirley as she stands in her kitchen. She knows herself to be biologically dead. Her spirit shudders: she has seen a vision, of waste matter, of meaningless after-life, of refuse, of decay" (200).

This vision of the void is dramatized in the murder of Jilly Fox, a tragic event which links the public and private realms of the novel and connects the characters in a macabre demonstration of "the kinship network" (221) and "the brotherhood of man" (361)—countered by the comic example of Drabble's complex social web, Leo Steen, Liz and Esther's high-flying Dutchman with a penchant for rites of passage (295, 314). As Alix sits stranded on the longest night of the year in her Renault—crippled because some witty Wandsworth wag has stuffed a bird's nest up its exhaust pipe (300)—the narrator comments, "No Good Samaritan paused for Alix, and Alix, still brooding on her cruelty to Jilly, felt she did not deserve one" (276). Alix acknowledges that "I have failed Jilly" (280), just as Esther failed Whitmore, who, Alix realizes, is the victim of Jilly's death wish: "Alix's mind wandered. Severed heads, floating wounds, teeth in pincers, cockatrices. Why did she not grieve, at the horror of Jilly's death? Because Jilly had willed it so. A martyr, she had become, and had died serenely. But a martyr to what?" (336).

Martyrdom is a favourite subject of religious art, as Alix and Esther acknowledge when they consider "the sado-masochistic content of Christian iconography," admitting that "all sacred art is full of wounds," especially in the erotic romanticism of Renaissance religious art. They contemplate the gaping wounds, "*vagina implorans*," of a *Pieta* and the "voluptuous disarray" of swooning saints from Renaissance Neapolitan religious paintings in a book of *Painting in Naples: from Caravaggio to Giordano* (329). The floating breast of Jilly's surrealistic decor recalls the severed breast of Saint Agatha in the twilight land between the erotic and the occult.

The head of Jilly Fox, loosely wrapped in muslin and reposing on the driver's seat of Alix's Renault, is clearly iconographic, with its staring ecstatic eyes, waxen skin and snake-like tresses—an image of death. Gazing at this death's head, Alix is not turned to stone, though Polly is "petrified" (334). But Alix does cross herself over Jilly's frozen body in the morgue—albeit the wrong way, "the Black Mass way?" (339). Believing, like Frances Wingate in *The Realms of Gold*, that this phenomenon is the creation of her own powerful imagination, Alix feels doomed to defeat:

> I see horrors, I imagine horrors. I have courted horrors, and they have come to greet me. Whereas I had wished not to court them, but to exorcize them. To gaze into their eyes and destroy them by gazing. They have won, they have destroyed me. There is no hope of a peaceable life, of a life for the people, of a society without fear. Fear grows, flourishes, is bred, blossoms, flames. . . . I am defeated, thought Alix. We are defeated. But how can I admit defeat? Is it the wrong battle I have been fighting, all these years? (337)

Alix requests, appropriately, that the hymn sung at her own funeral be Arthur Hugh Clough's "Say not the struggle naught availeth" from *The Hymns of Praise* (318).

When Esther tells the dying Claudio "the story of Jilly Fox and the cockatrice," he declares that it is not a private but a public act, not a mortal murderer, but a spirit, an emanation of his satanic *spiritus mundi*: "It is a mass hallucination, unleashed from the fear of the people. By disbelief you can disarm it. If you decide so, Esther, there will be no more deaths" (347). And Claudio is right, for after his own decease and the capture of the murderer, the image of death is exorcised. Jilly, the modern martyr, is a female scapegoat figure whose suicide, like that of Stephen Ollerenshaw in *The Realms of Gold*, purifies the spiritual disease which plagues the populace.

Thus, the death of Jilly constitutes the turning-point of *The Radiant Way*, as the focus shifts from public to private preoccupations (for redemption from evil must come through individual salvation), and from demonic darkness to radiant light. Once things have reached their nadir, in Drabble's novels, they must begin to improve. Characteristically, during one of the darkest days in the novel, Drabble portrays the first glimmer of light, as Alix, at her mother-in-law's funeral, has an idyllic vision of rural England—similar to Karel Schmidt's epiphany of pastoral Britain at the graveside of Frances Wingate's Aunt Constance in *The Realms of Gold*: "She went to the funeral, in the little church at the foot of the Downs. The leaves of the chestnut were unfolded. Broad green spring. There were bluebells in hedgerows. . . . What is it, this grace, wondered Alix. Is it natural? Is it of nature? Is it a free gift?" (345).

The characters also take this catastrophe as their cue to move on to a new life. Esther realizes, "I can't go on living here. It's like that story about the house with the Golden Windows. You know, where you find your own house is the one that shines in the distance. But this is the other way round. You find the rot was within" (371)—the reverse of the Golden Windows fable in *Jerusalem the Golden*. Liz, a white witch, complete with tabbycat, declares, "I banish the Harrow Road," and, indeed, the house with the leaden windows is totally demolished: "Utterly eliminated. As though it had never been. Cut out of the city, like a cancer" (376). Symbolically, Esther replaces her pessimistic palm tree, which perished appropriately along with Claudio and Jilly, by an optimistic "umbrella tree with big deep broad-fingered leaves and new delicate little opening pale-green uplifted hands at its crown: a more friendly plant, a less bristly plant" (365)—recalling the green bay tree that Kate Armstrong purchased as a pledge to the future at the conclusion of *The Middle Ground*.

Perspective is all, as even Jilly Fox realizes in this prophetic letter to Alix redeeming her apocalyptic imagery of evil in a transcendent vision of cosmic harmony:

> There is no death. There is death only of the body. This have I learned. I fly, I fly into the higher air, and I look down and see the small world turning. The upper reaches are thick with spirits. Perpetual life. The cry of the cockatrice is transformed into the music of the spheres. There is no evil: evil and good are one. At the extremities we meet. Crime is not: sin is not: evil is not: all is good, all is holy. The winter solstice is now, and for ever, and never, for the light shines for ever, in eternal glory, and we are consumed and not consumed in everlasting fire. (275)

Alix recalls Jilly saying that "evil and good are one," so she supposes that "light and darkness [another recurring motif of the novel] might be one" also (328). From her own pragmatic, psychiatrist's perspective, Liz also declares her own disbelief in evil: "I don't believe in good either. I believe in suffering, and the alleviation of suffering. I believe in pleasure. And I believe in death. I think belief in evil has caused immense suffering. I don't see the point of suffering. I'd like to do away with it" (390-91).

On the narrative level, the characters, relieved at last from the wicked spell by the martyrdom of the scapegoat Jilly and the death of the evil genius Volpe, embark on a new life in a new place. Even Alix feels "a sense of expectation . . . as she searched for the future" (374), when she and Brian go back to Brian's home town of Northam, where Brian will teach English literature and Alix will edit, in "an ivory attic," the papers of Northam's bard "Walrus Beaver," a cantankerous old "monster" (392-93).[13] "Alix is a hero," Liz declares, because "I love London" (375), she rhapsodizes, in a reprise of Clarissa Dalloway's rapture on London. Liz learns to relish her new-found independence in her new St John's Wood home, complete with a Drabblean garden for her to cultivate. Even Charles returns, abandoning Global International Network with its ironic initials, as well as Henrietta Latchett, to initiate a new creative enterprise, "Starting from scratch again. . . . Rejuvenated" (364). And Esther embarks on a new life in Italy with Claudio Volpe's sister Elena, concentrating on her professional love, Renaissance Italian art.

Finally the characters are all ready for the new life that they dreamed of at the outset of the novel. Liz thinks, "So Dirk Davis was dead, and Jilly Fox was dead, and Claudio Volpe was dead, and Rita Ablewhite was dead, and she, Liz

Headleand, was still alive" (388). The characters experience a change of heart as "they moved on from death to love" (372). This time they celebrate the New Year with a Twelfth Night party, a more auspicious celebration, for Twelfth Night marks the Feast of the Epiphany, commemorating the manifestation of Christ to the Magi. And indeed, the apotheosis of *The Radiant Way* is truly epiphanic.

Another mythic monster from the past remains to be vanquished, however, before the characters can discover the radiant way into the future. The classic example of the *bête humaine* is the minotaur, a mythological beast with the head of a bull and the body of a man. Imprisoned by King Minos in a labyrinth designed by the fabulous Greek artificer Daedalus, the minotaur was finally vanquished by Theseus. References to the monstrous minotaur abound in the novel, from Liz's lecture on *Theseus and the Minotaur: Spenser's Version of the Family Romance* (66), to the comparison of the paedophile's phallus to a "bull-headed minotaur" (390), linking sexuality and monstrosity.[14] The novel is also filled with mazes, from the Ablewhite prison on Abercorn Avenue (60), through executive toy mazes (155), to the urban labyrinth of London.

The minotaur who lurks in the midst of the maze is Liz's mysterious disappearing father, whose secrets Liz must unravel in order to discover her own identity.[15] "What does it matter who her father was?" is rephrased as "What does it matter who I am?" (385). Now that Liz has been betrayed and abandoned by "Charles the monster" (124), the sadistic lover who, Liz realizes, "had replaced the fantastic, punishing father of her childhood" (144), it becomes essential to discover the secrets of the father whose image Liz and her sister Shirley both superstitiously wear entrapped in silver lockets hanging about their necks, like the legendary albatross (or millstone): "She thinks of her father, whom she has never known, of whom she knows nothing, almost nothing, but whose image, it is alleged is in that locket: an image which also hangs in an identical locket at this moment around her sister's neck. A prized possession" (65).

Just as the quest for a spiritual mother informs *Jerusalem the Golden* and *The Realms of Gold*, so *The Radiant Way* is a mystery story structured around the the disappearance of Liz's father, the minotaur at the centre of the maze of memory, and Liz is the Theseus who holds the thread in her hands:

"She would turn back in order to leap forwards. She would dig up again her father's corpse, she would explore once more those dark labyrinthine strong-smelling chambers and passages. She would hold the string tightly as she made her way to meet the beast. She smiled at her own imagery" (145).

The opportunity to dig occurs when Liz's mother Rita Ablewhite, the evil genius of Abercorn Avenue, finally dies. Liz goes home again, like all of Drabble's protagonists—and like Drabble herself, whose own parents are recently deceased—to search for her own identity in her family home.[16] Digging, like Clara in *Jerusalem the Golden*, and Frances, the archaeologist, in *The Realms of Gold*, in a desk full of documents and hieroglyphics, Liz knows that "the end of the thread was in her own hand" (384). Instinctively, she realizes that her father's secret is also the source of her own shame: "Shame? Guilt? She was very near these monsters: she could smell them in their caves, she could smell them in the cave of her own body" (385). In her "desire to pursue the truth, in curiosity for truth" (223), Liz struggles to separate fact from fiction: "History, fact, memory, fantasy. Truth, belief, faith, delusion" (384). Surrounded by newspaper clippings about paedophiles and suicides, Liz knows that she possesses the pieces of the puzzle (one of Drabble's favourite symbols), if only she has the intelligence to assemble and the courage to interpret them accurately: "One could rearrange these pieces as one wished, like the jigsaw scraps of an experimental novel. . . . The story had a remorseless logic. It made narrative sense. . . . A great sun was burning dully, in the back of her mind, just beyond vision" (383-84).

The missing piece of the puzzle, significantly, turns out to be the source of the novel's title, *The Radiant Way*, a primer depicting "two children, a boy and a girl, running gaily down (not up) a hill, against a background of radiant thirties sunburst" (385)—also the source of the ironic title of television mogul Charles's utopian documentary on education in Britain during "The Brave New World" of the sixties (174). Delving inside the primer, Liz discovers her own name: "Elizabeth Ablewhite. *The Radiant Way, First Step*, 1933" (386). Gazing at the pictures of idyllic childhood and prim parents, Liz realizes the monstrous memories that she had concealed from her analyst and herself: "Father. Yes, she had sat upon her father's knee, learning to read from this very book. She had rubbed herself like a kitten up and down, sitting astride her child-molester father's knee. . . . Giggling as he tickled her and played with her. Damp between her innocent infant's legs." She recognizes in this repressed childhood secret the source of her own confusion between sex and sadism:

> Guilt. Shame. Infantile sexuality. Liz gazed at the white-ankle-socked children, in their sunny, monosyllabic garden. The children in the garden. The serpent hissed, sweetly. The children aged, slowly. They skipped downhill for ever, along the radiant way, and behind them burned for ever that great dark dull sun. (386)

The link between phallus and serpent, sex and evil, is forged.

The "skeleton in the cupboard" (388) is unlocked at last: Alfred Ablewhite was a paedophile who was arrested for exposing himself to children and who, though acquitted, committed suicide (389) out of shame—although the story told the daughters by their mother was that he had gone off to war, like Drabble's own father, and been killed (383). Once she faces the worst, Liz is relieved: she had declared, "Physician, heal thyself. Physician, know thyself" (144), but she feared the destructive power of knowledge, fearing that "Knowledge would be death" (384). But Liz recognizes that "the rational, radiant light" (331) of knowledge, however distasteful, is preferable to the darkness of ignorance. She acknowledges that it could have been worse: her father's shabby little sins are minor compared to the horrific crimes of his fellow sexual deviant, P. Whitmore. As Larkin wryly wrote and Alix quotes, "They fuck you up, your Mum and Dad" (212).

Now that she has discovered in the darkness of the past the light to illumine the future, Liz determines to lay her father's corpse back in its grave and go on with her own life, looking forward, not back: "She would no longer gaze at the past, she would no more question her own wicked heart. On she would go, relentlessly, into the dark-red sun, down the radiant way, towards the only possible ending" (389). Effort has been rewarded, and knowledge has enlightened the darkness of the past, illuminating the radiant way into the future.

Accordingly, Liz, happily reunited with her sister Shirley for the first time in the novel, commits the incriminating clippings to the "Ideal Boiler" (388), as they joyfully indulge in a ritual purgative house-cleaning of the Abercorn mausoleum (381)—like Kate Armstrong in *The Middle Ground*. The sisters learn that "Laughter was possible, *in ex-*

tremis" (380). Liz even discovers the identity and function of her *bête-noir*, the mysterious silver ornament which she was compelled to polish (along with her dead father's shoes) throughout her youth: amusingly, it turns out to be a wine-cooler, accessory to celebrations, and as she discovers its identity, the object is demystified—like the tulip-patterned slop bowl of Clara Maugham's home (314). Unlike the secret of Liz's father, however, the mystery of their mother's past secrets, suggested by this bizarre "symbol" (182), with its mailed fist and monogram, is never resolved.

In the apotheosis of *The Radiant Way*, dated June 1985, the trio of friends are reunited in a garden, under the aegis of "the solid fleshly apparition of their old Cambridge friend Flora Piercey" (394), the source of their original meeting, to celebrate Esther's fiftieth birthday—another momentous turning point. Named, like Emma Evans' daughter, for the goddess of flowers, Flora, conjured up by the remarkable powers of the witchlike Esther, "obeyed her summons and materialized at the garden gate, bearing a bunch of ragged white roses and a Camembert cheese" (394)—a benevolent deity. The next day, the friends are reunited in a "farewell party" (395), echoing in an optimistic manner the pessimistic farewell party which opened the novel, as they enjoy one of their ritual rural rambles and picnic—a matriarchal *déjeuner sur l'herbe*.

This reunion on the eve of their dispersal to their new lives takes on an idyllic quality, as they drowse together in the sunshine on this "perfect day" (394), even slumbering and perhaps dreaming in an echo of mediaeval romance allegory (395). Nature is portrayed in Edenic terms: "The green hill slopes up behind them to the brilliant azure. Large pink lambs, surreal, tinted from the red earth, stand outlined on the hill against the blue. An extraordinary primal timeless brightness shimmers in the hot afternoon air. A slight breeze moves the grass like waves on water" (395). Together, the friends experience an epiphanic vision of nature:[17]

> Esther describes to them the secrets of the landscape. She tells them of the snake by the trout pond. She tells them of the heron in the reeds. She tells them of the bleeding lamb. . . . She tells them of the primroses of March, of the rosebay willow herb of high summer, of the purple and gold of autumn. She tells them of the sliding fountain that appears, mysteriously, welling up in the green field, and disappears as mysteriously, regardless of rainfall. A secret spring, a hidden source,

a sacred fount. (395)

They have found their own secret spring of strength, their sacred fount of faith in the future. "Esther sticks a flower behind her ear," as the trio "make their way on, along the footpath, the devious way home. The sun descends" (396).

The final image is aureate, if ambiguous:

> At the top of the last steep, homeward ascent, they pause for breath, leaning on a gate. Below them lie the deep wood, the grove, the secret valley, the cottage, the wooden table, the cherry tree. Beyond are the hills, and beyond the hills, the sea. Where they stand it is still, but above their heads, high in the broad leaves of the trees, a high wind is passing. It shakes the leaves, the branches. The leaves glitter and dance. The spirit passes. The sun is dull with a red radiance. It sinks. Esther, Liz and Alix are silent with attention. The sun hangs in the sky, burning. The earth deepens to a more profound red. The sun bleeds, the earth bleeds. The sun stands still. (396)

Appropriately, the dustcover of *The Radiant Way* portrays the ambiguous symbol of a red sun—ambiguous because it may be either rising or setting.[18] But it does not really matter which, for the sun is an archetypal comic symbol of continuity, as well as enlightenment, since it sets only to rise again. Despite the serpent which always lurks in any garden, no matter how paradisal, the characters will all go on, "relentlessly, into the dark-red sun, down the radiant way, towards the only possible ending" (389). But the sun never really stands still, for, ever intent on writing "beyond the ending," Drabble is already producing the sequel to *The Radiant Way*.[19] As readers, we can only anticipate what golden realms the artist will illuminate at the heart of darkness.

NOTES

[1] Margaret Drabble, *Saturday Review*, vol. 11, no. 5, Sept./Oct. 1985. In a 1 November 1988 letter to Nora Stovel, Drabble amplifies: "I didn't take on the *OCEL* because of hostile critical reception of *The Middle Ground*—I agreed to do it in the summer of 1979, long before *The Middle Ground* was published, and was well into it by the publication date in

1980—I agreed rather because of my own doubts about fiction than those of others.

[2] Margaret Forster, "What Makes Margaret Drabble Run and Run," *Guardian Weekend*, 28 February 1981, p. 9.

[3] Margaret Drabble in a letter to Valerie Grosvenor Myer, September, 1983.

[4] A 19 April 1987 *Observer* Profile on Drabble is titled "Ambassadress of Literary London." One English diplomat in Canada accused Drabble in person, during her 1987 promotion tour, of being a poor ambassador for her own country by painting such a dark portrait of England in *The Radiant Way*.

[5] Phyllis Rose, "Our Chronicler of Britain," *New York Times Book Review*, 7 September 1980, p. 1. Joanne Creighton calls Drabble "a central chronicler of contemporary urban middle-class life" (*MD* 14).

[6] Margaret Atwood, *Chatelaine*, April 1987, p. 73.

[7] Margaret Drabble, *The Radiant Way* (McClelland and Stewart, 1987), 170. Subsequent references will be documented in the text.

[8] Margaret Drabble, quoted by Rupert Schleder in "The New Wasteland," *Books in Canada*, April 1987, p. 28. Drabble's latest novel approximates the ambitious social scope of her elder sister's, Antonia Susan Byatt's, projected trilogy of British social history over three decades, beginning with *The Virgin in the Garden* (1978) and *Still Life* (1985).

[9] Margaret Drabble, in conversation with Nora Foster Stovel, 15 April 1987, Edmonton, Alberta, Canada. Further references will be to this interview.

[10] The epigraph to *The Needle's Eye* is W. B. Yeats's "The Fascination of What's Difficult." Drabble approves that novel for its presentation of "people in a state of continual effort" (*AC* 35).

[11] Lindsay Duguid, "Icons of the Times," a review of *The Radiant Way*, *Times Literary Supplement*, 1 May 1987.

[12] This motif inevitably recalls Iris Murdoch's 1961 novel, *A Severed Head*. Liz opines that a "proper Freudian" would think that "this severed head business" has "something to do with fear of castration" (330) and says that Freud believed that "the Gorgon's head represented the castrating vision of female genitals" (249).

[13] Alix meets Beaver at Northam's Holroyd Gallery, the name of Drabble's husband, the noted literary biographer Michael Holroyd. Drabble refers to Harvey's *Oxford Com-*

panion to English Literature (266), which she reedited.

[14] Margaret Drabble, in "Child Abuse: When a Public Inquiry Isn't Enough," *Sunday Telegraph*, 2 August 1987, pp. 14-16, writes, "The novelist frequently ventures into [the psychotherapist's] territory, into the Minotaur's den" (16).

[15] This motif inevitably recalls Margaret Atwood's *Surfacing* (1972).

[16] Drabble's father died in 1982 and her mother in 1984.

[17] Esther has a similar idyllic vision of the English countryside (373).

[18] Ever ambivalent, Drabble remarked to me that she prefers to interpret this logo as ambiguous.

[19] See Rachel Blau DuPlessis, *Writing Beyond the Ending: Narrative Stratagies of Twentieth-Century Women Writers* (Bloomington: Indiana Univ. Press, 1985). Drabble began the sequel while *The Radiant Way* was still in press, because she knew that Alix would want to visit the murderer in prison. Drabble writes in a 1 November 1988 letter to Nora Foster Stovel: "The sequel to *The Radiant Way* is finished and is to be called *A Natural Curiosity*. It is a very odd book and I am sure it will mystify people, but never mind. On to the next, which I hope will take Stephen Cox to Kampuchea."

Chapter Twelve:

CONCLUSION

This study of Drabble's fiction has demonstrated that she is a moralist as well as a journalist, an artist as well as a realist, and that symbolism is her primary vehicle for conveying her moral vision. In taking an aesthetic approach to Drabble's work, the aim of this study has not been to contradict the prevailing realist or feminist criticism, but rather to complement its social focus with a more literary emphasis for a fuller appreciation of the artist. The critics are quite right to praise Drabble's social realism, for it is precisely the rooting of the ideal in the real that makes her vision convincing as well as inspiring. Realism provides the perfect vehicle for the artist's moral vision, for Drabble is aware that the more crass the actual, the more crucial the ideal. While the realist holds the mirror up to society, the idealist paints a vision of a golden realm to judge it by.

Tracing Drabble's literary progress throughout her fictional career has also revealed a distinct development in her moral vision and artistic vehicle. Just as her heroines progress from claustrophobia to community, so the author herself has broadened her horizons from private preoccupations to public responsibilities. Drabble summarizes her own development thus: "Her early novels deal primarily with the dilemma of the educated young woman caught in the conflicting claims of maternity, sexuality, and intellectual and economic aspiration; her later novels . . . have a broader canvas, a more ironic relationship with traditional narration, and a wider interest in documenting social change."[1] As we have seen, Drabble's symbolic, as well as her narrative, structures have developed to embody this widening scope in comprehensive patterns of imagery. The substructure of symbolism conveys the moral meaning that underlies the surface social realism, for the significant events in Drabble's novels are the invisible ones which cannot be realized on the narrative level, but only signified on the symbolic plane.

Drabble has declared that "I'm driven to look for another underlying meaning" because she is convinced that "a pattern will emerge. . . . I have this deep faith that it will all be revealed to me one day. One day I shall just see into the heart of the whole thing" (*BMI* 63-65). All of her mature protagonists strive to transcend the quagmire of the contemporary to achieve a vision of the design underlying the dither of detail. The true turning point of Drabble's novels is a movement of the spirit from paralyzing pessimism to guarded optimism, as the characters accept the reality of the present and the truth of the past and find the heart to travel the radiant way into the future.

A consideration of Drabble's development leads us naturally to speculation about the future of her fiction in the light of her past achievement. In *The Tradition of Women's Fiction*, Drabble entitles her chapter on her own fiction "The Search for a Future" because she believes that "writing fiction is a search for a future in that you are creating, as you go, the images that you can then pursue. . . . We are trying to imagine the impossible golden world, and into that we have to try to move" (*TWF* 91, 116). She insists that "The fiction creates the reality" (*BMI* 43), because she believes that "in writing novels we create not only a book but a future, we draw up through our characters our beautiful, impossible blueprints, and bring into being what we need to be."[2] Whatever blueprints Drabble creates, we can be sure that she will use her moral vision to imagine her realms of gold and her symbolic vehicle to take us there.

NOTES

[1] After reviewers complained that Drabble did not include an entry for herself in the first printing of *The Oxford Companion to English Literature*—since she made 1939, her birthdate, the cutoff point—this summary of her career on the dust jacket of a subsequent printing constitutes an entry on herself.

[2] Margaret Drabble, "Doris Lessing: Cassandra in a World Under Siege," *Ramparts*, 10 (January 1972), 54.

SELECTED BIBLIOGRAPHY

I WORKS BY MARGARET DRABBLE

A NOVELS

A Summer Bird-Cage. London: Weidenfeld and Nicolson, 1963.
The Garrick Year. London: Weidenfeld and Nicolson, 1964.
The Millstone. London: Weidenfeld and Nicolson, 1965.
Jerusalem the Golden. London: Weidenfeld and Nicolson, 1967.
The Waterfall. London: Weidenfeld and Nicolson, 1969.
The Needle's Eye. London: Weidenfeld and Nicolson, 1972.
The Realms of Gold. London: Weidenfeld and Nicolson, 1975.
The Ice Age. London: Weidenfeld and Nicolson, 1977.
The Middle Ground. London: Weidenfeld and Nicolson, 1980.
The Radiant Way. Toronto: McClelland and Stewart, 1987.

B NON-FICTION BOOKS

Wordsworth. London: Evans, 1966.
Arnold Bennett: A Biography. London: Weidenfeld and Nicolson, 1974.
For Queen and Country: Britain in the Victorian Age. London: Andre Deutsch, 1978.
A Writer's Britain: Landscape in Literature. New York: Knopf, 1979.
The Tradition of Women's Fiction: Lectures in Japan. Ed. Yukako Suga. Tokyo: Oxford Univ. Press, 1982.

C EDITIONS

Drabble, Margaret, and B.S. Johnson, eds. *London Consequences.* London: Greater London Arts Association, 1972.
Drabble, Margaret, ed. *Lady Susan, The Watsons, Sanditon.* Harmondsworth: Penguin, 1974.
Drabble, Margaret, ed. *The Genius of Thomas Hardy.* London: Weidenfeld and Nicolson, 1975.
Drabble, Margaret, and Charles Osborne, eds. *New Stories: An Anthology 1.* London: Greater Arts Council of Great

Britain, 1976.
Drabble Margaret, ed. *The Oxford Companion to English Literature*. 5th ed. Oxford: Oxford Univ. Press, 1985.

D PLAYS (produced but unpublished)

Laura. London: Granada, 1964.
Bird of Paradise. London: National Theatre, 1969. (British Library)
A Touch of Love. Screenplay, 1969. (based on *The Millstone*)
Isadora. Screenplay, 1969.

E SHORT STORIES

"Les Liaisons Dangereuses." *Punch*, 28 October 1964, pp. 646-48.
"Hassan's Tower." *Winter's Tales* 12. Ed. A. D. Maclean. London: Macmillan, 1966, pp. 41-59.
"A Voyage to Cytherea." *Mademoiselle*, December 1967, pp. 98-99.
"The Reunion." *Winter's Tales 14*. London: Macmillan, 1968, pp. 149-68.
"Faithful Lovers." *The Saturday Evening Post*, 6 April 1968, pp. 62-65.
"A Pyrrhic Victory." *Nova*, July 1968, pp. 80-84.
"Crossing the Alps." *Penguin Modern Stories 3*. Harmondsworth: *Penguin*, 1969, pp. 63-85.
"The Gifts of War." *Winter's Tales 16*. London: Macmillan, 1970, pp. 20-36.
"A Day in the Life of a Smiling Woman." *Cosmopolitan*, August 1973, pp. 90-91.
"A Success Story." *Ms.*, December 1974, pp. 52-55.
"Homework." *The Ontario Review* 7 (1977-78), pp. 7-13.

F ARTICLES

"The Unheroic Mode." (an unpublished essay submitted for the English Tripos at Cambridge University in 1960).
"The Month." *Twentieth Century*, 168 (1960), 73-78.
"The Sexual Revolution." *Manchester Guardian Weekly*, 12 Oct. 1967, p. 9.
"Slipping into Debt." *The Guardian*. 12 August 1968, p. 7.
"Money as a Subject for the Novelist." *Times Literary*

Supplement, 24 July 1969, pp. 792-93.
"The Author's Introduction." *The Millstone*. Ed. Michael Marland. Harlow: Longman, 1970, pp. vii-xiii.
"Doris Lessing: Cassandra in a World Under Siege." *Ramparts* 10 (January 1972), 50-54.
"A Woman Writer." *Books*, 11 (Spring 1973), 4-6.
"Virginia Woolf: A Personal Debt." London: Aloe, 1973.
"Once Again the Dark." *New York Times*, 6 January 1974, p. 15.
"Midway Through Motherhood." *Parent's Magazine*, April 1974, pp. 44-46.
"The Writer as Recluse: The Theme of Solitude in the Works of the Brontës." *Brontë Society Transactions*, 16 (1974), 259-69.
"Personal Matters." *New Statesman*, 89 (14 February 1975), 219-20.
"The Author Comments." *Dutch Quarterly Review of Anglo-American Letters*, 5 (1975), 35-38.
"Hardy and the Natural World." *The Genius of Thomas Hardy*. Ed. Margaret Drabble. London: Weidenfeld and Nicolson, 1975, pp. 162-69.
"Confessions of a Punster." *More Words*. London: BBC, 1977, pp. 43-44.
"The Fiendish Curse." *More Words*. London: BBC, 1977, pp. 45-48.
"Thinking About Rape." *New York Times*, 21 January 1979, p. 21.
"Introduction" to *Wuthering Heights* by Emily Brontë. London: Everyman, 1979, pp. v-xxii.
"Child Abuse: When a Public Inquiry Isn't Enough." *Sunday Telegraph*, 2 August 1987, pp. 14-16.
"Mimesis: The Representation of Reality in the Post-War Novel." *MOSAIC*, 20 (1987), 1-14.

II INTERVIEWS

Atwood, Margaret. *Chatelaine*, April 1987, p. 73.
Bergonzi, Bernard. "Novelists of the Sixties." London: BBC, 1968.
Clark, Diana Cooper. "Margaret Drabble: Cautious Feminist." *Atlantic Monthly*, 246 (November 1980), 69-75.
Creighton, Joanne V. "An Interview with Margaret Drabble." *Margaret Drabble: Golden Realms*. Ed. Dorey Schmidt.

Edinburg, Texas: Pan American Univ. Press, 1982, pp. 18-31.

Firchow, Peter. "Margaret Drabble." *The Writer's Place: Interviews on the Literary Situation in Contemporary Britain.* Ed. Peter Firchow. Minneapolis: Univ. of Minnesota Press, 1974, pp. 102-21.

Forster. Margaret. "What Makes Margaret Drabble Run and Run." *Guardian*, 28 February 1981, p. 9.

Gussow, Mel. "Margaret Drabble: A Double Life." *New York Times Book Review*, 9 October 1977, pp. 7, 40-41.

Hannay, John. "Interview with Margaret Drabble." *Michigan Quarterly*.

Hardin, Nancy S. "An Interview with Margaret Drabble." *Contemporary Literature*, 14 (1973), 273-95.

Higdon, David Leon. "An Interview with Margaret Drabble," September, 1979.

Horder, John. "Heroine in an Empty House." *The Times*, 21 May 1969, p. 12.

Household, Nicki. "Love Story: *The Waterfall*." *Radio Times*, 8 November 1980, pp. 23-27.

Le Franc, Bolivar. "An Interest in Guilt." *Books and Bookmen*, 14 September 1969, 20-21.

Milton, Barbara. "Margaret Drabble: The Art of Fiction LXX." *The Paris Review*, 20 (Fall-Winter 1978), 40-65.

Myer, Valerie Grosvenor. "Margaret Drabble in Conversation with Valerie Grosvenor Myer." London: The British Council, 1977.

Parker, Gillian and Todd, Janet. "Margaret Drabble." *Women Writers Talking.* Ed. Janet Todd. London: Holmes and Meier, 1983.

Poland, Nancy. "Margaret Drabble: 'There Must Be a Lot of People Like Me.'" *Midwest Quarterly*, 16 (Spring 1975), 255-67.

Powell, Marilyn. "An Interview with Margaret Drabble." Toronto: CBC, 22 February 1980.

Preussner, Dee. "Talking with Margaret Drabble." *Modern Fiction Studies*, 25 (Winter 1979-80), 563-77.

Rozencwajg, Iris. "Interview with Margaret Drabble." *Women's Studies*, 6 (1979), 335-47.

Stovel, Nora Foster. Margaret Drabble in Conversation with Nora Stovel. London, 17 May 1980. Edmonton, 15 April 1987.

Whitehall, Sharon. "Two for Tea: An Afternoon with Margaret Drabble." *Essays in Literature*, 11 (1984), 67-75.

III WORKS ABOUT MARGARET DRABBLE

A BOOKS

Creighton, Joanne. *Margaret Drabble*. London: Methuen, 1985.

Hannay, John. *The Intertextuality of Fate: A Study of Margaret Drabble*. Columbia: Univ. of Missouri Press, 1986.

Moran, Mary Hurley. *Margaret Drabble: Existing Within Structures*. Carbondale and Edwardsville: Southern Illinois Univ. Press, 1983.

Myer, Valerie Grosvenor. *Margaret Drabble: Puritanism and Permissiveness*. London: Vision Press, 1974.

Rose, Ellen Cronan. *The Novels of Margaret Drabble: Equivocal Figures*. London: Macmillan, 1980.

Rose, Ellen Cronan, ed. *Critical Essays on Margaret Drabble*. Boston: G.K. Hall, 1984.

Roxman, Susanna. *Guilt and Glory: Studies in Margaret Drabble's Novels 1963-1980*. Stockholm: Almqvist & Wiskell, 1984.

Sadler, Lynn Veach. *Margaret Drabble*. Boston: Twayne, 1986.

Schmidt, Dorey, ed. *Margaret Drabble: Golden Realms*. Edinburg, Texas: Pan American University, 1982.

B ARTICLES ON INDIVIDUAL NOVELS

A SUMMER BIRD-CAGE:

Davidson, Arnold E. "Pride and Prejudice in Margaret Drabble's *A Summer Bird-Cage*." *Arizona Quarterly*, 38 (1982), 303-10.

Nicolaisen. W.F.H. "'What a Name. Stephen Halifax: Onomastic Modes in Three Novels by Margaret Drabble." *Literary Onomastics Studies*, 10 (1983), 269-83.

THE GARRICK YEAR:

Preussner, Dee. "Patterns in The Garrick Year." *Margaret Drabble: Golden Realms*. Ed. Dorey Schmidt. Edinburg, Texas: Pan American Univ. Press, 1982, pp. 117-27.

Stovel, Nora Foster. "Staging a Marriage: Margaret Drabble's *The Garrick Year.*" *MOSAIC*, XVII/2 (1984), 161-74, reprinted in *"For Better or Worse": Attitudes Toward Marriage in Literature*, ed. Evelyn J. Hinz (Winnipeg, 1984), pp. 161-74.

THE MILLSTONE:

Butler, Colin. "Margaret Drabble: *The Millstone* and Wordsworth." *English Studies*, 59 (1978), 353-60.
Firchow, Peter. "Rosamund's Complaint: Margaret Drabble's *The Millstone.*" *Old Lines, New Forces: Essays on the Contemporary British Novel, 1960-1970*. Ed. Robert K. Morris (New Jersey: Associated Univ. Presses, 1976), pp. 93-108.
Hardin, Nancy. "Drabble's *The Millstone*: A Fable for Our Times." *Critique*, 15 (1973), 22-34.
Sherry, Ruth. "Margaret Drabble's *The Millstone*: A Feminist Approach." *Edda: Nordisk Tidsskrift for Litteraturforskning*, pp. 41-53.
Spitzer, Susan. "Fantasy and Femaleness in Margaret Drabble's *The Millstone.*" *Novel*, 11 (1978), 227-45.
Wikborg, Eleanor. "A Comparison of Margaret Drabble's *The Millstone* with its Vecko-Revyn Adaptation, 'Barnet Du Gav Mig.'" *Moderna Sprak*, 65 (1971), 305-11.

JERUSALEM THE GOLDEN:

Edwards, Lee. "*Jerusalem the Golden*: A Fable for Our Times." *Women's Studies*, 6 (1979), 317-34.
Johnston, Sue Ann. "The Daughter as Escape Artist." *Atlantis*, 9 (1984), 10-22.

THE WATERFALL:

Creighton, Joanne V. "Reading Margaret Drabble's *The Waterfall.*" *Critical Essays on Margaret Drabble*. Ed. Ellen Cronan Rose. Boston: G.K. Hall, 1984, pp. 106-18.
_____. "Sisterly Symbiosis: Margaret Drabble's *The Waterfall* and A.S. Byatt's *The Game.*" *MOSAIC*, 20 (1987), 15-31.
Rabinowitz, Nancy S. "Talc on the Scotch: Art and Morality in Margaret Drabble's *The Waterfall.*" *International Journal of Women's Studies*, 5 (1982), 236-45.

Rose, Ellen Cronan. "Feminine Endings—and Beginnings: Margaret Drabble's *The Waterfall*." *Contemporary Literature* 21 (Winter 1980), 81-99.

Rubenstein, Roberta. "Margaret Drabble's *The Waterfall*: The Myth of Psyche, Romantic Tradition, and the Female Quest." *Margaret Drabble: Golden Realms.* Ed. Dorey Schmidt. Edinburg, Texas: Pan American Univ. Press, 1982, pp. 139-57.

Skoller, Eleanor Honig. "The Progress of a Letter: Truth, Feminism, and *The Waterfall*." *Critical Essays on Margaret Drabble.* Ed. Ellen Cronan Rose. Boston: G.K. Hall, 1984, pp. 119-32.

Walker, Nancy. "Women Drifting: Drabble's *The Waterfall* and Chopin's *The Awakening*." *Denver Quarterly*, 17 (1983), 88-96.

Wyatt, Jean. "Escaping Literary Designs: The Politics of Reading and Writing in Margaret Drabble's *The Waterfall*." *Perspectives on Contemporary Literature*, 11 (1985), 37-45.

THE NEEDLE'S EYE:

Davidson, Arnold E. "Parables of Grace in Drabble's *The Needle's Eye*." *Margaret Drabble: Golden Realms.* Ed. Dorey Schmidt. Edinburg, Texas: Pan American Univ. Press, 1982, pp. 139-57.

Dixson, Barbara. "Patterned Figurative Language in *The Needle's Eye*." *Margaret Drabble: Golden Realms.* Ed. Dorey Schmidt. Edinburg, Texas: Pan American Univ. Press, 1982, pp. 128-38.

Lay, Mary M. "Margaret Drabble's *The Needle's Eye*: Jamesian Perception of Self." *College Language Association Journal*, 28 (1984), 33-45.

Mannheimer, Monica Lauritzen. "The Search for Identity in Margaret Drabble's *The Needle's Eye*." *Dutch Quarterly Review of Anglo-American Letters*, 5 (1975), 24-35.

Oates, Joyce Carol. "*The Needle's Eye*." *New York Times Book Review*, 11 June 1972.

THE REALMS OF GOLD:

Bromberg, Pamela S. "Romantic Revisionism in Margaret Drabble's *The Realms of Gold*." *Margaret Drabble: Golden Realms.* Ed. Dorey Schmidt. Edinburg, Texas: Pan

American Univ. Press, 1982, pp. 48-65.
Davis, Cynthia. "Unfolding Form: Narrative Approach and Theme in *The Realms of Gold.*" *Modern Language Quarterly*, 40 (1979), 390-402.
Kaplan, Carey. "A Vision of Power in Margaret Drabble's *The Realms of Gold.*" *Journal of Women's Studies in Literature*, 1 (Summer 1979), 233-42.
Little, Judy, "Humour and the Female Quest: Margaret Drabble's *The Realms of Gold.*" *Margaret Drabble: Golden Realms.* Ed. Dorey Schmidt. Edinburg, Texas: Pan American Univ. Press, 1982, pp. 158-67.
Rowe, Margaret. "The Uses of the Past in Margaret Drabble's *The Realms of Gold.*" *Margaret Drabble: Golden Realms.* Ed. Dorey Schmidt. Edinburg, Texas: Pan American Univ. Press, 1982, pp. 158-67.
Sale, Roger. "*The Realms of Gold.*" *Hudson Review*, 28 (1975-76), 21-23.
Sharpe, Patricia. "On First Looking into *The Realms of Gold.*" *Michigan Quarterly Review*, 16 (1977), 225-31.
Updike, John. "Drabbling in the Mud." *New Yorker*, 51 (12 January 1976), 88-90.

THE ICE AGE:

Goss, Margaret Hill. "Birds in Margaret Drabble's *The Ice Age.*" *Notes on Contemporary Literature*, 15 (1985), 10.
Bansen, Elaine Tuttle. "The Uses of Imagination: Margaret Drabble's *The Ice Age.*" *Critical Essays on Margaret Drabble.* Ed. Ellen Cronan Rose. Boston: G.K. Hall, 1984, pp. 151-68.

THE MIDDLE GROUND:

Amiel, Barbara. "Relentless Torment of Urban Souls." *Maclean's*, 93 (29 September 1980), 56.
Bromberg, Pamela S. "Narrative in Drabble's *The Middle Ground*: Relativity versus Teleology." *Contemporary Literature*, 24 (1983), 463-79.
Campbell, Jane. "Reaching Outwards: Versions of Reality in *The Middle Ground.*" *Journal of Narrative Technique* 14 (1984), 17-32.
Efrig, Gail. "*The Middle Ground.*" *Margaret Drabble: Golden Realms.* Ed. Dorey Schmidt. Edinburg, Texas: Pan

American Univ. Press, 1982, pp. 178-85.
Elkins, Mary J. "Alenoushka's Return: Motifs and Movement in *The Middle Ground*." *Critical Essays on Margaret Drabble*. Ed. Ellen Cronan Rose. Boston: G.K. Hall, 1984, pp. 169-180.
Glendinning, Victoria. "The New Matriarchy Reaches Middle Age." *Sunday Times*, 29 June 1980.
King, Francis. *Spectator*, 5 July 1980, p. 22.
Lucas, John. "Endlessly." *New Statesman*, 11 July 1980, p. 55.
Rose, Ellen Cronan. "Drabble's *The Middle Ground*: 'Mid-Life' Narrative Strategies.' *Critique*, 23 (Spring 1982), 69-82.
Rubenstein, Roberta. "From Detritus to Discovery: Margaret Drabble's *The Middle Ground*." *Journal of Narrative Technique*, 1984.
Sadler, Lynn Veach. "'The Society We Have': The Search for Meaning in Drabble's *The Middle Ground*." *Critique*, 23 (Spring 1982), 83-93.

C GENERAL ARTICLES AND REVIEWS

Apter, T. E. "Margaret Drabble: The Glamour of Seriousness." *Human World*, 12 (August 1973), 18-28.
Baker, Sheridan. "The Contemporary British Novel." *American Libraries* (October 1974), pp. 483-90.
Beards, Virginia K. "Margaret Drabble: Novels of a Cautious Feminist." *Critique*, 15 (1973), 35-47.
Bergonzi, Bernard. "Margaret Drabble." *Contemporary Novelists*. 2nd ed. Ed. James Vinson. New York: St. Martin's, 1976, pp. 371-74.
Bonford, François. "Margaret Drabble: How to Express Subjective Truth Through Fiction?" *Revue des Langues Vivantes*, 40 (1974), 41-55.
Bromberg, Pamela. "The Development of Narrative Technique in Margaret Drabble's Novels." *The Journal of Narrative Technique*, 16 (Fall, 1986), 179-91.
Burkhardt, Charles. "Arnold Bennett and Margaret Drabble." *Margaret Drabble: Golden Realms*. Ed. Dorey Schmidt. Edinburg, Texas: Pan American Univ. Press, 1982, pp. 91-103.
Campbell, Jane. "Margaret Drabble and the Search for Analogy." *The Practical Vision: Essays in English Litera-

ture in Honour of Flora Roy. Ed. Jane Campbell and James Doyle. Waterloo: Wilfrid Laurier Univ. Press, 1978, pp. 133-50.

_____ "Becoming Terrestrial: The Short Stories of Margaret Drabble." *Critique*, 25 (1983), 25-44.

Cunningham, Gail. "Women and Children First: The Novels of Margaret Drabble." *Twentieth-Century Women Novelists*. Ed. Thomas F. Staley. London: Macmillan, 1982, pp. 130-52.

Fox-Genovese, Elizabeth. "The Ambiguities of Female Identity: A Reading of the Novels of Margaret Drabble." *Partisan Review*, 46 (1979), 234-48.

Gindin, James. "Three Recent British Novels and an American Response." *Michigan Quarterly Review*, 27 (1978), 223-46.

Gullette, Margaret Morganroth. "Ugly Ducklings and Swans: Margaret Drabble's Fable of Progress in the Middle Years." *Modern Language Quarterly*, 44 (1983), 285-304.

Harper, Michael F. "Margaret Drabble and the Resurrection of the English Novel." *Contemporary Literature*, 23 (1982), 145-68.

Higdon, David Leon. "The Sense of Tradition in Margaret Drabble's Novels." *Conference of College Teachers of English of Texas Proceedings*, 50 (1985), 25-31.

Irvine, Lorna. "No Sense of an Ending: Drabble's Continuous Fictions." *Critical Essays on Margaret Drabble*. Ed. Ellen Cronan Rose. Boston: G.K. Hall, 1984, pp. 73-85.

Klein, Norma. "Real Novels about Real Women." *Ms.*, 1 (September 1972), 7-8.

Korenman, Joan. "The 'Liberation' of Margaret Drabble." *Critique*, 21 (1979), 61-72.

Lambert, Ellen Z. "Margaret Drabble and the Sense of Possibility." *University of Toronto Quarterly*, 49 (1980), 237-41.

Lay, Mary M. "Temporal Ordering in the Fiction of Margaret Drabble." *Critique*, 21 (1979), 73-83.

Levitt, Morton P. "The New Victorians: Margaret Drabble as Trollope." *Margaret Drabble: Golden Realms*. Ed. Dorey Schmidt. Edinburg, Texas: Pan American Univ. Press, 1982, 168-77.

Libby, Marion Vlastos. "Fate and Feminism in the Novels of Margaret Drabble." *Contemporary Literature*, 16 (1975), 175-92.

Mannheimer, Joan. "Margaret Drabble and the Journey to the

Self." *Studies in the Literary Imagination*, 11 (Fall 1978), 127-43.

Moran, Mary H. "Spots of Joy in the Midst of Darkness: The Universe of Margaret Drabble." *Margaret Drabble: Golden Realms*, Ed. Dorey Schmidt. Edinburg, Texas: Pan American Univ. Press, 1982, pp. 32-47.

Oates, Joyce Carol. "Bricks and Mortar." *Ms.*, August 1974, pp. 34-36.

Pickering, Jean. "Margaret Drabble's Sense of the Middle Problem." *Twentieth Century Literature*, 30 (1984), 475-83.

Rayson, Ann. "Motherhood in the Novels of Margaret Drabble." *Frontiers*, 3 (1978), 43-46.

Rose, Ellen Cronan. "A Farewell to Renunciations." *Nation* 215 (1972), 379-80.

_____ "Margaret Drabble: Surviving the Future." *Critique*, 15 (1973), 5-21.

_____ "Paradise Lost." *National Review* 29 (23 December 1977), 1504.

Ruderman, Judith. "An Invitation to a Dinner Party: Margaret Drabble on Women and Food." *Margaret Drabble: Golden Realms*. Ed. Dorey Schmidt. Edinburg, Texas: Pan American Univ. Press, pp. 104-16.

Sage, Lorna. "Female Fictions: The Women Novelists." *The Contemporary English Novel*. Ed. Malcolm Bradbury and David Palmer (London: Edward Arnold, 1979), pp. 66-78.

Schaefer, J. O'Brien. "The Novels of Margaret Drabble." *New Republic*, 26 April 1975, 21-23.

Spacks, Patricia Meyer. "Introduction." *Contemporary Novelists*. Ed. Patricia Meyer Spacks. Englewood Cliffs, N.J.: Prentice-Hall, 1977, pp. 1-17.

Stovel, Nora Foster. "Margaret Drabble's Golden Vision." *Margaret Drabble: Golden Realms*. Ed. Dorey Schmidt. Edinburg, Texas: Pan American Univ. Press, 1982, pp. 3-17.

_____ "The Aerial View of Modern Britain: The Airplane as a Vehicle for Idealism and Satire." *ARIEL*, 15 (Summer, 1984), pp. 17-34.

_____ 'A Feminine Ending?': Symbolism as Closure in the Novels of Margaret Drabble." *English Studies in Canada*, XV (March, 1989).

_____ "From Wordsworth to Bennett: The Development of Margaret Drabble's Fiction." *International Fiction Review* (1989).

_____ "From Victorian Lady through Modern Woman to Contemporary Female Person: Arnold Bennett's *Anna of the Five Towns*, D.H. Lawrence's *Lost Girl*, and Margaret Drabble's *Jerusalem the Golden*." *D.H. Lawrence's Literary Heritage*, Ed. Dennis Jackson and Keith Cushman (forthcoming).

Wilson, Angus. "Literary Landscapes." *The Observer*, 17 October 1979.

Wilson, Keith. "Jim, Jake and the Years Between: The Will to Stasis in the Contemporary British Novel." *ARIEL*, 13 (January 1982), 55-69.

D DISCUSSIONS OF DRABBLE IN BOOKS OF CRITICISM ON MODERN FICTION

Bergonzi, Bernard. *The Situation of the Novel*. London: Macmillan, 1970.

Higdon, David Leon. *Shadows of the Past in Contemporary British Fiction*. London: Macmillan, 1984.

Miles, Rosalind. *The Fiction of Sex: Themes and Functions of Sex Difference in the Modern Novel*. New York: Barnes and Noble, 1974, pp. 168-71.

Moers, Ellen. *Literary Women: The Great Writers*. New York: Anchor Books, 1977.

Raban, Jonathan. *The Technique of Modern Fiction: Essays in Practical Criticism*. London: Edward Arnold, 1968, pp. 162-68.

Ratcliffe, Michael. *The Novel Today*. London: Longmans, Green, 1968, pp. 14-16.

Showalter, Elaine. *A Literature of Their Own: British Women Novelists from Brontë to Lessing*. Princeton, N.J.: Princeton Univ. Press, 1977, pp. 298-319.

Sale, Roger. *On Not Being Good Enough: Writings of a Working Critic*. New York: Oxford Univ. Press, 1980.

Zeman, Anthea. *Presumptuous Girls: Women and their World in the Serious Woman's Novel*. London: Weidenfeld and Nicolson, 1977.

INDEX

Acting 47-48, 58-59
Academe 9, 46, 62-63, 65, 69
Aerial View 163, 178, 181
Albatross 68, 101, 198
Anthropology 138
Antigone 162
Apollo 150
Archaeology 12, 21, 130-38
Architecture 18-19, 21-22, 149, 155
Aristotle 65
Art 8, 13, 19-21
Atwood, Margaret 187, 203
    Surfacing 203
Austen, Jane 1, 8, 12, 21, 30, 40-41, 45, 47, 58, 93, 147
    Mansfield Park 47; *Sanditon* 93

Baker, Sheridan 1, 24
Balzac, Honore de 187, 192
Bennett, Arnold 10, 21, 41, 183
Bergonzi, Bernard 24-25
Bible 16, 68, 76, 109-13, 116, 121, 134
Birds 20, 29-30, 52, 153, 162
Boethius 162
Britain 149-65, 169, 187
Brontë, Charlotte 22, 107
    Jane Eyre 22, 107
Brontë, Emily 15
Bunyan, John 17, 64, 80, 113, 115, 123
    Pilgrim's Progress 113
Byatt, Antonia Susan 41, 183-4, 203
    The Game 41, 183; *The Virgin in the Garden* 183-84, 203;
    Still Life 203
Byron 62

Cambridge University 14, 41, 43, 45
Chekhov 31
    The Seagull 31
Clough, Hugh Arthur 195

Comedy 57, 142-44, 202
Community 6, 10-11, 67-69, 98, 110
Courtly Love 63-64
Culture 110, 155
Custody 109, 120

Daniel, Samuel 64
Daphne 34, 150
Dante Alighieri 192
Darwin, Charles 147
Dickens, Charles 127, 167, 182, 184, 187
  Our Mutual Friend 182
Dickinson, Emily 96-97, 101, 176
Donne, John 193
Drabble, Margaret
     Autobiography 9-10
     Development 10-12, 23-24
     Limitations 9-12, 55-56
Novels:
  The Garrick Year (1963) 1, 6, 8-9, 13, 19, 20-23, 40, 43-60, 83-84, 96
  The Ice Age (1977) 1, 6-7, 12, 19, 23, 130-48, 166, 177-78, 183
  Jerusalem the Golden (1967) 1, 6-7, 11-13, 17, 23, 78-79, 117, 131, 136, 173, 183, 196, 198-99, 201
  The Middle Ground (1980) 1, 6-7, 12, 19-23, 84, 149-66, 188-89, 196, 200
  The Millstone (1965) 1, 6, 9, 13, 16, 18, 21, 61-73, 95, 98, 108, 124
  A Natural Curiosity (1989) 204
  The Needle's Eye (1972) 1, 6-7, 11-12, 20-23, 109-29
  The Radiant Way (1987) 1, 6-7, 11-12, 22-24, 187-205
  The Realms of Gold (1975) 1, 6-7, 11-12, 17-19, 21-23, 130-48, 196, 198-99
  A Summer Bird-Cage (1963) 1, 6, 8, 13-14, 16, 20, 23, 29-42, 43-44, 47, 59, 183
  The Waterfall (1969) 1, 6-7, 9-10, 13, 16, 18, 20-23, 95-108
Critical Books:
  Arnold Bennett: A Biography (1974) 1, 92
  For Queen and Country: Britain in the Victorian Age (1978) 1
  The Tradition of Women's Fiction (1982) 1, 70, 206

   A Writer's Britain: Landscape in Literature (1979) 18, 97, 105
   Wordsworth (1966) 1, 5
  Editions:
   An Anthology I (1976) 1
   Jane Austen (1974) 1, 93
   London Consequences (1972) 1
   The Oxford Companion to English Literature (1985) 2, 186, 203, 205-06
   Thomas Hardy (1976) 1
  Short Stories:
   "A Pyrrhic Victory" 90, 94
   "The Reunion" 108
  Articles:
   "The Author Comments" 109
   "The Unheroic Mode" 45, 58
   "A Woman Writer" 4
Dunn, Nell 126

Eden 56-57, 135, 201
Eliot, George 99, 107, 187
  The Mill on the Floss 99, 107; *Middlemarch* 187
Eliot, T.S. 82
Elizabethan 62-63
Empedocles 140-41

Feminism 3-8, 109, 145, 170, 205
Fitzgerald, F. Scott 82
Flora and Fauna 20, 29-36, 110, 143
Forster, E.M.
  Howards End 152
Freud, Sigmund 99, 105, 203

Gardens 118-19
Garrick, David 43-47
  The Clandestine Marriage 45
Geology 134, 146
Gold 17, 130
Golden Windows 75-76, 87-89, 131
Goredale Scar 18, 97, 105, 107
Gould, Lois 170

Hamlet 160

Hardy 15, 18, 63, 65
  "Life's Little Ironies" 65
Hawthorne, Nathaniel
  The Scarlet Letter 63
Hill, Octavia 70
History 134
Holroyd, Michael 22, 203
Houses 21-22
Hugo, Victor 182
  Les Miserables 182
Hume, David 56

James, Henry 21, 116, 127
Job 68
Jonson, Ben 68
Journalism 12, 168-69, 170-75
Joyce, James 152

Landscape 18, 52
Larkin, Philip 200
Law 110-13, 124
Lawrence, D.H. 21, 53
Leavis, F.R. 7-8
Lessing, Doris 1, 206
Love 8, 36, 113, 124

Maternity 5, 18, 22, 55, 61, 67-70, 72, 98, 121, 175, 205
McCarthy, Mary 16
Metaphor 17
Methodism 79
Milton, John 149, 153, 162-63
  Aereopagitica 149, 153; *Paradise Lost* 162
Minotaur 198
Money 109
Montagu, Mary Wortley 47
Morality 4-12, 17, 36, 39, 109, 205
Murdoch, Iris 203

Names 18
National Health 66
Nature 18-21, 44, 51-57, 110, 149, 155

Oates, Joyce Carol 2, 7, 24, 109